Global Gender Issues in the New Millennium

Dilemmas in World Politics

Dilemmas in World Politics offers teachers and students in international relations a series of quality books on critical issues, trends, and regions in international politics. Each text examines a "real world" dilemma and is structured to cover the historical, theoretical, practical, and projected dimensions of its subject.

BOOKS IN THIS SERIES

THIRD EDITION

Global Gender Issues in the New Millennium

V. SPIKE PETERSON
University of Arizona

ANNE SISSON RUNYAN
University of Cincinnati

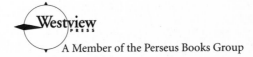

Westview
PRESS
A Member of the Perseus Books Group

Copyright © 2010 by V. Spike Peterson and Anne Sisson Runyan
Published by Westview Press,
A Member of the Perseus Books Group

Every effort has been made to secure required permissions to use all images, maps, and other art included in this volume.

Westview Press books are available at special discounts for bulk purchases in the United States by corporations, institutions, and other organizations. For more information, please contact the Special Markets Department at the Perseus Books Group, 2300 Chestnut Street, Suite 200, Philadelphia, PA 19103, or call (800) 810-4145, ext. 5000, or e-mail special.markets@perseusbooks.com.

Library of Congress Cataloging-in-Publication Data
Peterson, V. Spike.
    Global gender issues in the new millennium / V. Spike Peterson, Anne Sisson Runyan. —
3rd ed.
        p.   cm.
    Rev. ed. of: Global gender issues. 2nd ed. 1999.
    Includes bibliographical references and index.
    ISBN 978-0-8133-4394-5 (pbk. : alk. paper)
    1. Women in politics.   2. World politics—21st century.   I. Runyan, Anne Sisson.
II. Peterson, V. Spike. Global gender issues.   III. Title.
    HQ1236.P45 2010
    305.42—dc22

                                                                                2009020172

10 9 8 7 6 5 4 3 2 1

To our sisters,
for all that we share

Contents

Acknowledgments to the Third Edition

Far from being merely a third edition, this book is a significantly new treatment of global gender issues for the new millennium. The events on the ground and the massive shifts in feminist inquiry and theory to analyze and respond to them since our second edition have necessitated an almost total rereading and rewriting of the relationship between gender and world politics in the new millennium. Our task has been eased by, and our text is highly reflective of, the contemporary feminist international relations (IR) scholarship that is now regularly represented in the pages of the *International Feminist Journal of Politics,* which arose out of the Feminist Theory and Gender Studies (FTGS) Section of the International Studies Association (ISA). The advances in such scholarship that this journal has fostered enabled our own re-thinking and re-representation of both gender and world politics. The major advances in transnational feminist inquiry in general, which have been influenced by, intersected with, and contributed to feminist international relations (or feminist world politics) scholarship, have also lighted our way. These two connected, expanding, and varied bodies of knowledge have enabled us to document, analyze, and respond to the full-fledged crises of the incendiary violence unleashed by the global "war on terror" and economic and planetary meltdowns resulting from unbridled global capitalism. As contributors to these bodies of knowledge, we hope we have done justice to the theories and research of our many feminist colleagues around the world.

Many of these colleagues are also our friends who have supported our work since the late 1980s when we began working together to produce early feminist interventions in IR. We have returned to our collaboration once more to produce what we hope is one of the latest words (but far from the last or most exhaustive word) on the state of world politics from feminist perspectives.

To faithful readers and users of our previous editions, please note that gone are almost all the illustrations, graphs, and tables, as well as the glossary and questions for discussion, that were useful in early stages of teaching feminist IR and prior to the world of images now available on the Internet. We have concentrated instead on text that attempts to illuminate the complexities of injustice in and resistance to world-politics-as-usual, in language friendly to a range of levels but representing some of the most sophisticated analyses in feminist postcolonial and post-structural thought. We hope it will be as useful and used as previous editions. We thank Westview for its continued commitment to this endeavor and its staff who ably assisted us this time around.

We are indebted to so many colleagues and friends that we cannot possibly list them all here. However, we would first like to thank two students who served as research and manuscript production assistants and without whose help this would have been a much harder undertaking. Marjon Kamrani, doctoral candidate in Political Science and Women's Studies graduate certificate student at the University of Cincinnati (UC), provided the front-end research assistance for this endeavor. Marjon has become a part of our FTGS community as she produces her own feminist IR dissertation. Holly McEntyre, who has almost completed her joint MA/JD in Women's Studies and Law at UC, has provided the lion's share of the back-end work, carefully and professionally tracking the back-and-forth production of the text and helping us pull together the final manuscript. Holly has been Anne's right hand throughout her studies, serving as Anne's graduate assistant through most of the years Anne headed and served as graduate director of what is now the Department of Women's, Gender, and Sexuality Studies at UC. She cannot be thanked enough for all this support. As we noted in the acknowledgments to the previous editions of this text (which we retain in this edition to sustain the memories and threads of our running collaborations on this project), we do this, first and foremost, for the students—ours and yours—in the hope that commitments to social justice are reproduced and extended in the process.

Anne also thanks her department members and staff for their support, and especially Deb Meem, Amy Lind, and Michelle Gibson for taking on leadership roles in her department so that Anne could take the long-awaited sabbatical needed to work on this third edition. Feminist community is so important in our "neoliberalized" work environments, and Anne is fortunate to have so much of it.

For their friendship as well as their exceptional scholarship, Spike thanks the community of academic activists centered around the Department of Women's Studies and Institute for LGBT Studies at the University of Arizona, and the Gender Studies Institute at the London School of Economics where she greatly enjoyed being a Visiting Scholar in 2007 and 2008. Among many, Spike appreciates two recent graduate students—Amber Ussery and Kara Ellerby—for their teaching skills and critical scholarship. As ever, Spike is indebted to friends and family— near and far—whose love, laughter, partying, and passionate activism "keep her keepin' on." Her heartfelt thanks to these and all who dare to imagine—and create—a world with less pain and much more dancing.

Many of the members of our wider feminist community are reflected in this book, but we especially acknowledge those who have been among our longest-term mentors, collaborators, friends, and sister-partiers (!): Cynthia, Ann, Jindy, Marianne, Jane, Marysia, Cindy, Sandy, Lily, Anna, Simona, Carol, Francine, Deborah, Gillian, Berenice, Val, Shirin, Kathy, Judy, and Laila. There are so many more who have inspired us, changed us, and supported us. Thanks to you all.

We also pay tribute to our families for nurturing our feminist sensibilities as they nurtured us. Anne especially dedicates this edition to her sister, Margery, who is among the many sisters to whom it is broadly dedicated. Our partners, Al and CJ, sustained us through this project (as well as much else over time), providing the care and emotional support that are always so desperately needed by anyone writing a book (as they have repeatedly learned and have so lovingly accepted time and time again).

Finally, we take this opportunity to "hug" each other. Although separated by space and somewhat differing trajectories over time, we have maintained our intellectual and affective connections and lovingly supported each other through thick and thin. The depth of our friendship defies description, but it has made possible so much and has given us so much.

V. Spike Peterson
Anne Sisson Runyan

Acknowledgments to the Second Edition

Contrary to common assumptions and our expectations, a second edition can be more difficult than the first. In this case, we faced the challenge of both documenting how the world has radically changed and reflecting how the field of gender and international relations has substantially grown since the early 1990s. When our first edition appeared, the Cold War had barely subsided and the process of globalization or global restructuring was only beginning to be analyzed. There were also few book-length treatments of gender and world politics available. Unfortunately, the few hopeful signs that the world was changing for the better in the early 1990s dissipated quickly. Encouragingly, however, the reassertions of oppressive world-politics-as-usual have been met by the broadening and deepening of local, national, and transnational women's and other gender-aware social movements committed to political, economic, social, cultural, and ecological justice. Feminist challenges to the study of international-relations-as-usual have also proliferated, within as well as outside of the discipline. We take particular pleasure in noting the extensive book and journal literature produced by members of the now ten-year-old Feminist Theory and Gender Studies section of the International Studies Association.

It is these women and men, struggling in progressive social movements and doing critical work in academe, whom we especially thank for continuing to build supportive, caring, and joyous communities that enlarge the space for feminist transformations of the international relations field and world politics more generally. We cannot do justice to the breadth and complexity of their work, but we do acknowledge how crucial these communities of activists, scholars, teachers, and friends are to our well-being and that of the planet.

Thanks also go to the many teachers around the world who have used the first edition of our book to introduce the study of gender and international relations to students in their undergraduate and graduate courses. It is for them and for their (and our) many students—who are the future of feminist international relations thought and feminist world politics practice—that we prepared this second edition. We can only hope it will continue to serve this important purpose and its readers well.

In addition, we wish to thank the many people who suggested changes to and provided new materials for this second edition. They include Marianne Marchand, Sandra Whitworth (and her students), Margaret Leahy, Laura Parisi, Cynthia Enloe, and several anonymous reviewers. We could not address all of their insightful comments without producing an entirely new book, but we have accommodated many of their suggestions and are grateful for the time and energy they invested. Many thanks, too, go to the numerous artists, cartoonists, and photographers whose images of gender injustice and women's struggles enliven the pages of this book.

We also acknowledge Westview Press for seeing the need for and encouraging us to produce a second edition. Thanks in particular go to the series editor, George Lopez; the Westview editorial staff in New York, including Leo Wiegman, Adina Popescu, and Kwon Chong; and Jane Raese and Kristin Milavec as well as other Westview production staff members in Boulder. Special thanks go to Christine Arden for competent and insightful copyediting. We all weathered the storms of ownership and staffing changes at Westview and look forward to its continued commitment to publishing progressive texts on world politics.

More personally, Anne is indebted to her support staff at Wright State University, including Joanne Ballmann for her extraordinary manuscript production skills and many kindnesses; Women's Studies secretary Pamela Mondini and Women's Studies student assistant Jacqueline Ingram for their help with correspondence, research, and photocopying; and graphic artist Bruce Stiver for the production of charts and graphs. Anne is also grateful for the faculty development grant and other travel and research funds that were provided by Wright State University's College of Liberal Arts to subsidize the preparation of the manuscript.

Anne further thanks family, friends, and colleagues nearby and far away for nurturing and nourishing her feminist ideals and work. Although her sister, Malinda, did not live to see the first edition and her father passed away during the preparation of the second, they live on in her commitments to social justice, which they shared. Her mother, whom she now can take care of, continues to teach her and her remaining sisters to remember. To her husband, Albert Adrian Kanters, she owes her deepest gratitude for his loving support of her work and her life for so long. And to Spike go love and sisterhood always.

Spike is indebted to a number of overlapping communities. Closest to her heart, because they provide affirmation, sustenance, and partnership-in-partying, are close friends: especially rosie, eva, paula, and jane. A wider circle of feminists in Tucson, family in Illinois, and friends around the world constitute a community of support and inspiration for which Spike expresses deep gratitude and affection. Students make a different difference. Their questions, insights, challenges, contributions, and, often, friendship make academe a place worth being. Friends among the Feminist Theory and Gender Studies section constitute another special community. Their personal support, solidarity of spirit, and professional interventions in the field of international relations make it, too, a place worth being. Less concrete but equally crucial, the scholarship and activism of feminists around the world are sources of inspiration to Spike. Being critical of domination takes courage; doing it with love in your heart and in your strategies takes much more. Spike honors and thanks the loving radicals who combine these traits, and especially the many who face dire consequences for doing so.

Finally, Spike is still learning to decipher Anne's handwriting—and still learning from her how to love better. But the best part is how they laugh together.

V. Spike Peterson
Anne Sisson Runyan

Acknowledgments to the First Edition

Venturing into new terrain requires vision as well as commitment. Our thanks go first to George Lopez, the series editor, for recognizing the importance of gender as a dilemma in world politics. Jennifer Knerr's professional guidance and personal warmth were invaluable for keeping not only our efforts but also our enthusiasm on track. Of the many other people at Westview who eased our task, and editorial board members who supported our project, we thank especially Marian Safran, Libby Barstow, Deborah Gerner, and Karen Mingst. From start to finish, the farsightedness and expertise of Lev Gonick and Mary Ann Tetreault have enhanced this project and its product.

Exploring new terrain requires bold spirits and reliable support systems. Among the bold spirits, we thank our foremothers, who took great risks to clear new paths, and our feminist colleagues, who also take risks in order to pursue and expand those paths. Our support system is the global community of feminists who refuse to separate theory and practice. Of the countless women and men who make up this community, we thank especially our friends in the Feminist Theory and Gender Studies section of the International Studies Association, who have given us invaluable support, encouragement—and permission to party. In particular, because the integrity of their energy makes such an important difference, we acknowledge our appreciation of Simona Sharoni, Theresa Scionti, and Judy Logan.

More personally, Anne thanks her secretary, Jackie Brisson, and her student assistants, Michele Sylvestri and Mary Burns, for their tremendous assistance with research, photocopying, mailings, and tracking down addresses and phone numbers (mostly of illustration copyright holders, many of whom were very gracious and helpful). It was, indeed, an all-women struggle at SUNY-Potsdam that brought Anne's part of the book to fruition. She also thanks her husband, Al Kanters, who, as always, lovingly cared for her basic needs throughout this project. It is the reproductive work of men like him that makes the productive work of women possible. She is also grateful to family members, friends, and colleagues, close by and far away, who have so strongly supported her feminist ideals and her feminist work. Finally, she offers her heartfelt appreciation to Spike, who has been not only an intellectual partner but a dear friend and true "sister."

Spike leaned heavily on the research assistance and emotional support so effectively rendered by graduate students Stacey Mayhall, Jacqui True, and Anwara Begum. Words only begin to convey how the community generated during the states seminar has enhanced Spike's quality of life. She is indebted to this group especially—and students more generally—because they not only make the hard work worthwhile but also keep her mentally and physically dancing. "It doesn't get any better than this." Her deepest thanks, as ever, go to family and friends whose love, affirmation, and inspiration keep her going—and growing; to those whose ways of being, loving, and knowing offer a lighted path: thanks especially to beryl, eva, rosie, and ozone. Finally, she wants to let Anne know that the best part of this project, like their friendship, was/is learning to love better, for which Anne gets the credit.

V. Spike Peterson
Anne Sisson Runyan

Acronyms

ICC International Criminal Court
ICERD International Convention on the Elimination of All Forms of Racial Discrimination
ICJ International Court of Justice
ICTs information and communications technologies
ICTR International Criminal Tribunal for Rwanda
ICTY International Criminal Tribunal for the former Yugoslavia
IDPs internally displaced persons
IFIs international financial institutions
IGOs intergovernmental organizations
ILO International Labor Organization
IMF International Monetary Fund
IPE international political economy
IPU Inter-Parliamentary Union
IR international relations
IRA Irish Republican Army
IWPR Institute for Women's Policy Research
IWRAW International Women's Rights Action Watch
LGBTQ lesbian, gay, bisexual, transgender, transsexual, queer, questioning
MDGs United Nations Millennium Development Goals
MPs members of parliament
MST military sexual trauma
NAFTA North American Free Trade Agreement
NGOs nongovernmental organizations
OECD Organization for Economic Cooperation and Development
OSAGI United Nations Office of the Special Adviser to the Secretary-General on Gender Issues and Advancement of Women
PR proportional representation
PTSD post-traumatic stress disorder
R&R rest and recreation
RAWA Revolutionary Association of the Women of Afghanistan
SAPs structural adjustment programs

SERNAM Servicio Nacional de la Mujer/National Office for Women's Affairs

SOFAs Status of Forces Agreements

TFNs transnational feminist networks

TNCs transnational corporations

TRIPs (Agreement on) Trade-Related Aspects of Intellectual Property Rights

TSNs transnational social networks

UK United Kingdom

UN United Nations

UNAIDS Joint United Nations Program on HIV/AIDS

UNDAW United Nations Division for the Advancement of Women

UNDP United Nations Development Program

UNEP United Nations Environment Program

UNESCO United Nations Educational, Scientific, and Cultural Organization

UNFCCC United Nations Framework Convention on Climate Change

UNFPA United Nations Fund for Population Activities

UNHCR Office of the United Nations High Commissioner for Refugees

UNICEF United Nations Children's Fund

UNIFEM United Nations Development Fund for Women

UN-INSTRAW United Nations International Research and Training Institute for the Advancement of Women

UNITAR United Nations Institute for Training and Research

US United States (of America)

WCAR United Nations World Conference Against Racism

WEDO Women's Environment and Development Organization

WHO World Health Organization

WID women in development

WIIS Women in International Security

WILPF Women's International League for Peace and Freedom

WREI Women's Research and Education Institute

WTO World Trade Organization

1

Introduction

Gender and Global Issues

Not long ago, gender was not considered a legitimate category of analysis for the study of world politics. Today, gender analysis constitutes an accepted and burgeoning part of international relations (IR) inquiry and a significant international policy tool. These advances in taking gender seriously as a lens on, or explanatory framework for, world politics and in incorporating gender as a matter of international policymaking resulted primarily from the work of feminist IR or feminist world politics scholars and activists over the past few decades. They began gender inquiry by asking "Where are the women?" in international affairs. Although this was an important starting point, it is important to recognize that gender inquiry in IR is not reducible to it.

In this introductory chapter, we set out our basic premises for the present examination of the relationship between gender and world politics. The emphasis here is different from in the first two editions of this text, which were generated at earlier stages of feminist IR inquiry. This selective survey of feminist perspectives on world politics shifts from a focus on the positions of women in world affairs as state, antistate, and transstate actors to a focus on the *re-positionings of both women and men* in the face of the changing nature of global governance, global security, and global political economy. This emphasizes, on the one hand, the gains made in international and national gender policymaking that elevate some women, and, on the other hand, the setbacks to achieving greater social equality and justice arising from a series of contemporary global crises. As in earlier editions, we invoke the concept of the *power of*

1

gender, but this time to account particularly for the contemporary contradiction between increased attention to gender equality and "women's issues" in international politics inquiry and policy and the worsening of global crises. We retain the notion of gender as a lens on world politics, but we emphasize that the power of gender acts as a *meta-lens* that fosters dichotomization, stratification, and depoliticization in thought and action, sustaining global power structures and crises that prevent or mitigate against meaningful advances in social equality and justice. Also as in previous editions, we employ the matrices of the *gendered divisions of power, violence,* and *labor and resources* not only to track the positioning and re-positionings of diverse women and men in relation to global governance institutions, global security apparatuses, and global political economy formations, but also to show how the power of gender operates in these contexts to maintain interlocking inequalities based on gender, race, class, sexuality, and nationality (including inequalities among nations and with respect to national origin). We argue that inattention to the interlocking nature of these inequalities—an insight derived from intersectional analysis—has resulted in problematic gender equality policymaking. Such policymaking tends to target only women and fails to take into account inequalities among women. It further deflects attention from such interlocking forces as neoliberal governmentality, militarization, and globalization, which undercut equality and social justice efforts. These forces are responsible for what we refer to as the *crises of representation, insecurity,* and *sustainability* that diverse women and men are resisting at local, national, and transnational levels.

GENDER AND GLOBAL CRISES

Gender "is not synonymous with women" (Carver 1996). Rather, it generally refers to the socially learned behaviors, repeated performances, and idealized expectations that are associated with and distinguish between the proscribed gender roles of masculinity and femininity. As such, it is not the same as and may be wholly unrelated to sex, which is typically defined as the biological and anatomical characteristics that distinguish between women's and men's bodies. Contemporary feminist analysis argues that sex, too, is socially constructed because it is only through the meanings given to and the marshaling of particular biological and anatomical characteristics that sex difference, as an unequivocal binary, is naturalized and enforced, including surgically when children born with ambiguous sexual organs are made into either "girls" or "boys" to sustain the idea that there are only two sexes (Fausto-Sterling 1992 and 2000). Gender analysis includes challenging not only the biologically determinist idea that dualistic gender identities and roles arise from natural sex difference, but also the notion that sex difference itself is natural and dualistic, calling into question even our assumptions about a world made up of only "females" and "males," "girls" and "boys," "men" and "women." Thus, gender is as much about the socially constructed categories of "men" and masculinity as it is about the socially constructed categories of "women" and femininity. It also recognizes that there are multiple genders, as well as sexes, because race/ethnicity, class, sexuality, and other cultural variations shape gender identities and performances.

Moreover, gender analysis reveals that masculine and feminine "natures" are not simply inscribed on what are assumed to be distinct male and female bodies, but also are applied to other objects, including things, nonhuman beings, groups, institutions, and even nations and states. Consider references to a ship or car as "she," invocations of "mother nature," characterizations of opposing sports teams as "wimpy" while one's own is "mighty," notions of "motherlands" and "fatherlands," and categorizations of "strong" and "weak" states. Everyday parlance is rife with gender appellations and metaphors. As we discuss at great length in Chapter 2, this constant gendering of natural, artificial, and social worlds through language and, thus, thought is no trivial matter. Gendering operates to set up and reinforce dualistic, dichotomous, or either-or thinking, but it also fosters hierarchical thinking in which those people and objects assigned masculine qualities are valued or given power over those assigned feminine qualities. Thus, as part of feminist IR inquiry, our approach is foremost about how gender, as a meta-lens that orders thinking and thus social reality and action, serves as a major source of power projections and inequalities in world affairs. We refer to this as the *power of gender*. Making the power of gender visible, however, first depended on making women and their positionings visible in international politics.

Tracking the positionings of women in world affairs became possible when governments around the world—since the first United Nations (UN) conference on women in 1975—committed to provide data regularly to the UN that disaggregated the roles men and women play in state governance, militaries, diplomatic machineries, and economies. By the end of the last millennium, the data regarding how men and women are situated differently around the world revealed, starkly, the extent of gender inequality. In 1997 the UN Development Program (UNDP) unequivocally concluded that "no society treats its women as well as its men" (UNDP 1997: 39). Such a conclusion was based on reports to the UN Committee on the Status of Women that although women composed one-half of the world's population, they performed the majority of the world's work hours when counting unpaid labor, yet in aggregate were poorer in resources and poorly represented in elite positions of decision-making power (Tickner 1993: 75). As we point out in this chapter and in others to follow, little has changed in these material conditions for most women, but much has changed in terms of the attention brought to the issue of gender in the international community. For example, over the past decade or two and as a result of both feminist IR inquiry and activism by feminist international nongovernmental organizations (NGOs), such policies as gender quotas (to get more women into elective office) and gender mainstreaming (designed to avoid building gender discrimination into any government policy) have been heavily promoted and used by the UN and other international governmental organizations (IGOs), causing their adoption across many parts of the world. Such gender gains have had a modicum of effect on the *re-positionings* of some women.

Despite these recent gender gains in terms of the legitimation of gender inquiry and policy at the international level, particularly in relation to re-positioning (some) women in world politics, it is also the case that global crises have worsened at the same time. While previous "hot" and "cold" wars since the times of the first colonial conquests have wreaked considerable havoc and violence that continue to this day, the current rise in international violence is often pegged as a "post-9/11" phenomenon following the September 11, 2001, terrorist attacks on the United States. The Bush administration chose to respond to this through wars in Afghanistan and Iraq, as well as a legitimation of torture and rendition in the name of national security and the global "war on terror," thereby justifying any violence across the globe done in its name.[1] The recent upsurge of a global economic crisis is tied to the deregulation and manipulation of financial markets in the North with reverberations in the South, but these have earlier roots in neoliberal restructuring at least since the 1970s. At the same time, past colonizations and imperialisms continue to exert effects materially and ideologically, whether in the forms of gross economic inequalities, civil wars, ethnic cleansing, or the rise of a range of fundamentalisms. The planetary crisis of global warming has its roots in the industrial revolution, although the poisoning of the atmosphere has certainly accelerated as global capitalist-led industrial production has permeated the globe in more recent years.

Such crises are undermining modest gender gains as they worsen economic, political, and social inequalities, ratchet up violence, and threaten the very foundations of human and other life on the planet. We refer to these interacting global crises throughout the text as the *crises of representation, insecurity,* and *sustainability*. The crisis of *representation* entails inequalities not only in political representation in formal power structures but also in NGOs and social movements, which can hamper more complex and fuller analyses of "global" problems that can take different forms in "local" contexts. Without a range of perspectives from varying social locations, proposed solutions by the few (and most privileged) can do more harm than good. Moreover, the crisis of representation refers to how groups are "framed" in problem analysis and solutions. For example, if "Third World women" are constructed "under Western eyes" as only "victims," then they are denied agency and the ability to exercise their own approaches to local and global problemsolving (Mohanty 1991). The crisis of *insecurity* relates to not only the direct violence of international and intranational conflict, but also to the structural violence of political, economic, and social priorities and inequalities that leave wide swaths of people subject to unemployment, underemployment, poverty, disease, malnutrition, crime, and domestic and sexual violence. The crisis of *sustainability* refers to a crisis both of social reproduction and of resource depletion. The former is shorthand for the systematic disabling of households and human communities to cope and care for each other and future generations, whereas the latter is shorthand for the systematic disabling of the environment to sustain human communities. Both are the result of narrow constructions and obsessions with "growth," the pursuit of which enslaves all and mitigates against reprioritizations that are not market-based. We relate these crises to gendered divisions of power, violence, and labor and resources (described at the end of Chapter 2) from which they arise and that sorely limit the re-positionings of women and other subjugated people(s) to have a say in world politics and to resist global power structures and the crises they induce.

The seeming contradiction between rising international attention to ameliorating gender inequality—which is now seen by many UN agencies and many member states as a significant source of global political, economic, and social problems—and the deepening of global crises that are undermining this acknowledgment and its implementation constitutes our central theme. This contradiction relates to some current conundrums in feminist IR inquiry. Whereas prior editions of this book were devoted to introducing the case for the relationship between gender inequality and global crises that was featured in initial feminist IR inquiry, the problem now is somewhat different. First, despite some gender policy gains at international and national levels, attention to the relationship between gender inequality and global problems is still insufficient. Second, policymaking bodies have interpreted gender equality narrowly to mean only raising the status of women relative to men, without regard to inequalities among both women and men that arise from class, ethnicity/race, sexuality, and national divisions. Just as problematically, such bodies have used stereotypes of women and men to promote raising the status of women so that women are cast—whether as peacemakers, responsible debt-payers, or innocent victims—as the solutions to global problems, while certain men—usually lower-class men and men of color or of the global South—are cast as backward, violence-prone rogues who stand in the way of gender equality and constitute the main sources of global problems. Some feminist scholars and activists have sometimes contributed to this kind of stereotyping or "framing," for example, when arguing for women's empowerment on the world stage. But this stereotyping is more pernicious when taken up by policy-making power structures to deflect attention away from larger causes and results of gender and other inequalities, which include militarization and global capitalism.

In our previous editions, we connected the dominant world political commitments to militarization and global capitalism, on one hand, to the power of gender to sustain dichotomous and hierarchical worldviews, on the other. In this edition, we emphasize even more that the power of gender in world politics remains intact despite policy and positional gains for women. In doing so, we complicate the category of "women" and the notion of "gender" by engaging more consciously in "intersectional analysis" in order to minimize reproducing stereotypes of women and men that can be deployed by policymakers to avoid the more complex challenges of changing world-politics-as-usual.

Intersectional analysis holds that there are no generic women and men; our gender identities, loyalties, interests, and opportunities are affected by intersecting and cross-cutting gender, race, class, national, and sexual identities. Whereas some parts of our identities may confer privilege, others may serve to disadvantage us. For example, a white American working-class lesbian would be privileged by race and nationality but not by class, gender, and sexuality. This has implications for theorizing about the gender categories of masculinity and femininity but also for analyzing inequalities. It is now accepted that there are multiple forms of masculinity that not only vary over time and across cultures but also confer different levels of power. What is referred to as "hegemonic masculinity" (Connell 1987 and 1995) is the ideal form of masculinity performed by men with the most power attributes, who not incidentally populate most global power positions—typically white, Western, upper-class, straight men who have conferred on them the complete range of gender, race, class, national, and sexuality privileges. "Subordinated masculinities" (Connell 1987 and 1995) are embodied by those who lack one, some, or all of these privileges and thus are rendered "feminized" on these scores. Although all femininities are subordinated to all masculinities, it is also the case that some femininities are subordinated more than or differently from others. The idealized image of Western femininity remains associated with Victorian notions of womanhood that celebrated the gentility, passivity, decorativeness, and asexuality that was imposed on white, middle- to upper-class women who were the only ones who could enact such standards. Working-class women, women of color, and/or lesbians are either denied the (dubious) status of feminine because they cannot meet these standards, or are feminized (that is, devalorized) in other ways through processes of racialization and/or sexualization. For example, since the times of slavery and colonization, women of color have been labeled as naturally oversexual, thereby not only being unworthy of (white) male protection but also particularly open to (white) male sexual exploitation.

This form of analysis will guide our examination of the power of gender to naturalize inequalities and power relations not only between and among women and men, but also between and among states, cultures, institutions, organizations, policies, practices, and even ideas and perspectives in the global system. As laid out in the map of the book that concludes this chapter, our examination will show the power of gender at work in the lenses we use to analyze world politics in the contexts of global governance, global security, and global political economy. In the process, we will explore what it would take to de-gender world politics.

GENDER GAINS: RE-POSITIONINGS OF WOMEN AND MEN IN WORLD POLITICS

Gender and International Relations Inquiry

Gender analysis in IR inquiry has become a subfield of the discipline, and feminist perspectives on world politics now appear alongside or in combination with other, longer legitimated ones, such as (neo)realism, idealism or (neo)liberalism, and (neo)Marxism, and more recent ones, such as constructivist, poststructuralist, and postcolonial perspectives. We explore gender as a lens on world politics in Chapter 2 in significant detail, but here we briefly introduce the development of gender inquiry in IR and its impact on giving gender substantive consideration in world politics thinking.

As already noted, gender inquiry in IR began with the question "Where are the women?" in international affairs, as they appeared absent in typical accounts of the rise of great powers, their leaders, their weaponries, and their wars, as well as dominant theories about the nature of and interactions among states and their economies. This seemingly simplistic question has yielded many insights. First, it has revealed that women are not absent in world affairs, even though they are rarely present in the top echelons of states, corporations, and IGOs. Instead, they tend to play roles that (1) grease the wheels of world politics, such as military or diplomatic wives who enable men to make war or peace by taking care of men's needs through freeing them for combat or creating social environments for men to negotiate, or sex workers who provide R&R to combat troops in service to sustaining militaries; (2) produce the wheels of world politics by sustaining everyday life in households and serving primarily as low-paid workers in defense plants, assembly work, agribusiness, and domestic, sexual, social, and clerical service industries—thereby undergirding the world's production of weapons, goods, and services—while also being situated as the predominant consumers of goods for households; and/or (3) derail the wheels of world politics through social movements and NGOs that protest world-politics-as-usual, whether in resistance to dictators, global capitalism, nuclear weapons, or natural resource depletion and destruction (Enloe 1989). Such observations have led to an understanding that women are, in fact, central to the operations we associate with world politics, but their centrality in relation to greasing and producing the wheels of world-politics-as-usual rests upon their invisibility and conformity to "acting like 'women'"—that is, subservient to men. Second, the positioning of women in world affairs has also illuminated the positionings of men. Prior to gender inquiry in IR, the fact that men dominated positions of power in world politics remained unremarked upon. It was just assumed that men would hold such positions of power, and there was no interest in why or with what effects. Asking the "man question" in international relations (Zalewski and Parpart 1998; Parpart and Zalewski 2008) draws attention to what "acting like 'men'" means for the conduct and outcomes of international politics.

Acting like "women" and "men" is central to (but does not exhaust) what is meant by gender, referring here to an acquired identity gained through performing the proscribed gender roles of femininity and masculinity. Moreover, because societies place different values on masculinity and femininity, gender is also the basis for relations of inequality between men and women. Finally, as we explore more thoroughly in Chapter 2, gender is a particularly powerful lens through which all of us see and organize reality.

We learn, through culturally specific socialization, what characteristics are associated with masculinity and femininity and how to assume the identities of men and women. In this sense, "gender refers to characteristics linked to a particular sex by one's culture" (D'Amico and Beckman 1994: 3). The specific meanings of and values given to masculinity and femininity vary dramatically over time and across cultures. For example, Western ideals of "manliness" have undergone historical shifts: From the early Greeks through the feudal period, the emphasis of idealized masculinity was on military heroism and political prowess through male bonding and risk-taking, whereas more modern meanings of masculinity stress "competitive individualism, reason, self-control or self-denial, combining respectability as breadwinner and head of household with calculative rationality in public life" (Hooper 1998: 33). Moreover, not all cultures have associated either of these conceptions of masculinity with leadership qualities: "Queen mothers" in Ghana and "clan mothers" in many Native American societies have been accorded power and leadership roles in these matrilineal contexts on the basis of the feminine quality of regeneration of the people and the land (Okojo 1994: 286; Guerrero 1997: 215). Furthermore, there is some play in gender roles even within patrilineal or patriarchal cultures, given that men are not exclusively leaders and warriors, and women are not exclusively in charge of maintaining the home and caring for children. Due to the variation in meanings attached to femininity and masculinity, we know that expressions of gender are not "fixed" or predetermined: The particulars of gender are always shaped by context. However, these variations still rest on concepts of gender differences and do not necessarily disrupt gender as an oppositional dichotomy and as a relation of inequality.

A focus on gender in IR arose not because other axes of difference and bases of inequality (e.g., race/ethnicity, class, religion, age) are less important than—or even extricable from—gender, as we discuss later in this chapter. Rather, gender became a significant lens through which to view world politics as feminist researchers and social movement activists increasingly documented the worldwide institutionalization of gender *differences* as a major underpinning of structural inequalities of significance to world politics. Through a complex interaction of identification processes, symbol systems, and social institutions (explored in subsequent chapters), gender differences are produced—typically in the form of a *dichotomy* that not only opposes masculinity to femininity but also translates these oppositional differences into *gender hierarchy*, the privileging of traits and activities defined as masculine over those defined as feminine. Thus, although it is important to recognize the cultural variation in how gender differences are formed and expressed, it is also important to stress the political nature of gender as a system of difference construction and hierarchical dichotomy production that constitutes virtually all contemporary societies. Gender is about power, and power is gendered. How power operates in this way starts to become visible in an examination of the relationship between masculinity and femininity.

Here we make two points in regard to this relationship in order to elucidate what is meant by gender dichotomy and hierarchy. First, masculinity and femininity are not "independent" categories, such as fruit, children, or labor, but are defined in oppositional "relation" to each other: More of one is understood to mean less of the other—as with ripe versus unripe fruit, active versus passive children, mental versus manual labor. Specifically, the dominant masculinity in Western culture, what we referred to earlier as "hegemonic masculinity," is associated with qualities of rationality, "hardheadedness," ambition, and strength. To the extent that a man displays emotionality, "softheadedness," passivity, and weakness, he is likely to be identified as nonmasculine, which is to say, feminine. Similarly, women who appear hardheaded and ambitious are often described as masculine.

Second, the relationship between masculinity and femininity shows considerable constancy in greater value being assigned to that which is associated with masculinity and lesser value to that which is associated with femininity. Again, the terms are not independent but form a hierarchical (unequal) relation that we refer to as a *dichotomy* (explored further in Chapter 2). Thus, in most—but not all—situations, rationality, hardheadedness, ambition, and strength are perceived as positive and admired traits that are in contrast to less desirable feminine qualities. This hierarchy is readily observed. Consider (in the United States) how different our response is to women wearing pants and even business suits compared with our response to men wearing dresses, ruffles, or flowery prints. Similarly, girls can be tomboys and adopt boyish names, but boys avoid behaving in ways that might result in their being called "sissies" or girlish names. We applaud women who achieve success in previously male-dominated activities (climbing mountains, becoming astronauts, presiding over colleges), but men who enter traditionally female arenas (water ballet, child care, nursing) are rarely applauded and often treated with suspicion. Females who dress or act like males appear to be copying or aiming for something valued—they are attempting to improve their status by "moving up." But because feminine characteristics are less valued, boys and men who adopt feminine dress or undertake female roles are more likely to be perceived as failing in their manhood or "moving down."

Gender shapes not only how we identify ourselves and view the world but also how others identify and relate to us and how we are positioned within social structures. Gender divisions of labor particularly exemplify the either-or construction that constitutes the dichotomy of masculine and feminine. Consider that women are traditionally associated with childbearing, child rearing, emotional caretaking, and responsibility for the physical maintenance of the household. In contrast, men are associated with the activities of wage labor, physical prowess, intellectual achievements, and political agency. This gender labeling is so strong that even when women work for wages (and women have been wage workers as long as men have), they typically do so in areas regarded as "women's work": taking care of others and providing emotional and maintenance services (counseling, welfare services, clerical support, cleaning).

Labor markets are thus segregated horizontally by gender, with women and men clustered in different occupational roles. They are also segregated vertically, with women concentrated in the lowest-paid, least-protected, and least-powerful positions. And when individual women move up corporate ladders, they often run into a "glass ceiling" that obstructs their access to the most powerful positions. This horizontal and vertical gender segregation accounts in part for the fact that women in the paid labor force worldwide earn about two-thirds of what men earn (NCRW 2006: 28).

The point is that stereotypes of gender (masculinity and femininity) have consequences for the difference between men's and women's experience in, for example, earning money and exercising public power. The disproportional presence or absence of women or men in a given activity does not suggest gender neutrality but in fact demonstrates the personal, political, systemic, and structural effects of hierarchical gender differentiation. The latter involves defining different qualities, roles, and activities for men and women and ensuring the reproduction of these discriminatory structures.

Because of the interdependent nature of this relationship, we learn about both women and men—femininity and masculinity—when we study gender. When we look at activities associated with masculinity (e.g., competitive sports, politics, militaries), it appears simply that men are present and women are absent. Moreover, it appears that we can explain this result simply by attending to the men engaging in these activities. Gender analysis, however, offers a more complex and comprehensive explanation; it enables us to "see" how women are in fact important to the picture (enabling men's activities, providing reasons for men to fight), even though women and the roles they are expected to play are obscured when we focus only on men. Through a gender-sensitive lens, we see how constructions of masculinity (agency, control, aggression) are not independent of, but rely upon, contrasting constructions of femininity (dependence, vulnerability, passivity). In an important sense, the dominant presence of men and the overvaluing of masculinity depend on the absence of women and the devaluing of femininity. Because of this interdependence, using gender analysis in IR does not merely reveal heretofore unseen conditions and roles of women in world politics, but "transforms" what we know about men and the activities they undertake in international affairs. Hence, the study of gender alters our understandings of the conventional foci of IR—power politics, war, and economic control—by exposing what more deeply underpins them and why they are given such prominence over other ways of thinking about and acting in the world.

In general, gender analysts in IR operate from feminist perspectives, which, although varied, share minimally a concern with the problem of gender inequality as a motivation for research. They have found in their examinations that individuals, institutions, and practices associated with masculinity (men, states, war-making, wealth production) are highly valued in political and world political thought, whereas those individuals, institutions, and practices associated with femininity (women, local or international political formations, peace-making, and poverty reduction) are more typically devalued and even dismissed in such thinking. This is key to what we mean by the power of gender—the pervasiveness of gender as a filtering category or meta-lens. That is, gender-sensitive research does more than document the pattern of excluding or trivializing women and their experiences while inflating men's experiences and power. It documents how gender—characterizations of masculinity and femininity—can influence the very categories and frameworks within which scholars work.

In short, how we understand and value masculine and feminine characteristics profoundly shapes how we care about, perceive, understand, analyze, and critique the world in which we live. Gender thus influences not only who we are, how we live, and what we have, but also how we think, order reality, and claim to know what is true, and, hence, how we understand and explain the social world as well as what alternative realities could be created in that world.

Although the power of gender continues to structure and limit our vision, in recent decades feminist IR researchers—whether in academe, NGOs, or IGOs—have accumulated increasing evidence that gender equity is strongly related to the quality of life for everyone in every country (Eisler, Loye, and Norgaard 1995; Eisler 2007). The fundamental message from this research has been that "empowering women and improving their status are essential to realizing the full potential of economic, political and social development" (UN 1995: xvii). Hence, all those who seek a better world have been advised to take seriously the bettering of women's positions. These findings and arguments have not fallen on deaf ears. IGO and state policymakers—facing new challenges in the post–Cold War and post-9/11 contexts that feature widening violent conflicts, economic inequalities, social and cultural divisions, and environmental breakdowns—have become increasingly open to accepting that the improvement of women's positions can bring improvements in world conditions. This acknowledgment was hard won by scholars and social movement actors who have built access to and influence on UN and member state governments since the beginning of the UN Decade for Women in 1975. From this acknowledgment has flowed an unprecedented array of national and international gender policies, referred to by one feminist IR specialist as "the new politics of gender equality" (Squires 2007). This shift in policymaking, which constitutes in a sense the re-positioning of gender on the world politics agenda from relative absence to increasing presence, relates to the re-positionings of women (and men) that constitutes a running theme in this text.

Gender in International Policymaking

Angela Merkel of Germany, Michelle Bachelet of Chile, Ellen Johnson-Sirleaf of Liberia, Benazir Bhutto of Pakistan (assassinated in 2007), and

Hillary Rodham Clinton of the United States—these are only a few of the women who most recently have become or sought to become heads of state and/or government. Although 2008 was the first time that a woman was taken seriously as a candidate for U.S. president, some fifty-eight other women have been elected as presidents or prime ministers during the twentieth and twenty-first centuries in almost as many countries (Hoogensen and Solheim 2006: 15). Albeit comparatively late, Clinton's historic candidacy in the United States did serve to make gender—for a time—a major political topic in the country. Their numbers are still comparatively very low, but arguably women as world leaders have become slightly less anomalous. Nevertheless, severe barriers remain (discussed in Chapter 3).

Among the recent developments that could significantly increase the numbers of women heads of state and governments is the adoption of some form of gender quota in at least 90 countries (Dahlerup 2006b: 3). Drude Dahlerup identifies this as "a global trend" stretching back to 1990 when the UN Economic and Social Council (ECOSOC) supported the goal lobbied for by women's movements to have 30 percent of world decision-making positions held by women by 1995 (2006b: 6). As of 2005, only 16 percent of the world's parliamentarians were women; however, 17 countries had reached or exceeded the 30 percent target, with postgenocide Rwanda topping the list at 48.5 percent (and in 2008 becoming the first country with more female than male legislators), followed by the Nordic countries, and a mix of Latin American and other northern European and African states (Dahlerup 2006b: 6–7). Almost all of these had legal or party gender quota systems in combination with proportional representation systems (defined and discussed in Chapter 3). Although quota systems vary in form and efficacy, they were specifically promoted in the Platform for Action[2] arising from the UN World Women's Conference in Beijing in 1995, which was unanimously supported by the world's governments, as the "fast-track" way to increase women's political representation. Following that conference, in Latin America alone, 11 out of 19 governments had adopted either constitutional or legal gender quotas by 2000 (Araújo and García 2006: 83). There are many reasons for this recent "contagion" of gender quotas, but among them is a growing international consensus or norm, advocated by women's movements worldwide and supported by feminist scholarship, that gender equality in the form of women's greater political representation, ideally to the point of parity with men, is necessary for polities claiming or aspiring to be modern and democratic.

Gender mainstreaming also gained momentum and increasing acceptance during the same period that gender quotas were advancing. Although definitions vary somewhat, gender mainstreaming refers generally to integrating the principle of gender equality into any (inter)governmental policy (not just those associated with so-called women's issues, such as family and violence against women) to ensure that in practice it does not, wittingly or unwittingly, increase or sustain inequalities between women and men (Squires 2007: 39–40). It was first advocated in the context of economic development policies where it was found by feminist research from the 1970s onward that approaches taken by bodies like the World Bank, such as the promotion of capital-intensive agriculture for export, tended to privilege men who had or were given more access to capital, agricultural inputs and machinery, and land ownership. Women, although heavily involved in subsistence agriculture that is the main source of family food consumption, were not seen as farmers or landowners and, thus, did not benefit from this kind of World Bank funding. This disparity not only increased men's power over women in agricultural work and families, but also contributed to producing more hunger and malnutrition when women's work of subsistence farming was increasingly so devalued and unsupported. The World Bank and a number of other supranational institutions, ranging from the UN and the Organization for Economic Cooperation and Development (OECD) to the European Union (EU), as well as many development agencies within states in the North, have been convinced by such findings to adopt gender mainstreaming, also called for in the Beijing Platform for Action (BPA), to try to avoid such outcomes (Squires 2007: 42). There have been numerous downsides to this approach (which we address in Chapter 3), but its institutionalization represents a sea change in its recognition that gender is infused in all (world) political issues and legitimizes the need for "gender experts" in world politics.

No less than the UN Security Council, arguably the most male-dominated and masculinist body in the world (that is, steeped in the most hegemonic masculine values associated with power politics), has also acquiesced to giving some attention to gender. For example, Security

Council Resolution 1325,[3] passed in 2000, calls for women to be present at peace negotiating tables, a goal long advocated by women's peace movements that have claimed women have greater interests and different stakes in ending war. As we explore in Chapter 4, it is not that women are inherently more peaceful, but rather their predominantly civilian status means that they are increasingly bearing the high structural costs of modern warfare. With the rise of "total" wars in the twentieth century, wherein there is little separation between the battlefront and the home front, civilians are an increasing proportion of those left homeless, diseased, and hungry, turned into refugees, and made victims of sexual and domestic assault (by enemy and "friendly" combatants). Although combatants still die in greater numbers from direct violence, civilian deaths from direct violence and more often indirect violence continue to rise (Goldstein 2001: 400). The majority of civilians are women and children (both female and male), despite some increases in women in state and nonstate militaries and in child soldiers (both male and female) pressed into combat. Women, as can be seen in the case of postgenocide Rwanda, also are critical to the mending of postconflict societies as they tend to be the backbone of civil society, most centrally recreating households and communities.

Predating this Security Council resolution was a significant codification and prosecution of rape as a war crime following the highly visible use of systematic rape in the early 1990s in the wars in the former Yugoslavia and in Rwanda. Systematic wartime rape not only neutralizes women as threats, but also seeks to weaken men's resolve to fight by "soiling their women" while also trying to wipe out an enemy culture or ethnicity by impregnating women with "alien" seed or keeping them from reproducing altogether. The assumption that rape was merely a natural "spoil of war" (for men) had kept it from being fully recognized as an international war crime until feminist activists and events in Bosnia and Rwanda made it clear that rape was a direct violation of women's human rights, rising to the level of torture as an instrument of warfare.

The ideas that women have human rights and that women's human rights expand traditional definitions of human rights were significantly advanced by the UN Convention on the Elimination of All Forms of Discrimination against Women (CEDAW),[4] initially adopted in 1979 following the UN Decade for Women and going into force in 1981. By

2000, only 25 countries (including most glaringly the United States, as well as a smattering of Muslim and least-developed countries) had failed to ratify CEDAW, making it the second most widely ratified human rights convention (UN 2000: 151). As of 2009, only eight countries, including the United States, remain nonsignatories, although the Obama administration supports CEDAW and is seeking congressional approval for it. Through CEDAW and subsequent UN conferences on human rights, particularly throughout the 1990s, women's movements and NGOs made the case that "women's rights are human rights," achieving international recognition that reproductive and, to some degree, sexual rights were just as important as and connected to political and economic rights. As long as women are denied choices about if, when, and under what conditions they bear children or terminate pregnancies, are subject to sexual and domestic abuse, and are limited in their sexual expressions and orientations, they will not be able to exercise their political and economic rights. Although women's and other human rights continue to be violated on a massive scale, the widespread ratification of CEDAW has given women's movements throughout much of the world a major tool through which to hold their governments accountable for continued abuses.

GLOBAL CRISES:
RE-MASCULINIZATIONS OF WORLD POLITICS

Just as women were gaining voice and ground in international forums and policymaking arenas, particularly in the first decade of the post–Cold War period, a series of political, economic, cultural, and environmental shocks heightened both direct and structural violence in world politics. While so-called hot wars raged in the global South (often as a result of East-West conflict) throughout the Cold War period and into the post–Cold War time (including conflicts in the global North arising out of the unraveling of the former Soviet Union as well as the first U.S.-waged war against Iraq), decisions made in the aftermath of 9/11 produced not only wars in Afghanistan and Iraq waged largely by the United States, but also the so-called global "war on terror." Far from reaping the substantial peace dividend hoped for by this point in the post–Cold War era, world military spending has skyrocketed, reaching almost $1.5 trillion in 2008, with U.S. military spending accounting for 48 percent of the total (Center for Arms Control and Non-Proliferation 2008). Although there was a reduction in military spending primarily by former Warsaw Pact countries in the 1990s, military spending has returned to Cold War highs (WCC 2005: 4). Even more problematic in the U.S. case are the facts that, as of 2004, nine times more was spent on the U.S. military than on homeland security and other nonmilitary security programs with additional evidence that military spending had "tightened spending on social services such as education, health care, and environmental protection" (WCC 2005: 9–10).

This latter effect of military spending is what is referred to as structural violence, or making populations more vulnerable to social, economic, health, and environmental harms. Not only has the United States increased structural violence against its own population in favor of waging direct (and structural) violence abroad, but also a number of other countries, some of which have the weakest social safety nets, have made similar choices, given that most "developing" countries spend as much or more on militaries than on basic social services (WCC 2005: 18). Moreover, nonsecurity-related foreign aid has also been sacrificed to military spending, with almost no "developed" country giving the UN-recommended minimum of .07 percent of GDP annually for this purpose (WCC 2005: 20).

Another major source of structural violence is neoliberal globalization, or the expansion (and imposition) of global capital interconnecting the world's economies, which, in its contemporary form, began in the 1970s and accelerated in the 1990s onward (Peterson 2003). As we write this, the world is gripped in an economic crisis precipitated by poor and poorly regulated lending practices by U.S.-based transnational banks and investment firms, which, for a time, artificially propped up the global capitalist economy in which almost all countries and many of their peoples were expected to become deeply enmeshed. Critics of globalization have long argued that extremely unregulated capital flows render the global capitalist system unstable. Advocates of deregulation argued that an unfettered market would raise all boats, but it has, in fact, only enriched the few at the top; created unprecedented income and wealth gaps between the rich and the rest; shifted sites of industrial production to places with minimal or no labor and environmental standards and enforcement; and based wealth production not on the production of goods and services but on risky, faulty, and even fraudulent financial-sector mechanisms. Another net result of unbridled global industrial capitalism is global warming, around which there is finally close to world consensus that it is "man-made" and is threatening polities, economies, and life as we know it on the planet as a result of climate change and the "natural" disasters it accelerates.

Undergirding globalization is the economic philosophy or ideology of neoliberalism that was developed by economists in the global North and imposed there and on the global South. Critics refer to this as a form of economic or market "fundamentalism" (Klein 2007), as it represents a total faith in the market, unfettered by state regulation and protections for citizens, and a total belief in the dismantling of the welfare state through the privatization for profit of public services, leaving no accountability or universal access to satisfaction of basic needs. The ensuing economic insecurities have also unleashed a variety of other fundamentalisms, including political, religious, ethnic, and other cultural ones. Neoconservativism combines a neoliberal faith in the market with the view that the only role for the state is a coercive one: first, to control other states through strong national defense and offense (which is part and parcel of a militarist ideology), and second, to control populations through the imposition of laws that limit civil liberties and human rights, insisting that people conform to a particular set of behaviors deemed "moral." The rise of neoconservativism is closely related to the rise of patriarchal religious fundamentalisms—whether Christian, Judaic, or Islamic—especially when they are espoused by state elites and determine the "moral" codes upon which they seek to order and control society. Ethnic and other cultural fundamentalisms, whether they are based on conceptions of the "traditional" or the "modern," when espoused by elites, produce similar intolerances for those who are "different" or dissent from the imposed social order. All these fundamentalisms result in structural and/or direct violence, ranging from political, economic, and social discriminations to ethnic cleansing and religion-based wars.

What is less acknowledged as a fundamentalism—and is an ideology that feeds and cuts across all other fundamentalisms—is masculinism, which justifies and "naturalizes" gender hierarchy (that is, makes it seem natural rather than socially and politically constructed and thus subject to change). As a number of feminist scholars (Faludi 2007; Joseph and Sharma 2003; Hawthorne and Winter 2002) observed in the aftermath of 9/11, women virtually disappeared as expert commentators on world affairs, particularly in the U.S. media, where talking heads became almost exclusively military men who controlled the public discourse and espoused aggression—a decidedly masculine value—as the only acceptable course of action. Feminists and other critics from the academy and social movements of the ensuing wars were feminized—that is, portrayed as weak, naive, and dangerous—and many received death threats to further silence them. A similar pattern emerged in the United States in the post–Vietnam War period, during which we saw what Susan Jeffords (1989) called the "re-masculinization of America" as neoconservatives took power under Ronald Reagan in the 1980s. Seeking to put behind them the defeat in Vietnam that led to a more chastened view about the value of military conflict to solve problems and secure geopolitical objectives, neoconservatives—through public discourse and policy and even popular culture—rehabilitated the Rambo-esque masculinist and militarist values of might makes right, unfettered by "feminine" considerations about the costs and usefulness of war. The post-9/11 re-masculinization of America under yet another neoconservative government has been justified with resort to the necessity of war arising from some inevitable "clash of civilizations" in which one ethnic and religious fundamentalism must combat another (the West/Christianity against the East/Islam), but also with resort, at least for a short time, to the claim that the war in Afghanistan was about civilized men (in the West) saving women from barbaric men (the Taliban).

As Susan Faludi (2007) has observed, this latter justification has a long pedigree in U.S. history, naturalizing, for example, the European colonists' genocide of Native Americans. Moreover, as others have observed, the voices of Afghan women went unheeded, although they warned that the invasion and new government installed would simply put another set of violent patriarchs (or male rulers who believe in the subordination of women) in charge (Russo 2006; Farrell and McDermott 2005). Thus, they and other outside observers concluded that women's human rights were neither a reason for the war, despite the early rhetoric about this from the Bush administration, nor could they be achieved by war, which most often vastly increases insecurity for women. A more comprehensive examination of gender and global security appears in Chapter 4, but suffice it to say here that masculinism is deeply implicated in increasing militarization and silencing alternatives to armed conflict and resolving conflict nonviolently.

Masculinism has also shaped and propelled globalization. Charlotte Hooper's (2001) study of the discourse, or language, used by Anglo-American neoliberal economists and leaders to promote globalization in the 1990s revealed a new kind of hegemonic masculinity emerging: It combined older forms of "hard" masculinity that celebrated war heroism and risk-taking frontiersmanship with newer forms of relatively "softer" masculinity that applauded rational calculus, technological prowess, and global networking. This new model served to elevate global capitalist development to the most manly pursuit, even over war, to which all men and manly countries should aspire. Those (whether women or men, movements, organizations, institutions, or states) who were concerned with what globalization was doing—the loss of industrial jobs and the shift to low-wage service economies in the global North, the exploitation of labor and the environment in the global South, the decline of the welfare state and the privatization of social services, and the disinterest in human development and environmental protection in favor of only capital accumulation that went to the very few—were seen as anachronistic (feminine) and thus should be brushed aside as being unready for the brave new world of the "new economy." Infusing martial values into the global capitalist cause, already replete with competitiveness values, encouraged the hubris that enabled the risky ventures that have currently brought the world economy to its knees.

Long preceding this economic crisis, however, evidence had been piling up that most women were bearing the brunt of the new economy (Marchand and Runyan 2000). For example, as reproductive workers in the voluntaristic economy, or household members given by gender ideology the most responsibility for the creation and care of family and community members on an unpaid basis, women—who are also the largest consumers and providers of social services because of their reproductive roles—have lost the most with the reduction or privatization of social services. The retreat of the welfare state has meant that women have had to take on additional roles in the private or domestic sphere that used to be public services, for which women also used to be paid or paid better. As productive workers in the cash economy, women, who have been rendered as "cheap" labor by gender ideology, became the preferred labor force in low-wage service and light-industrial assembly work created by offshore production. Some women have benefited to a degree from this newfound employment, but their working conditions—including low wages, lack of union protections, poor health and safety regulations, sexual harassment, and polluted and dangerous workplaces and living spaces—have kept them in subordinate and precarious positions. Subordinate men, such as those in the working classes, have suffered as well, having their skills, wages, and jobs "feminized" (devalued or eliminated). But this effect, too, boomerangs on women in such forms as enduring higher incidences of domestic violence, taking full responsibility for both wage and reproductive work, and/or being left behind to sustain the household alone when men migrate for jobs elsewhere or having to migrate themselves to find work, thus leaving their families behind. Chapter 5 more fully addresses the impact of gender on the global political economy, and the impact of the global political economy on gender, and this analysis will promote our thinking alternatively about how to make more sustainable and just economies.

So how do we make sense of the contradiction of the rise of the new global politics of gender equality (or the re-positionings of women and men) at the same time that re-masculinizations of states and economies have been in ascendance? Our short answer is the power of gender, the principle concept informing this book and the other running theme of it. As a filtering and organizing mechanism that produces both worldviews and world structures, the power of gender is particularly resilient and adaptive, accommodating some changes in the positionings (or re-positionings) of women and men, while sustaining, through shifting formations of what constitutes ideal forms of masculinity and femininity, masculinist values in world politics that devalue other ways of identifying, seeing, structuring, and acting in the world. Our somewhat longer explanation in the following pages lies in the interactions of gender with the other identity markers and power relations of race, class, nation, and sexuality. These provide more complicated pictures of social orders, enabling us to see how even the concept of gender equality is manipulated to privilege some women over other women and some men over other men—with the result being a general continuation of unjust social orders and political and economic relations. These also bring our attention to how divisions and inequalities created among women and among men have disabling effects on resistances and alternatives to world-politics-as-usual unless all inequalities are confronted in those resistances and alternatives.

GENDER AND INTERSECTIONAL ANALYSIS IN IR

Feminist IR scholars generally do not subscribe to the conventional definition of international relations as being the power struggles between sovereign states in an anarchic world in which there is no supranational government to control state behaviors through the rule of law. Rather, these scholars favor an alternative definition of IR: "the identification and explanation of social stratifications and of inequality as structured at the level of global relations" (Brown, S. 1988: 461). In this sense, feminist perspectives on IR understand power in broader and more complex terms than more traditional IR scholars and have sought to put the relations of people, as agents and within social structures, back into international relations. To do so, they have relied on feminist sociopolitical theorizing in other disciplines, including the now well-developed (inter)discipline of women's and gender studies. The concept of intersectional analysis emerged within these studies as a result of the work of black U.S. feminist theorists in the 1980s and beyond (Collins 1991) who recognized that the lives and experiences of women of color were underrepresented in dominant Western feminist theories about women's subordination that were based on the experiences of largely white, Western, middle-class and/or working-class women. Intersectional analysis holds that gender is always raced, classed, sexualized, and nationalized, just as race, class, nationality, and sexuality are always gendered.[5]

These premises of intersectional analysis mean several things. First, women and men have multiple identities simultaneously, describing themselves or being described not only by gender but also by race, class, sexual, and national markers, such as a black, American, working-class, gay male. Second, these identity markers, however, are not just additive, merely descriptive, or politically or socially neutral. As noted at the out-set of this chapter, some parts of our identities carry privilege and others do not. In the example given, male privilege, which an individual may be able to exercise in the home over women and children, is offset in other, more public arenas if the individual is a racial minority in the larger de-mographic and thus subject to racism; a sexual minority within the per-son's own race or a wider demographic and thus subject to homophobia; and/or not a member of the owning or managerial class and thus subject to classism. Being an American may confer some privileges, such as citi-zenship rights, including voting rights, that are denied to nonnaturalized immigrants (of color or not), but we also know that racism (and clas-sism) can trump those formal citizenship rights, as in the case of black Americans who were routinely kept from voting through Jim Crow laws, poll taxes, and literacy tests long after they won the formal right to vote.

Third, different parts of our identities become politically salient at dif-ferent times. This casts us into pigeonholes that deny the complexity of our identities, and when some aspects of our identities are given rights but others are not, it can create a kind of schizophrenia within the indi-vidual and divisive mentalities within and between seemingly cohesive social groups. Consider the case of suffrage for African American women. The common notion is that African Americans were given the vote before women in the United States, but in fact only African Ameri-can men were enfranchised first, whereas African American women had to await enfranchisement of women generally. Thus, their gender sepa-rated them from the category of "African American," which was coded as meaning only black men. At the same time, although many white women suffragists had been abolitionists, their anger over the enfran-chisement first of only black men prompted racist arguments as to why white women were better entrusted with the vote to uphold white civi-lizational values. This effectively discounted black women, who had to organize separately. Thus, because of their race, African American women were also separated from the category of "women," which was coded as meaning only white women (Giddings 1984). A more contem-porary example is the documented resistance of many leaders of the U.S. black community (along with many others from majority communities) to recognize sexual minorities, particularly gay men, within their com-munity. The idea that a man can be both black and gay is perceived as an oxymoron because dominant constructions of black men's sexuality, foisted by whites and internalized by blacks from slavery on, are so tied to images of aggressive heterosexuality.

This brings us to the fourth meaning of intersectional analysis— namely, the kind of masculinity or femininity one is assumed to have rests on the meanings given to one's race, class, sexuality, and nationality. For example, Africans brought as slaves to the Americas were defined by their captors as subhuman with largely animal instincts, which included the assumption that animals mate indiscriminately. The idea that slaves, whether men or women, were "oversexed" was a convenient mythology for male slaveholders who could thereby justify their sexual assaults on female slaves while upholding slavery and later lynchings in the name of protecting white women from "naturally" sexually predatory black men. The contemporary terms for this kind of thinking are the gendered racialization and sexualization of groups to render them as "other" or different and less than the groups doing the labeling. As raised earlier, hegemonic masculinity—currently identified with and exercised by those individuals, groups, cultures, organizations, and states coded with the full privileges of Western-ness, whiteness, wealth, and maleness born out of long histories of conquest and colonization—carries the highest representational (or labeling) power to render others "other." If we focus only on a narrow definition of gender or singular notions of masculinity and femininity, we miss the complexity of unjust social orders and fail to see how they are upheld often by pitting subordinated groups against each other, especially when such groups are coded as homogeneous without both cross-cutting and conflicting interests within them that hold potential for coalitions and more comprehensive resistance to un-just social (and world political) orders.

Contemporary feminist scholars engage in intersectional analysis to avoid the practice of "essentialism," or the assumption that, for example, all women or all men or all those within a given race or class share the same experiences and interests. Only by recognizing how, for example, some women have benefited by the racial, class, sexual, and national origin oppression of other women, whereas many men subordinated by these very characteristics still exercise gender oppression, can we advance a more comprehensive notion of gender equality that sees it as indivisible from racial, class, and sexual equality and equality among nations. Unfortunately, the new politics of gender equality observable at the international level has largely separated gender equality from these other forms of equality. As a result, international efforts to increase gender equality can fail to address other sources of inequality (such as race and class discrimination) that disadvantage certain groups of women. At the same time, when such efforts blame only men, and mostly nonelite men, for gender inequality, and fail to address forms of discrimination that subordinated men experience (based on class, race, and/or sexuality), then subordinated men may withhold support for gender equality. It also maintains the power of gender even as the socioeconomic positionings of women and men may be somewhat altered.

Another reason to avoid essentialism is also to avoid "universalism," or universal prescriptions for how to achieve comprehensive gender equality. Not only do women not share the same experiences or interests as a result of their multiple identities derived from their differing social locations in the world, but also the sociopolitical, cultural, and historical contexts in which women live vary significantly, requiring varying strategies for social change. These complex realities have made many feminists skeptical of resorting to "global" solutions just as they have recognized that "global" problems take many and differing "local" forms to which agents of social change must be attentive to create context-specific and context-sensitive solutions that do not backfire (Grewal and Kaplan 1994). This skepticism also extends to global actors, whether IGOs or NGOs, because they tend to be among the elite whose interests and analyses may reproduce inequalities on the local level even as they purport to be ameliorating them (Spivak 1998). Thus, global norms and global actors are double-edged swords that can both reduce and reproduce inequalities. On the other hand, local efforts to reduce inequalities at the local level that are not attentive to how those inequalities may be, at least partially, the result of more global processes that produce similar inequalities across locales risk failing to see these interconnections, thereby leaving inequalities largely intact or simply shifting them to "other" places.

Such insights that arise from intersectional analysis help us to make sense of the paradox between increased global attention to gender equality and increased global crises associated with reassertions of masculinism and other subordinating fundamentalisms. These insights also inform this book, which we map here in concluding this chapter.

MAPPING THE BOOK

Why "Global Gender Issues"?

We share skepticism about invocations of "global" problems and solutions for several reasons: They can erase differences in social locations, experiences, and interests that must be recognized to unravel the depth, breadth, and multiplicity of power relations in world politics; they may privilege global actors as the only meaningful ones in world politics; and they often misrepresent world political inequalities and the crises that arise from them as being produced and experienced in the same ways across the globe, when in fact some actors are more responsible than others for such problems. The manifestations of such problems differ in kind and degree in varying local contexts, and the experience of such problems depends on one's social location, so that some people are more insulated from and some are more exposed to them. We retain the term "global" in this third edition, however, to foreground not only the interrelationships between the conventional constructs and practices of global governance, global security, and global political economy inequalities they both engender and rest upon, but also the interconnections between differing "local" (including national) manifestations of inequalities as a result of these "global" constructs and practices.

We also share skepticism about a narrow, overarching, and unitary conception of gender and reject essentialist approaches to and universalist claims about it. We retain the term "gender," however, to signify gender as a power relation that is inextricable from other power relations and significantly affected by and affecting them. Early feminist IR scholars have been taken to task for not attending enough to the intersections of gender, race, class, sexuality, and nation (Chowdhry and Nair 2002), but we use gender—specifically in our concept of the power of gender— to refer to a hegemonic (or dominant) worldview or meta-lens that produces and reproduces these intersecting oppressions. The latter, in turn, enables the production and reproduction of hegemonies in world politics, that is, the extraction of consent (or tacit acceptance) by dominated groups to unjust social orders maintained by dominant groups.

Our continued use of the term "issues" (in combination with "global" and "gender") is not intended to mean that there is a homogeneous set of interests and issues that all women share globally. Nor is it meant to reduce the global politics of inequality to "women's issues." Rather, it is suggestive of a different and wider conception of not only what *issues from* global processes, namely, savage and interconnected inequalities and injustices, but also why these are world political issues, that is, subject to political debate and change, not the result of some inexorable, natural, or necessary processes that cannot be questioned. We organize our investigation of global gender issues according to major lines of inquiry in IR—global governance, global security, and global political economy—not to suggest that these are the only ways to think about world politics or to categorize knowledge about world politics, but rather to show how gender, in an intersectional sense, is deeply implicated in these "global issues" and the crises they induce.

The (Re)Positionings of Women, Men, and Gender

As we have begun to argue, gender is salient both as a substantive (empirical, concrete) topic in world politics and as a dimension of how we study (analyze, think about) world politics. The former we characterize as the effects of world politics on gender. In subsequent chapters, we provide data on women's positions (or roles) relative to men's in the contexts of global political, security, and economic structures and organizations. But we emphasize *re-positionings of women and men* (including re-positionings among groups of women and among groups of men) where these have occurred, as the result either of recent global attention to gender policymaking or shifts in the nature of war-making and the global economy. These data flesh out what we refer to as the gendered (understood intersectionally) divisions of power, violence, and labor and resources, which are addressed respectively in the chapters on global governance (power), global security (violence), and global political economy (labor and resources). Although overall patterns continue to show that men in aggregate hold more privileged positions in global power structures, whereas women in aggregate are subordinated in and by those structures, there is evidence that some women in some national and sectoral contexts are advancing (i.e., moving "up"), and more men are becoming more vulnerable to the vicissitudes of violent conflict and economic change. These (still overall limited) shifts show that gender roles are far from static, but they also reveal that other power relations such as race, class, sexuality, and nationality play significant roles in determining which women "move up" and which men stay down or "move down."

Another common feature of our "issues" chapters (3, 4, and 5) is attention to the *re-positioning of gender* in global policymaking. Not long ago, gender was absent as an explicit focus of policymaking by IGOs. Today, gender—either referring to women or to gender equality between women and men—is on the agenda of many IGOs in relation to a range of political, security, economic, and social issues. We address recent key gender policies, but also critique them in terms of, on the one hand, their appropriations and depoliticizations of gender analysis and demands and, on the other, their insufficiencies in re-positioning women and men, attending to inequalities not only between but also among women and men, and alleviating the global crises to which they acknowledge gender is related.

The Power of Gender

As our other recurring theme, we deal with gender as a dimension of the way world politics is studied, thought about, and thus conducted by referring to the effects of gender on world politics, or the power of gender as a meta-lens, or mental ordering and filtering system, that produces and reproduces global inequalities, injustices, and crises. Chapter 2 elaborates the power of gender as a meta-lens; other chapters reveal how it operates to perpetuate inequalities between and among women and men, insufficiencies in the re-positionings of diverse women and men, and appropriations of equality, nonviolence, social justice, and environmental sustainability demands. Thus, the (re)positionings of women and men and the power of gender are two *interacting* themes—two sides of the same coin—that frame and cut across the material presented in this text.

These interacting phenomena provide a *gender-sensitive* lens on global processes that foregrounds the relationship between gendered thinking and actors and gendered actions and consequences. Those consequences have most severely culminated in what we refer to as the interlocking global crises of representation, insecurity, and sustainability throughout the text, but we also deal with them serially and in more depth in the issues chapters. Such a lens alters both the "what" of world politics and "how" we view it. We see the extent and structure of gendered inequalities, the role of gender in combination with other inequalities in structuring the experience of women *and* men worldwide, the significance of gender in relation to other power relations in shaping how we think about world politics, and the process by which gendered thought shapes world politics itself. In shifting our vision, a gender-sensitive lens, which is most concerned with uprooting the power of gender from which inequalities and injustices flow, also shifts our attention from questions of order, control, and growth at any cost (which are ostensibly best left in the hands of experts at the top) to questions of representational equity, nonviolent security, and human and ecological sustainability that actually require multiple voices from multiple social locations to address.

Gender Lenses in World Politics Inquiry

Although a gender-sensitive lens on world politics alerts us to the power of gender as a hegemonic worldview or meta-lens, there are multiple gender lenses, or feminist perspectives, in world politics inquiry. These are addressed in Chapter 2, but here it is important to point out that we will be applying a range of these lenses in our engendered examinations of traditional categories of world politics inquiry: global governance (Chapter 3), global security (Chapter 4), and global political economy (Chapter 5). The employment of multiple feminist perspectives foregrounds the substantial body of work that now exists in feminist IR, affords more complex and sometimes conflicting analyses of these world political constructs, and ensures no single or hegemonic analysis that produces fixed or static approaches that foreclose debate within gender inquiry. At the same time, we point to weaknesses in and appropriations of gender inquiry and policy when they fail to address the power relations among women and among men that forestall more comprehensive critiques and resistances to processes that widen and deepen global and local inequalities. Our final chapter (6) examines some resistances that seek to change the inequalities between and among women and men and/or transform perspectives on world politics. Although varied, incomplete, and sometimes conflictual, resistance strategies attempt to confront the crises of representation, insecurity, and sustainability through enabling more participatory and nonhegemonic governance, nonviolent forms of security, and more just and environmentally sustainable economies.

Clarifications of Terms

Recognizing that readers of this text will come from differing disciplines and educational levels, we offer some clarification of terms we use that may be less familiar. This is less of a glossary, which assumes agreed upon and fixed meanings, and more a clarification of how we use terms whose meanings are multiple and sometimes contested. Where appropriate, less familiar terms not addressed here are defined where they first appear in the text.

For additional clarity, we note that when we use "gender" as a noun or adjective, we are most often foregrounding the masculine-feminine dynamic conventionally emphasized in feminist and gender-sensitive accounts. When we use "gender*ed*" as an adjective we intend something more complex and intersectional, referring not only to masculinity-femininity, but also to how gender is always cross-cut by other axes of difference. We sometimes list these dimensions—race, ethnicity, class, religion, sexuality, nationality, age, ability, and so on—but at other times prefer "gendered" as a less cumbersome shorthand signaling intersectionality without listing specific differences.

Similarly, although we largely refer only to "women" and "men" or "males" and "females" or use notions like "both genders," we understand, as indicated in the beginning of this chapter, that there are multiple sexes and genders and that "women" and "men" are themselves socially constructed and nonhomogeneous categories (Fausto-Sterling 2000). Implied or explicit references to "elites" in the text signify those privileged in the particular context by (especially but not exclusively) gender, class, ethnicity/race, sexuality, and nation.

We often refer to the ideologies of heteronormativity and heterosexism that assume an essentialized (natural, universal) binary of sex difference (male and female only), that privilege exclusively heterosexual desire (for the "opposite" sex), and that maintain the only natural and hence appropriate or respectable expressions of desire, intimacy, sexual identity, marriage, and family formation are heterosexual. The rigid gender dichotomy presumed in both ideologies promotes masculinism, devalues that which is feminized, and fosters the demonization and even criminalization of nonheterosexual relations. We most often use "sexual minorities" to signify individuals and groups who contest or do not conform to heteronormativity. Although "LGBTQ" can capture an array of sexual minority identifications (lesbian, gay, bisexual, transgender, transvestite, transsexual, queer, questioning), we note here that engaging in particular sexual practices need not constitute assuming a particular sexual identity, that these Western-originating terms are less widely circulated elsewhere, and that those who engage in same-sex or other minority sexual practices do not necessarily identify as LGBTQ. Moreover, gender "queer" can refer to a range of sexual minority identities, but "queering" more typically refers to analytical processes and social practices that defy heteronormative readings of social reality and performances of normative gender identity. Heteronormative "patriarchy" refers not only to male-dominated or masculinist rule but also to rule that enforces heterosexual norms to achieve that end.

Although we have addressed sexualization and racialization definitionally to some degree, we want to stress that they carry two meanings that are often in tension. They refer in one sense to processes of identifying an individual or group as one or another sexuality (straight, gay, queer) or race (white, black, Asian) by attributing to them particular and often stereotypical ideas and practices associated with that label. In a second sense, the attributing process often emerges from a position of normative privilege and presumed superiority, which effectively stigmatizes (or "others") the objects of attribution, especially by constructing them unidimensionally—as "only" their race, class, or sexuality. It is in this sense that privilege permits whites to be both less aware of "having a race" themselves and more often to be those who "racialize" others, even as the social construction of "race" permits some who are excluded from "whiteness" through economic or religious discrimination at one juncture to be "whitened up" by altered alignments at another (southern Europeans, Jews, Irish). References to "white," then, also can refer to those who gain the status of "whiteness," regardless of actual skin color, as a result of class and other privileges.

Racialization is also historically inextricable from the expansionary and colonizing practices of European elites who deployed Enlightenment ideas ("reason," "science") and new technologies (gun powder, steam engine) to enhance their power over foreign populations, thus enabling the extraction of resources and labor to fuel European "modernization" and geopolitical dominance. "Eurocentrism" is an ideology of

European superiority that arose from this conquest and is often used interchangeably with "Western-centrism" in more recent times. "Orientalism" (Said 1979) is one effect of Eurocentrism (or "Occidentalism"), consigning the "non-West" to the status of cultural, political, economic, and technological backwardness. Such backwardness is assumed, in Eurocentric and Orientalist thinking, to need stimulation from the West to "develop" or "modernize" or "progress." It is for this reason that we try to resist such labels as "developed" versus "developing" countries or the oft-used terms of First and Third Worlds, as they maintain notions of upward continuums and hierarchies. Moreover, like "industrialized" and "nonindustrialized," they are not accurate because there are postindustrial, industrial, and nonindustrial formations in most countries. We instead use, where possible, the terms "global South" and "global North" to denote social locations of subjugation and privilege respectively. At times we invoke the global North or North or the global South or South to refer to the geographic locations associated with First and Third worlds, but at other times, we mean to include nonprivileged groups in both the geographical South and North when we refer to the global South. We also remind readers that there are elites in the South who share the privileges of the global North.

Although after World War II, resistance to direct colonial rule was largely successful, the global North continues to exploit the global South through less direct and differently manipulated forms of "neocolonial" or "neoimperial" rule (sometimes referred to as "recolonization"). Most recently, "neoliberal governmentality," or the marketization of all life, has been put forward as the current form of neoimperialism. "Neoliberalism" refers to what we earlier called market fundamentalism, and "governmentality" is a form of governance that posits a right or normative order and entails a range of often noncoercive disciplinary mechanisms that enable conformism of human subjectivities to it (Foucault 1991). Neoliberal governmentality is sometimes used interchangeably with a contemporary notion of "Empire." Empire today refers not to sovereign actors pursuing economic and military power beyond their territories but a deterritorialized, decentered apparatus of rule operating across all dimensions of the social order and constituting the paradigmatic form of "biopower" in which subjectivities inculcate "self-discipline" to conform to market and other dominant logics (Hardt and Negri 2000: xiixv). The United States leads but does not (cannot) control this new form of rule. The Bush administration, however, forcefully promulgated a cultural logic and normative order presupposing global capitalism and the "war on terror" as inseparable components of the only "right" conceptualization of democracy and world order—an orientation that is somewhat changing under the Obama administration but may not significantly or sufficiently disturb the dynamics of Empire. This contextualizes what we mean by "the imperial(ist) impulse": the practice of thinking and acting from a position of presumptive power and moral superiority in ways that reproduce essentialized and oppositional categories that silence, condemn, or preclude alternative ways of thinking and acting, and do so in the name of knowing unequivocally the one "best" answer, policy, or global project. It is a key argument of this text that the "power of gender" constitutes just such an imperial(ist) impulse by underpinning, naturalizing, and reproducing it.

Notes

1. The new Obama administration is taking a strong stand against lax definitions of torture enabled under the Bush administration, planning to close the military prison for terrorist suspects at Guantánamo Bay and retreating from the terminology "war on terror." The implementation and effects of these policy shifts remain to be seen.

2. See Web Resources listed at the end of this text for the online location of the full text of the Beijing Platform for Action (BPA). A list of acronyms and to what they refer is also provided at the front of this text for handy reference.

3. See Web Resources listed at the end of this text for the online location of the full text of UN Security Council Resolution 1325.

4. See Web Resources listed at the end of this text for the online location of the full text of the UN Convention on the Elimination of All Forms of Discrimination Against Women (CEDAW). On women's rights and/as human rights see Cook 1994; Peters and Wolper 1995; Peterson and Parisi 1995; Ackerly 2008; and UNDAW in the Web Resources section of the text.

5. Crenshaw (1991) is credited with introducing intersectionality as an analytics. Recent discussions include McCall 2001; Brah 2002; Knapp 2005; Phoenix and Pattynama 2006; Yuval-Davis 2006.

2

⋖○⋗

Gendered Lenses on
World Politics

In Chapter 1, we presented an apparent contradiction. On the one hand, attention to gender inequality has expanded dramatically in the past decade, as evidenced in global activism, national and international policies, and academic studies. In this sense, and especially in relation to re-positioning (some) women in world politics, it appears that gender equality is being taken seriously in the international community. On the other hand, what we refer to as crises of representation, insecurity, and sustainability have worsened in the past decade, evidenced not only by continued inequalities between and among women and men, but also by a re-masculinization of global governance, international security, and global political economy (GPE). In this sense, and especially in relation to realizing a transformation in gendered ideologies, practices, and structures, it appears that gender analyses are being selectively embraced and problematically implemented. How do we make sense of this paradox?

Our answer to this question foregrounds the *power of gender* as an especially resilient and adaptive filtering and organizing mechanism, a meta-lens that produces particular ways of seeing, thinking, and acting in the world. Gender may feature in policymaking, women and men may be re-positioned, and ideal forms of masculinity may shift, but we argue that as long as the power of gender as a meta-lens continues to operate, it will produce and reproduce inequalities, injustices, and crises of global proportion. In this book, we aim to make sense of and substantiate this claim.

This chapter begins with an account of how lenses work and why they matter in a general sense. Next we provide clarification of these claims with reference to more familiar world politics lenses, and consider how stereotypes, dichotomies, and ideologies have political effects. We then turn to feminist inquiry and politicizing gender, revealing its historical construction and ever-changing expressions, and clarifying our reference to the power of gender as a meta-lens, or hegemonic worldview. Following is a section introducing feminist IR lenses that will be drawn upon in subsequent chapters. The concluding section considers how gendered divisions of power, violence, and labor and resources (the themes of Chapters 3, 4, and 5) are cross-cut by ethnicity/race, class, sexuality, and nation-based inequalities, and how the systemic reproduction of these interlocking inequalities generates global crises of representation, insecurity, and sustainability.

HOW LENSES WORK AND WHY THEY MATTER

In simple terms, lenses operate at various levels or scales. The single words or short phrases that constitute *stereotypes* focus our attention on particular aspects or characteristics of groups of people. *Dichotomies* order our thinking in asymmetrical, either-or terms whose apparent opposition obscures how they depend on each other. Typologies, academic disciplines, and theoretical schools of thought frame our thinking by linking multiple concepts to constitute a lens. *Ideologies* are even more encompassing lenses, affording legitimacy to a wide range of beliefs and practices in support of maintaining particular social orders. The key point in each case is that any lens focuses our attention selectively.

Selective attention is a necessary feature of making sense of any particular subject, practice, paradox, or social order. Because it is not physically possible for any human to see or comprehend everything at once, we rely on conceptual filters—lenses—that enable us to see some things in greater detail, more accurately, or in better relation to certain other things. Lenses simplify our thinking by focusing our attention on what seems most relevant. They "order" what we see and provide direction for subsequent actions. In this sense, lenses are like maps: They frame our choices, expectations, and explorations, enabling us to take advantage of knowledge already gained and, presumably, to move more effectively toward our objectives. Like maps, lenses enable us to make sense of where we are, what to expect next, and how to proceed. From the conceptual ordering systems available to us, we choose the lens we assume is most appropriate for a particular context—a lens that we expect will enable us to make sense of and act appropriately in that context.

Lenses are thus indispensable for "ordering" what we see and orienting our responses. But their filtering function is also problematic. Because we cannot focus on everything, any particular lens directs our attention to some features of a context, which unavoidably renders other features out of focus—filtered out—by that lens. In short, lenses both include and exclude, with important and often political implications.

By filtering our ways of thinking and ordering experience, the lenses we rely on have concrete effects. We observe this readily in the case of self-fulfilling prophecies: If we expect hostility, our own behavior (acting superior, displaying power) may elicit responses (defensive posturing, aggression) that we then interpret as confirming our expectations. It is in this sense that we refer to lenses and "realities" as interactive, interdependent, or mutually constituted. Lenses shape who we are, what we think, and what actions we take, thus shaping the world we live in. At the same time, the world we live in ("reality") shapes which lenses are available to us, what we see through them, and the likelihood of our using them—or adjusting them—in particular contexts.

In general, as long as our lenses seem to work, we continue to rely on them. The more useful they appear to be, or the more accustomed to them we become, the more we are inclined to take them for granted and to resist making major changes in them. We forget that a particular lens is a choice among many alternatives. Instead, we tend to believe we are seeing "reality" as it "*is*" rather than as our language, culture, or discipline interprets reality. It is difficult and sometimes uncomfortable to reflect critically on our assumptions, to question their accuracy or desirability, and to explore the implications of shifting our vantage point by adopting a different lens. We argue in this text that the power of gender is a meta-lens that frames our thinking and hence our realities in ways that are deeply problematic. Although we take it very much for granted, and resist changing it, the power of gender as a meta-lens does *not* work for pursuing social justice; rather, we must reflect critically on its assumptions and expose its implications so that we can more effectively move beyond it.

We acquire our lenses, or learn our conceptual ordering systems, in a variety of contexts, but early childhood is especially consequential. From infancy on, we are socialized into and internalize ways of thinking and acting that enable us to perform appropriately within a particular culture. This involves acquiring an identity that constitutes subject formation— "who I am"—and assimilating cultural codes that provide meaning for "what I do." Socialization processes are embedded in wider social relations of power that determine which codes are dominant. These include familial, linguistic, cultural, economic, educational, religious, political, and legal institutions that stabilize particular symbolic and social orders and orderings. Dominant codes are infused with normative and ideological beliefs that constitute systems of meaning and valorization, and these can have significant effects on world politics. For example, in complex relationships with governmental, economic, and patriarchal power, religious institutions have historically promoted particular worldviews that guide human action in its most passionate expressions and normative investments—not least, the willingness to die and/or kill others in the name of a cause.

What we learn at an early age is psychosocially formative: The conceptual ordering system (language, cultural rules) we uncritically absorb in childhood is especially resistant to transformation. This is not simply a matter of accustomed habits but of psychic coherence and the security of "knowing" how to act appropriately and effectively in the world. Hence, we are intensely invested in identities and cultural codes learned in early childhood, and challenges to the meaning and order they afford are experienced as particularly threatening.

Whatever their institutional forms, parenting practices are embedded in and reinscribe power relations, because infants are helpless and children are variously dependent. Family life is where we first learn about and observe gender differentiation, its respective identities, and its divisions of labor. It is also where we begin to internalize beliefs about race/ethnicity, age, sexuality, class, religion, nationality, and other axes of difference. Historically sedimented conventions of masculinist language, religion, and worldview inscribe the heteronormative gender order as foundational and nonnegotiable, while predominately heterosexual family life ensures that heterosexual identities, roles, and practices are the only apparent options. The effects of this ordering system, and psychic acceptance of it, are manifested throughout social relations, not simply contained in early childhood or family dynamics. In these multiple senses, we are exposed to, and typically internalize, the dichotomizing and ordering power of gender as a meta-lens from infancy onward, which enhances its apparent "given-ness" and makes resistance to it especially difficult.

Of course, the world we live in, and therefore our life experiences, are constantly changing, prompting changes in our lenses as well. The modifications may be minor: from liking one type of music to liking another, from being a high school student in a small town to being a college student in an urban environment. Or the changes may be more profound: from casual dating to parenting, from the freedom of student lifestyles to the assumption of full-time job responsibilities, from Newtonian to quantum physics, from conditions of relative peace to the direct violence of war. To function effectively as reality changes, we must modify our thinking as well. This is especially the case to the extent that outdated lenses or worldviews distort our understanding of current realities, placing us in danger or leading us away from our objectives. As both early explorers and contemporary drivers know, outdated maps are inadequate, and potentially disastrous, guides. We argue in this text that the power of gender is indeed a disastrous guide.

WORLD POLITICS LENSES

Educational systems tend to reproduce an orientation to learning that divides topics according to apparently differentiated tasks, for example, "reading, writing, and arithmetic." College students are taught the distinctions appropriate to particular disciplines (psychology, anthropology, political science) and particular schools of thought within them (behavioralism, psychoanalysis, structuralism, liberalism). There are many lenses (or theoretical perspectives, explanatory frameworks) through which world politics has been viewed historically and in the contemporary context (idealism, liberalism, realism, and so on). How to label lenses is always controversial, and most lenses are continually changing in response to both analytical debates and real-world developments.

Ideologies

(Neo)realist lenses bring the conflictual behavior of states to the fore, whereas (neo)liberal lenses focus attention on interstate cooperation and organization. (Neo)Marxist lenses direct our gaze to class inequalities and conflicts within and across states, and postcolonial lenses call attention to racial inequalities, nationalist identities and conflicts, and imperialist practices within and across states. Constructivists foreground the interaction of agency and structure and include ideas and culture in IR theorizing. Poststructuralists emphasize the politics of symbolic ordering, language, and discursive practices to illuminate how power operates in knowledge production. Feminists focus on gender inequalities and the political effects of masculinist ideologies.

As these examples suggest, lenses often vary by what aspects of reality they find problematic—which involves normative (evaluative) as well as substantive (material) commitments—and, relatedly, by what conceptual schema they find useful in explaining particular problematics. At the same time, topics and commitments may be variously mixed and comprise elements of several lenses. For example, because Marxists focus on economic inequalities, their conceptual frameworks privilege economic variables and practices, although these are inextricable from political dimensions, and some Marxists pay particular attention to culture. Both neorealists and neoliberals assume a model of human nature that views emotion and subjectivity—rather than rationality and objectivity—as problematic, although their different foci lead them to different expectations about behavior. Institutionalists share a focus on institutions, but may be liberal or conservative, and interested in foreign policy or labor markets.

Stated simply, different world politics lenses direct our attention and orient our research in particular ways. They shape, for example, our assumptions about who are the significant actors (individuals, states, multinational corporations, social movements), what are their attributes (rationality, self-interest, power, activism), how are social processes categorized (politics, cooperation, dependence), and what outcomes are desirable (peace, national security, welfare provisioning, global equity).

When considering different theoretical lenses, it helps to make a further distinction: between *what* objects (variables, topics, issues, levels of analysis) are focused on, and *how* knowledge/truth about those objects is produced (empirically, analytically, comparatively, intuitively). Stated another way, the former refers to *ontology* (the nature of "being," i.e., *what* is reality) and the latter to *epistemology* (the study of truth claims, i.e., *how* do we know?), and they are always intertwined, because claims about "what *x* is" are necessarily also claims about how we know what *x* is. We cannot engage these issues in depth, but they are important for comprehending the complexity and range of theories (or lenses) in both IR and feminism. They also are key to appreciating current theoretical debates, which center on how we understand the relationship between knowledge and power.

Epistemological preferences cut across both normative/political commitments and substantive foci (objects of inquiry), though they often go unacknowledged. As a starting point, the most salient epistemological distinction in world politics lenses is between *positivist* (sometimes called modernist, Enlightenment, rationalist, empiricist) and *postpositivist* orientations (including critical, interpretive, reflexive, postcolonial, poststructuralist, most of these feminist, and some constructivist perspectives).[1] We simplify the discussion by noting two assumptions associated with positivist orientations: First, through the application of scientific method, facts can be separated from values; second, subjects (knowers, observers) and objects (that which is known, observed) can also be categorically separated. Hence, positivists assume that the subject/knower is independent of—can stand "outside of"—the reality being observed, and that the observer can see this reality objectively (separating fact from value) by employing the scientific method to control for bias or other emotional investments. Similarly, positivists assume that social reality is "given" (separate from the knower) and is the product of identifiable "laws" of (human and physical) nature and rational action.

A key point is the extent to which positivists assume a referential view of language, understanding it as a neutral, transparent medium that corresponds to, and therefore simply reflects or refers to, the "objective" world "as it is." The claim here is that objects (horses, trees, rights, power) have some central essence or timeless form that can be captured and conveyed linguistically in a word, or signifier, that simply refers to that essence. This orientation tends to essentialize—to understand as timeless, unchanging, and independent of context—the meaning of terms (power, rationality, human nature) and hence what they refer to (capacity to enforce compliance; logically determined relationships;

atomistic, self-interested, acquisitive). It assumes that the meanings of and the differences between terms can be clearly specified and will remain constant across contexts, thus suggesting order, continuity, and stability.

In contrast, postpositivists argue that "reality" is *socially constructed*, in the sense that humans/subjects create meaning and intelligibility through the mutual constitution of symbols, languages, identities, practices, and social structures. This is decisively *not* to argue that the physical world does not exist independent of humans/subjects, but rather that it has no social meaning independent of that which is constructed through human thought and interaction. In other words, there is no pre-social or prediscursive meaning (or essence) to things, but only the meanings produced by social subjects, inevitably reflecting their specific contexts, interests, and objectives. Recall the discussion of lenses: Humans depend on selective attention to make sense of and act in the world. Lenses are drawn from the conceptual ordering systems and languages available to us, and these do not predate culture and social relations, but instead are produced by them. The conditions of human existence and the successful reproduction of social formations *require* some stable ordering—of meaning systems *and* of social practices. Yet, we often forget that the conceptual systems, social identities, and institutionalized practices that humans have constructed are historically specific and contingent. They "lack any essence, and their regularities merely consist of the relative and precarious forms of fixation [stabilization, normalization] which accompany the establishment of a certain order" (Laclau and Mouffe 1985: 98). Moreover, power relations operating in all historical contexts have shaped which and whose ordering preferences dominate. Those who have more access to and control over symbolic and material resources have more opportunities and capabilities for stabilizing and institutionalizing particular symbols, meanings, lenses, norms, rules, and practices. In this sense, elites draw on particular lenses to construct more encompassing belief systems—or ideologies— to normalize, legitimate, and reproduce their privileged positions. As with all lenses, these reflect selective attention and interests that entail devaluing, marginalizing, or excluding alternatives.

We expand on the concept of ideologies later, but here the key point is that knowers cannot stand "outside" of the reality they observe, because their participation in that reality is a necessary condition for the object observed to have any meaning; both subject and object gain their meaning and intelligibility by reference to their locations in a system of meaning (language, discourse, norms, rules) that encompasses them both. In this view, subjects and objects are not categorically separate, but rather exist in a relationship and in a historically specific context that shapes what we wish to know (what questions we ask, etc.), how we go about knowing (what methods we use, etc.), and whose knowledge counts (whose "truth claims" are included or excluded). As a consequence of questioning the positivist lens, objectivity must be rethought, the relationship between power and knowledge becomes central, and language becomes political insofar as it constitutes the meaning system of intelligibility and order.

By denying the categorical separations (fact from value and subject from object) that are assumed by positivists, then, postpositivists—and especially poststructuralists—challenge conventional claims about scientific objectivity and spurn either-or thinking (dichotomies) as a distortion of social reality. Because constructivism has become so influential in IR, we make note here of its ambiguous location "between" positivist lenses, which share commitments to rationalism and foundationalism (belief that knowledge claims can ultimately be judged true or false), and postpositivist lenses, which reject these commitments. All constructivists take ideas and norms seriously, and their contributions in the past decade have dramatically and productively shifted IR thinking to better appreciate the roles of symbols and subjectivities in *constituting* world politics. At the same time, constructivists differ in the extent to which they retain rationalist and foundationalist commitments and essentialist understandings of language. The appeal of these commitments presumably has to do with retaining an unambiguous notion of "reason" and enabling some version of objectivity; both are understood to require access to some unmediated (prediscursive) reality that can "ground" knowledge claims.

[margin annotation: critique of constructivism]

In this text we refer to poststructuralists as postpositivists who identify more closely with antifoundationalist positions and Foucauldian interpretations of the nexus of power and knowledge operating through language and discursive practices (Edkins 1999). In contrast to (rationalist) constructivists, poststructuralists deny the possibility of either absolute certainty regarding the meanings of terms (as unambiguous, timeless) or absolute objectivity regarding knowledge claims (as independent of participation in mediated—social, discursive—realities). From this perspective, mainstream constructivists in IR may aspire to a middle-ground between—or even bridging—foundationalism and antifoundationalism, but their commitments to essentialized rationality and objectivity render them problematically positivist. Although their interventions have expanded IR inquiry, they resist a more radical interrogation of language that exposes its power-laden effects. The point here is that the presumed certainty and objectivity of positivist foundational claims renders them politically suspect. Because observers are always implicated in the context of their observations, the pursuit of absolute objectivity is illusory, and no inquiry is value-free, nor could it be. What questions we ask, problems we focus on, methods we use, resources we commit, and emotional investments we make in our pursuit of knowledge are *all* shaped by the meaning systems and social contexts—therefore power relations—in which they occur.

Accepting that knowledge is socially situated and thus productive of, at best, only partial accounts of reality does not entail a position of absolute relativism—that "anything goes" or that no criteria for comparative assessments can be substantiated. That conclusion reflects a positivist lens of *either* we have "real truth" *or* complete relativism; but the either-or cage is rejected by postpositivists who insist on thinking not in oppositions but relationally. Sandra Harding has proposed an alternative lens: Practicing "strong objectivity" that permits one "to abandon notions of perfect, mirror-like representations of the world, the self as a defended fortress, and 'the truly scientific' as disinterested with regard to morals and politics, yet still apply rational standards to sorting less from more partial and distorted belief" (Harding 1991: 159). In other words, we must give up pursuit of an Archimedean standpoint, the "God's-eye view," or the illusion that certainty is attainable, and recognize instead that all perspectives, problems, and methods are context-specific and value-laden (shaped by power and commitments). This does not mean that they are all equally valid, or that we cannot comparatively assess them. It does mean that all claims must be situated, and any absolute, transcendent, universal claims—because they deny context and the politics of their making—are inherently suspect and politically problematic. Because inquiry is a social practice and so is always value-laden, it is incumbent on inquirers to critically examine their social locations and the values that arise from them. In this way, normative commitments that underlie inquiry are made visible and can become the subject of political debate about what values inquiry should advance.

POLITICIZING STEREOTYPES, DICHOTOMIES, AND IDEOLOGIES

Stereotypes

Stereotypes function as simple lenses: They filter our seeing, thinking, and responding. In one sense, they are like words—simply generalizations that have been stabilized—and our conceptual systems rely on such generalizations to ease the challenge of "making sense" of complex and constantly changing phenomena. We focus here, however, on stereotypes that constitute differential valorizations. We can picture them as composite images that attribute—often incorrectly and always too generally—certain characteristics to whole groups of people. In this way, groups—and individuals "perceived" to fit group stereotypes—are seen as others want or expect to see them, not necessarily as they are. It is not only that stereotypes foreground a negative characterization of groups, but also that they homogenize all members of the group, erasing the differences and complexities that actually exist within—not simply between—groups.

Studies show that we tend to see what we expect to see, and stereotypes "frame" how we see individuals and groups in particular ways, even—especially—when we actually know little about them. Like all lenses, the simplifying effect of stereotypes encourages us to ignore complexity and contradictory signals that are rendered out of focus. This tends to reproduce stereotypical thinking and operates to sustain status quo orderings. In the process, stereotypes become "common sense" and the particular characteristics and behaviors they project are essentialized: appearing as natural, "given," and unchanging, rather than as socially constructed, in historically specific and power-laden contexts.

By providing unquestioned and apparently unambiguous categories that prompt unreflective responses, stereotypes play a key role in legitimating discrimination and reproducing hierarchical relations of power. For example, poverty and low academic performance among poor and/or ethnically subordinated groups may be "explained" by stereotypes of their being lazy, incompetent, or irresponsible. The underrepresentation of women in political office may be "explained" by the stereotype of their being uninterested in power and politics. In this way, stereotypes "blame" individuals for their "failures" and divert attention from institutionalized practices and social structures that shape *everyone's* personal abilities, social opportunities, and realization of preferred objectives.

Because they oversimplify and overgeneralize, promote inaccurate images, and are resistant to change, stereotypes significantly affect how we see ourselves, others, and social ordering generally. Stereotypes that value some groups and devalue others are inherently political, operating to normalize (depoliticize) and thus to reproduce unequal power relations. They reproduce inequalities by being taken for granted and self-fulfilling: If we expect certain behaviors, we may act in ways that in fact create and reinforce such behaviors. (Expecting girls to dislike mechanics and hate math affects how much encouragement we give them; without expectations of success or encouragement, girls may avoid or do poorly in these activities.) Furthermore, stereotypes depoliticize inequalities by naturalizing and essentializing negative images of subordinated groups as inferior, undesirable, or threatening. When members of such groups internalize oppressive stereotypes, they typically hold themselves—rather than social structures—responsible for undesirable outcomes. (Females are more likely to blame themselves for ineptness or poor grades rather than to ask how social structures discourage girls from exploring mechanics and favor boys in regard to educational and career goals.) Those who believe they are acting out the inevitable are, in effect, reconciled to discriminatory treatment.

Dichotomies

Stereotypes, like generalizations, are present in all cultures and communication systems. In this section we focus on the lens of dichotomies, which tends to reproduce essentialized and stereotypical thinking that is key to the power of gender (addressed in detail later). Here we examine both the structure and the status of dichotomies to illuminate how they shape relations of power.

The simplifying, reductionist, and parsimonious quality of dichotomized, either-or thinking is notoriously "efficient." It enables us to reduce (order) complex phenomena into discrete categories that afford calculability and instrumental manipulation. This has played a crucial role in advancing scientific knowledge for several centuries. A contemporary example is our global—though varying—reliance on computer technologies. In effect, computerization involves the translation (reduction) of symbolic and material goods—images, data, information, designs, literature, music, machines—into a binary code of ones and zeros that can be read, manipulated, and communicated by information and communication technologies (ICTs). Digitization permits traditionally disparate and experientially dense phenomena—the textures of a tapestry, the violence of war, the multiple sensory dimensions of seduction—to be converted into binary codes available to anyone with the relevant reading capacity. Not only are these many and diverse phenomena reduced to a common, universal code, but in coded form they are available around the world, virtually without the constraints of time and space.

As this example suggests, the application of binary thinking is not inherently pernicious, and we need not spurn positivist orientations and dichotomized thinking in every context. As with all lenses, evaluating the outcome of their application depends on multiple factors that are specific to objectives and context. We argue, however, that in the study, analysis, and explanation of *social relations,* the structure of dichotomies severely compromises our thoughts and—therefore—actions. In regard to social phenomena, we suggest that although dichotomized thinking is not inherently pernicious, it is inescapably political.

Dichotomies divide concepts (terms, ideas, characteristics) into two, mutually exclusive, ontologically separate poles: paired opposites that share nothing in common, because whatever qualities each depicts must belong only to one but not the other. The binary logic underpinning dichotomies results in either-or thinking, an essentializing of terms, and an exclusion of meanings (and thus awareness of ambiguity) that would otherwise complicate polarities by revealing overlaps or continuities between the terms. In this important sense, dichotomized terms are not simply "independent" concepts (A and B) but defined in oppositional relation to each other (A and not-A). The meaning of one determines the meaning of the other, and more of one is less of the other.

The image of only two mutually exclusive choices keeps us locked into those—and only those—choices. Polarities (right versus wrong, rational versus emotional, strong versus weak) forestall our consideration of nonoppositional constructions (right in relation to plausible, persuasive, preferable, viable; rational in relation to consistent, instrumental, coherent, reductionist; strong in relation to effective, principled, respected, sustainable). Dichotomies thus exclude any middle, "maybe," mixing of terms, or alternative constructions. Similarly, by denying any overlap or commonalities between terms, the polarizing structure of dichotomies puts oppositional differences in focus, at the expense of viewing terms *relationally*. As humans, our commonalities and even mutual interests are extensive. Differences matter and warrant analysis, but there is always a trade-off in what focus we choose. There are political consequences when we unreflectively depend on patterns of thinking that emphasize our differences—especially essentialized, stereotyped, and devalorized differences—at the expense of our commonalities and shared interests.

Because dichotomized terms are assumed to be categorically separate, their meanings appear fixed, timeless, and independent of context—as if they are givens of logic and language rather than social conventions.[2] All ambiguity, complexity, and shifts in meaning constituted by differing contexts simply disappear as they are rendered out of focus through a dichotomizing lens. In this sense, dichotomies contribute to conservative rather than critical analyses: They tend to essentialize either-or categories and polarized thinking (and ordering), at the expense of critical reflection on the meaning of terms and status quo hierarchies. In reality, meanings and social reality are complex, dynamic, and shaped by crosscutting variables. Categorical oppositions misrepresent (distort) social relations by eliminating this complexity, dynamism, and interdependence of terms. They offer a "too simple" picture.

For example, in IR, we often posit state sovereignty as independence and autonomy, the opposite of dependence and constraints. Until recently, this dichotomy prevented our seeing interdependence as a third option and a more accurate picture of actual relationships between states. Similarly, when we define the field's theoretical debates as "idealism versus realism," we make it impossible to address how virtually all theorists in fact adopt a mixture of idealist and realist positions. The dichotomies of sovereignty-anarchy, politics-economics, war-peace, and core-periphery similarly structure how we think about and therefore act in the world. The terms emphasize polarized and hierarchical differences rather than how states, transnational processes, and people are embedded in complex and ever-changing relationships that are inadequately characterized or analyzed in either-or terms.

As the preceding points suggest, essentialized categories and polarized opposites present what appear to be unambiguous, inevitable, and "logical" ways of categorizing. They filter our thinking processes in ways that may be efficient for some purposes, but they severely constrain how we understand social reality. In sum, the structure of dichotomies promotes patterns of thought and action that are stunted (too reductionist; unable to acknowledge complications and consider alternatives), static (too ahistorical; unable to acknowledge or address change), dangerously oversimplified (too decontextualized; unable to accommodate the ambiguities and complexities of social reality), and politically problematic (too essentializing; reproducing oppositional ordering and disabling critical reflection).

Whereas the *structure* of dichotomies is constraining and problematic, the *status* of dichotomies in Western modernist thought poses additional problems. Although all cultures employ generalizations, categories of comparison, and patterned thinking processes, Western thought is distinctive in the extent to which binary logic (thinking in either-or oppositions) is taken for granted and privileged. This is, in large part, due to the prominence of positivist modes of analysis associated with the development of science and rationalism in the context of Western modernity. The positivist dichotomies separating fact from value, and knower (subject) from that which is known (object), are deeply embedded in Eurocentric thinking and accorded elevated status, because of their association with scientific advances and with claims to "objective knowledge" and "Truth." The privileged status of binary logic, however, is not confined to scientific analyses of material phenomena. Rather, the privilege and power accorded to dualistic thinking extend to a litany of dichotomies stabilized over millennia in Western discourse, and especially in dominant narratives of philosophy and political theory. Take a moment to examine and reflect on the dichotomies presented in Table 2.1.

Consider both how familiar these dichotomies are and how frequently they are deployed in our thinking about the world. Consider also how the essentialized oppositional meanings they constitute have become "common sense" and operate across multiple contexts. Now also reflect

TABLE 2.1 **Hierarchical Dichotomies**

Subject (Masculine)	Object (Feminine)
Knower/self/autonomy/agency	Known/other/dependence/passivity
Objective/rational/fact/logical/hard	Subjective/emotional/value/illogical/soft
Order/certainty/predictability/ control over	Anarchy/uncertainty/unpredictability/ subject to control
Mind/abstract/transcendence/ freedom/intellectual	Body/concrete/contingency/necessity/ manual
Culture/civilized/exploiter/ production/public	Nature/primitive/exploited/ reproduction/private

on how the polarized terms are not equally valorized but are hierarchical: Those in the first column are typically considered desirable, admirable, and preferred. Those in the second column are variously understood as less desirable, inferior, and/or threatening to the esteemed qualities of those in the first column. You may also notice how these dichotomies carry gendered and racialized meanings: The first column reflects masculinist and Eurocentric qualities; the second column reflects qualities associated with femininity and subordinated groups. We return to these issues later in this chapter.

Ideologies

As used in this text, *ideology* refers to systems of belief—including notions of human nature and social life—that operate to justify status quo sociocultural, economic, and political arrangements. In Margaret Andersen's words: "Ideologies serve the powerful by presenting us with a definition of reality that is false [partial, self-interested] and yet orders our comprehension of the surrounding world. When ideas emerge from ideology, they operate as a form of social control by defining the status quo to be the proper state of affairs" (1983: 213).

Ideologies are thus political: They order ways of thinking about social relations and operate to legitimate particular relations of power.[3] Whereas stereotypes are essentialized expectations about certain groups of people, and dichotomies promote either-or thinking, ideologies are beliefs about the nature of social systems and the relationships among groups of people within them. They buttress the effects of stereotyping by further filtering our perceptions and actions in ways that reproduce discrimination by "naturalizing" social hierarchies. Ideologies constitute lenses that are more encompassing; they typically bring stereotypes and other differentially valorized generalizations into more systematic and apparently coherent ordering of assumptions, beliefs, and preferences. Insofar as ideologies serve the interests of the powerful, they promote political agendas that sustain the authority and power of elites and obscure the interests of others.

Political theorists have argued for millennia that ideologies are most stable and effective when most taken-for-granted and therefore not questioned. One of the most successful strategies is to draw on biological determinism, arguing that social hierarchies are the result of "natural" biological differences.[4] The classic example is "social Darwinism," which emerged in the context of European developments in science, industrial capitalism, and colonial expansion. This ideology drew on aspects of the theory of natural selection to posit, in effect, narrow genetic or biological causes for complex social behaviors. In actuality, human behavior is always mediated by culture—by systems of meaning and the values they incorporate. The role that biology plays varies dramatically and can *never* be determined without reference to cultural context. Social Darwinism was used to justify the presumption of moral superiority and accumulation of wealth by powerful (European) men, while fostering a racist belief that ethnic and cultural inferiority—rather than the direct and indirect violence of imperialism—explained the subordinated status of non-Europeans. Ideological beliefs may exaggerate the role of biological factors (arguing that men's upper-body strength explains their political domination) or posit biological factors where none need be involved (arguing that because some women during part of their life bear children, all women should care for children and are unfit for political power).

Reliance on biological determinism means that such ideologies tend to flourish, or be rejuvenated, in periods of disruption or transition, when uncertainties and insecurities can fuel excessive desires for stability. Partially responding to (and taking advantage of) the turbulence and uncertainty associated with dramatic changes in recent decades and, in particular, the post-9/11 environment, right-wing activists and religious fundamentalists in many countries have crusaded for a return to "traditional values." Implicitly, and sometimes explicitly, the policies they

promote rely on and reproduce ahistorical stereotypes (of groups, cultures, religions, nations) and polarized thinking (right-wrong, patriots-
traitors, believers-infidels). In this sense, an understandable desire for
security and stability in the face of disturbing changes is translated into
an incitement of essentializing and oppositional thinking that tends to
exacerbate crises of insecurity.

Although they appear timeless, ideologies are context-dependent and
alterable to suit the interests of those with power. For example, as conditions change, gender ideology may promote women as physically strong
and capable of backbreaking work (slave women, frontier women), as
dexterous and immune to boredom (electronics assembly industries), as
competent to do men's work (women as industrial workers during war),
or as full-time housewives and devoted mothers (postwar demands that
women vacate jobs in favor of returning soldiers and focus on repopulating the nation). The point is that ideologies are often reconfigured to
suit the changing interests of those in power, though rarely the interests
of subordinated groups.

In sum, ideologies make the status quo appear natural, as "the way
things are," rather than as the result of human intervention and practice.
Like stereotypes and dichotomies, they oversimplify what are, in fact,
complex processes and obscure differences in power that serve some
more than others. Insofar as elites dominate religion, myths, educational
systems, advertising, and the media, these institutionalized practices are
variously involved in reproducing stereotypes and ideologies that make
the crises in the world we live in seem inevitable and, for some who
profit from these crises, even desirable. Conditions in the world are indeed very bad, but the point here is that ideologies present only a partial
and particular view of the world that favors those already enjoying disproportionate power. Most important, dominant ideologies obscure the
reality of structural inequalities, how they impoverish the majority and
threaten all of us, and how we can act to resist and change them.

It is important also to consider how in the absence of critique and reflection, much of our behavior *unintentionally* reproduces status quo inequalities and oppressive ideologies. We cannot simply locate an "enemy" to
blame for institutional discrimination and its many consequences. Although there are, of course, individuals who actively pursue discriminatory
policies and the perpetuation of injustice, few of us positively identify with

such characterizations. Most of us wish to be and think of ourselves as good family members, friends, neighbors, and citizens. Most of us express a commitment to the ideals of equality, equity, democratic principles, decreasing violence, and ensuring the sustainability of the environment.

But stereotypes, dichotomies, and ideologies play a particular role in shaping our expectations and behaviors. We begin to be socialized into dominant belief systems early in life, well before we have the capacity to reflect critically on their implications for our own or others' lives. Hence, for the most part we internalize these beliefs and do not think to question them. This is especially true of childhood socialization regarding gender, sexuality, ethnicity/race, class, and national distinctions and ordering systems. Our internalization of these belief systems subsequently disciplines our thoughts and actions, without our even being aware of this. As Allan Johnson has noted, most of the time we are simply following "paths of least resistance" (2005: 80)—conforming to cultural expectations and rules that appear to be common sense. Using the example of being in a movie theater, he points out that in any particular situation there are unlimited things we *might* do (sing loudly, throw objects, light a fire), but a smaller range of things we are *likely* to do, because they are the "obvious" options (sit quietly, be polite); they will encounter the "least resistance" because they are the most taken-for-granted behaviors. Typically, we follow a path of least resistance because it is the only one we are aware of, or the one we consciously prefer (sitting quietly). Other times, we do so because doing otherwise would create resistance in the form of negative responses, the extent and intensity of which vary. For example, a critical remark might generate feelings of discomfort, a scolding look, a verbal rebuke, social ostracism, getting arrested, or physical violence.

The point here is to recognize how, typically, our behavior is shaped by unconscious conformity to internalized "rules" and/or by conscious preference for "going along to get along," conforming simply because it is easier than not doing so. On the one hand, it is not possible to be continually and consciously examining every possible choice, and patterns in our actions are a necessary component of individual sanity and social order. On the other hand, when we follow paths of least resistance in contexts of institutionalized inequality and oppression—that is, conditions of structural violence—we effectively contribute to the reproduction of these practices, *whether intended or not*. Laughing at racist or sexist humor, assuming your audience is heterosexual, not questioning the demonization of someone or some group, perpetuating excessive consumption, failing to protest discrimination and exploitation, and remaining silent or taking no action in the face of government (and other) abuses of power—all in small and large ways sustain unjust power relations. Although not the same as direct and intentional harms, taking these paths of least resistance nonetheless perpetuates harms. By "going along" we further the stabilization—rather than disruption or contestation—of beliefs, stereotypes, assumptions, privileging, orderings, marginalizations, and devalorizations that perpetuate and "naturalize" inequalities and oppression, that is, conditions of structural violence. In Johnson's words, "We don't have to be ruthless *people* in order to support or follow paths of least resistance that lead to behavior with ruthless *consequences*" (2006: 86). A crucial dimension of transforming systems of power—rather than perpetuating them—is that we be more consciously aware of buried assumptions, damaging stereotypes, and arrogant presumptions that have become institutionalized as "the way things are" and "how things are done."

Complicating the picture is our tendency to be unreflective about structural hierarchies and how they confer privilege—"unearned advantages"—on some people by denying it to others. Most males are privileged by gender and enjoy advantages denied to most women, though this is complicated when men are gay and hence not privileged by sexuality. Anyone who is identified by others as belonging to a privileged group has privilege conferred on them, whether or not that individual seeks it, or even if they are activists resisting such institutionalized privilege. For example, whites who are active against racism still enjoy the privilege of not being treated suspiciously when they enter a store to shop. It is in this sense that social hierarchies are structural—about group stereotypes and institutionalized practices—and not simply individual or idiosyncratic. Peggy McIntosh (2007) has provided telling examples of how much those who enjoy privileged statuses can take for granted, how much they do not have to think about (or be angered, hurt, or impoverished by) the effects of structural hierarchies (see Box 2.1).

Being held accountable and subject to sanctions is appropriate in regard to intended and specific harms. But this addresses only the individualized aspect of the problem and tends to be counterproductive and

BOX 2.1 **Illuminating Invisible Privilege**

Privilege constitutes an "invisible package of unearned assets" that can be counted on and about which the privileged are encouraged to remain oblivious. It is hard not to desire and to enjoy privilege. We are not trained to see ourselves as oppressors, as unfairly advantaged, or as participants in damaged cultures. Hence, we often unintentionally participate in reproducing oppression simply by taking our privilege—and the culture and structures that sustain it—as "normal." The following examples suggest everyday ways in which the privileged can take for granted advantages that are denied to others. This is the nature of structural oppression: Advantages to some are premised upon their denial to others.

White/Anglo Privilege
(many of the following apply to elite privilege more generally)

1. I can turn on the television or read the paper and see people of my race/ethnicity widely and positively represented. I can be sure that my children will be given educational materials that testify to the existence and value of their race, and I do not have to teach them about systemic racism for their own daily protection.
2. I am never asked to speak for all the people of my racial group. I can behave in an unconventional or unattractive manner without people attributing these "faults" to my race. I am not made acutely aware that my shape, mode of dress, abilities, or body odor will be taken as a reflection on my race. When I perform well, I am not called a credit to my race.
3. I can remain oblivious to the language, customs, desires, and injuries of persons of color (who constitute the majority of the world). Within my culture, I suffer no penalty for this ignorance and insensitivity. If I do protest racism, my efforts are not disparaged as self-interested or self-seeking.
4. I can be confident that if I seek accommodation, a job, social services, legal help, or medical care, my race will not work against me.
5. I can count on the presence of English-speakers even in foreign countries, and that most professional meetings I attend will be conducted in English.

Male Privilege

1. I can watch, listen to, and read multiple media and count on most of the actors, directors, athletes, speakers, authors, teachers, politicians, scientists, religious leaders, and corporate decision-makers to represent my gender and interests. At school, I can count on learning (and my children learning) about what men find interesting, what they have said and done (mostly about and with other men) throughout history and across cultures, and how men's ideas, theories, discoveries, conquests, experiments, and conquests have determined "human" history and progress.

2. I can go walking, drinking, working, and playing wherever I want to without fear of violence on the basis of my sex. I can dress as I like without being held responsible if I am harassed or attacked. If I behave assertively, aggressively, dogmatically, and/or unsympathetically, I will usually be applauded for "taking control."

3. I can attend religious services and count on celebrating the experiences, authority, power, and spiritual teachings of men. I can readily access visual and written materials that objectify women and cultivate male dominance.

4. Aside from personal relationships (and often even then), I can remain oblivious to the fantasies, life experiences, health concerns, distresses, and injuries of women (who constitute more than half the world's population). I rarely suffer any penalty for this ignorance and insensitivity. If I protest sexism, I am not dismissed as being self-interested.

5. I can choose not to participate in parenting without being branded unnatural or immoral.

6. If I am successful and single, it is assumed to be my choice rather than my inability to attract women.

Heterosexual Privilege

1. I can enjoy virtually all popular cultural media as a celebration of desires, humor, stories, relationships, intimacy, romance, and family life that I participate in and identify with. My children are exposed to cultural and educational materials that support our kind of family unit and do not turn them against my choice of domestic partnership. I can enjoy the taxation, legal, health insurance, adoption, and immigration benefits of being able to marry.

2. I have no difficulty finding neighborhoods, schools, jobs, recreational activities, or travel arrangements where people approve of our family unit. I can express feelings of affection for my partner in public, without fear of censure or physical attack.

3. If in my work or play I spend time with children of my sex, my motives and actions are not treated with suspicion. If I am critical of heterosexism, I am not dismissed as self-interested.

4. I, and my children, can talk about our home life or the social events of the weekend without fearing most listeners' reactions. I am not asked to deny or hide who I am, in the important sense of my sexual identity, desires, and loving relationships.

5. If the person I love does not share my citizenship, we have the option of marriage, which permits us to live together and have a family.

Adapted from McIntosh 2007: 9–15. We have expanded and revised
McIntosh's examples, in particular, to reflect our global focus.

backward looking in relation to structural oppressions and hierarchies, which are sustained less by explicit and intentional harms than by continual, unconscious, and cumulative repetition of conformity (taking the path of least resistance) to historically institutionalized practices that we inherit. Similarly, a further problem with sanctioning individual behavior is the setting up of disciplining and punishment systems that privilege coercive approaches to solving social problems. Structural oppressions and hierarchies are, by definition, the effect of institutionalized practices and social ordering, hence not reducible to individual acts or ameliorated by individual punishments.

We emphasize two points. Once they are historically in place, institutionalized hierarchies generate paths of least resistance that "automatically" reproduce structures of inequality. Hence, the perpetuation of many oppressions is less a matter of intentionally promoting harms than unintentionally (unconsciously) reproducing (going along to get along) the institutions we inherit—what (unreflectively) appears to be "the way things are." Once in place, structural privilege confers power on those with privilege, whether desired or not. Hence, privileged individuals are not to blame for (inherited) institutional hierarchies; but the privileged in every hierarchy have greater power *and therefore greater responsibility* for transforming those and related hierarchies. Rather than be caught up in blaming and its defensive responses, our objective here is to increase awareness of these opaque issues and promote less *unintentional* participation in reproducing inequalities and structural oppressions, that is, taking paths of least resistance, when these are actually part of the problem.

Oppressive hierarchies are not in fact inevitable. If we are to change the world, we must change ourselves, as well as the social structures that both produce and are produced by those selves. We cannot change either without changing how we think. In that regard, understanding the role of stereotypes, dichotomies, and ideologies is crucial. We turn next to how these are gendered.

FEMINIST INQUIRY AND POLITICIZING GENDER

In this section we shift from lenses in general to gender-sensitive lenses. We draw on feminist analyses to politicize gender by denaturalizing it:

Drawing attention to cross-cutting dynamics of culture, ethnicity/race, class, sexuality, nationality, age, and other axes of difference reveals many variations of gender. Its particular manifestations do vary, but we argue that gender operates pervasively to constitute systems of structurally significant power. Gender is thus unequivocally *political*. We next turn to clarifying what we mean by the power of gender as a hegemonic worldview—in our account, a meta-lens or meta-narrative—by providing a more detailed account of the social construction of gender and gendered hierarchies and the political work that feminization does.

DENATURALIZING GENDER

Today there are many complexities in defining sex—conventionally understood as the biological distinction between embodied females and males—and gender. References to gender have proliferated in recent decades, as feminists worldwide drew attention to the unequal positions of women and men. Two unintended effects of this shift in discourse have been to think, typically and erroneously, that gender is a synonym for "women" and to assume that women constitute a homogeneous category. We argue, instead, that gender refers to the dichotomous and hierarchical relationship between the social constructions of masculinity and femininity as a major source of power projections and inequalities in world affairs. Hence, gender is a social, not physiological, construction; it is not the same as, and may be wholly unrelated to, sex; it is not a synonym for women, but rather a hierarchical relationship between constructions of masculinity and femininity; hence, men and masculinity are as important as women and femininity are for analyzing gender.[5]

The particular characteristics associated with femininity and masculinity vary significantly across cultures, races, classes, and age groups. As we emphasize throughout this text, there are no generic women and men; our gender identities, loyalties, interests, and opportunities are affected by countless dimensions of "difference," and especially those associated with ethnicity/race, class, national, and sexual identities. "Acting like a man" (or a woman) means different things to different groups of people (e.g., heterosexual Catholics, Native Americans, British colonials, agriculturists versus corporate managers, athletes versus orchestra conductors, combat soldiers versus military strategists) and to the same group of people at different points in time (e.g., nineteenth- versus twentieth-century Europeans, colonized versus postcolonial Africans, prepuberty versus elderly age sets, women during war versus after war). Men may be characterized as feminine (e.g., Mahatma Gandhi; "flamboyant" gay men) and women as "masculine" (e.g., Margaret Thatcher; "butch" lesbians). Gender is shaped by race (models of masculinity and femininity vary among Africans, Indians, Asians, Europeans), and race is gendered (gender stereotypes shape racial stereotypes of Africans, Indians, Asians, whites). Moreover, because masculinities and femininities vary (by class, race/ethnicity, sexuality, age), some expressions of gender (Hispanic in the United States, Muslim in India, Turkana in Kenya) are subordinated to *dominant* constructions of gender (Anglo, Hindu, Kikuyu). There are thus multiple masculinities, although an idealized model often dominates in representations of masculinity. Even within dominant masculinities, particular characteristics may be more or less valued in particular contexts (aggressive masculinity may be good for fighting but less desirable as a management style and inappropriate in conflict-resolution processes).

Because models of appropriate gender behavior are diverse, we know that femininity and masculinity are not timeless or separable from the contexts in which they are embodied, acted out, and observed. This illustrates how gender rests not on biological sex differences but on *interpretations* or constructions of behavior that are culturally specific, that shift as contexts change, and that typically have little to do with biological differences. In short, there are multiple gender orderings, and gender is always raced, classed, sexualized, and nationalized, just as race, class, sexuality, and nationality are always gendered. Hence, our analytical lenses must avoid essentializing singular identities and instead adopt intersectional analyses to make sense of our multiple, cross-cutting, and differentially valorized identities.

Although the specific traits that mark gender-appropriate behavior vary cross-culturally, they constitute systems of politically significant structural power in the following interacting ways. First, males are expected to conform to models of masculinity (that are privileged) and females to models of femininity (that are subordinated). There are multiple models of masculinity within cultures, but one typically has hegemonic status as the most valued and esteemed model that is associated with elite (class, race, and culturally privileged) males. Within particular cultures, these expectations are taken very seriously, because they are considered fundamental to who we are, how we are perceived by others, and what actions are appropriate. In this sense, gender ordering is inextricable from social ordering of power, authority, work, leisure, and pleasure. (We expand on the importance of gender to subject formation later.)

Second, because masculine activities are more highly valued or privileged than are feminine activities in most of the world most of the time, the identities and activities associated with men and women are typically unequal. Thus, the social construction of gender is actually a system of power that not only divides the world into "men" and "women" and masculine and feminine, but also typically places some men and masculinity above most women and femininity. Consider, for example, how consistently institutions and practices that are male-dominated and/or representative of hegemonically masculine traits and style (politics, making money) are valued more highly and considered more important than institutions and practices associated with femininity (families, caring labor).

Third, because the dichotomy of masculine and feminine constructs them as polarized and mutually exclusive (A and not-A), when we favor or privilege that which is associated with masculinity, we do so at the expense of that which is associated with femininity. Politics, as conventionally defined, is about differential access to power—about who gets what and how. Therefore, the privileging of masculinity is political insofar as relations of inequality, manifested in this case as gender inequality, represent men's and women's unequal access to power, authority, and resources. In this sense, the power of gender is effectively masculinist, which refers to individuals, perspectives, practices, and institutions that embody, naturalize, and privilege the traits of masculinity at the expense of feminized and other alternatives, and are thus engaged in producing and sustaining relations of gender inequality.

Like other social hierarchies, gender inequality is maintained by various means, ranging from psychological mechanisms (sexist humor, blaming the victim, internalizing oppressive stereotypes), sociocultural practices (objectifying women, "chilly climates," sexual harassment, trivializing women's concerns), structural discrimination (denial of equal rights, job segregation, marginalizing reproductive health issues) to direct violence (domestic battering, rape, homicide). Also, like many social hierarchies, gender inequality is "justified" by focusing on physical differences and exaggerating their significance as determinants of what are in fact socially constructed, learned behaviors. Thus, Arthur Brittan has argued that by denying the social construction of gender, masculinism serves to justify and "naturalize" (depoliticize) male domination because "it takes for granted that there is a fundamental difference between men and women, it assumes that heterosexuality is normal, it accepts without question the sexual division of labor, and it sanctions the political and dominant role of men in the public and private spheres" (1989: 4).

Like the abstract concepts of family, race, and nation, gender "in the real" sense is always inflected by such dimensions as race/ethnicity and class that vary depending on culture and context. What does not appear to vary is the power of gender to conceptually and structurally organize not only identities and sexual practices, but virtually all aspects of social life in all cultures. In one sense, we see this in how gender pervades our naming, clothing, speaking, working, entertainment, sports, religious authority, knowledge production, militarization, and governance. In another sense, the power of gender operates as a meta-lens to continually normalize—hence depoliticize—essentialized stereotypes, dichotomized categories, and hierarchical arrangements. In these multiple and overlapping ways, gender is political: It operates pervasively to produce and sustain unequal power relations. Hence, lenses that obscure how gender operates systemically and structurally are politically inadequate and obstruct the pursuit of social justice.

Masculinism is arguably the dominant mode of gender ideology: valuing what is characterized as masculine at the expense of what is feminine, with the material effect of elevating the positioning of men in general above and at the expense of the positioning of women in general. But masculinism also operates to materially exclude or marginalize all those who are feminized, whether women or men. Understood as a key "move" in producing, reproducing, and naturalizing gender hierarchy, masculinism and masculinist lenses are political and deeply implicated in exclusionary practices.

Feminism, in contrast, is a more complicated and contested term. There are, in fact, many forms of feminism, and these are discussed later in this chapter. Here we suggest that the common thread among feminisms is an orientation valuing women's diverse experiences and taking seriously women's interests in and capacities for bringing about social and political change. (Because ideologies are not given biologically but are socioculturally and politically constructed, we note here that masculinist perspectives can be held by women and feminist perspectives can be held by men.) As an aspect of making change, many feminists advocate shifting attention away from men and their activities so that women and their lives come into clearer focus. The objective is to increase awareness of and take more seriously women's diverse ways of identifying, acting, and knowing—and especially—women's agency. This may involve revaluing feminized characteristics—affect, connectedness, sensitivity to others and the self—that have traditionally (through masculinist lenses) been romanticized, trivialized, or deemed inferior. But we note here that the ultimate objective is not a simplistic role reversal in which women gain power over men or femininity becomes more valued than masculinity. Rather, a range of feminist individuals, organizations, perspectives, practices, and institutions seek an end to social relations of gender inequality in recognition that class, race, sexuality, and national origin inequalities exist among women and men and between them. Such recognition arose from the question of which men women want to be equal to given the many inequalities among men. This, in turn, prompted the understanding that economically and racially privileged women can oppress less economically and racially privileged (or feminized) men. Thus, gender equality has been rethought to entail transforming the stereotypes and polarization of gender identities and contesting how masculinity is privileged in concepts, practices, and institutions. For us, this also entails transforming the masculinist and imperialist ways of thinking and acting that produce global crises of representation, insecurity, and sustainability. Doing so requires a gender-sensitive lens that reveals not only the (re-)positionings of women in relation to men but also how the power of gender operates to re-position some women at the expense of other women and to continually disempower the majority of men—and women. While gender-sensitive lenses are now familiar in feminist accounts and appear increasingly in studies of world politics, the power of gender as we deploy it in this text is less familiar, and hence is the focus of the next section.

THE "POWER OF GENDER" AS A META-LENS

We make numerous claims about the power of gender as a lens because this lens involves numerous dimensions, most of which are so taken for granted (normalized) that they operate below a conscious level. We argue that the constellation of these interactive dimensions (our meta-lens) has become a hegemonic worldview that is rarely acknowledged, therefore not analytically or critically addressed, and hence often unintentionally reproduced. In this section we "unpack" these dimensions to bring into sharper focus the many ways in which gender operates to normalize hierarchical thinking and ordering and effectively disable more complex intersectional analyses that are crucial to "seeing" and addressing crises of representation, insecurity, and sustainability.

The questions we address in this section include these: How does gender become so deeply internalized, so taken for granted, and so embedded in social relations? How are gendered identities constructed so that we are deeply invested in them and enact them pervasively in social life? How are stereotypes and dichotomized thinking gendered in ways that deepen the normalization and unreflective reproduction of the power of gender? How has the power of gender become so pervasive and potent yet so invisible and marginalized in accounts of world politics?

To clarify the power of gender as a meta-lens requires mapping the social construction of gender and gendered hierarchies. We do so by examining social formations from several vantage points: the formation of gendered identities (subjectivities) and internalization of hierarchical gender coding, the operation of gender coding throughout social relations, and the institutionalization and reproduction of gendered social structures. The map thus covers *socialization:* how individuals are taught and internalize culturally appropriate gendered ways of identifying, thinking, and acting. Families, schools, religious institutions, and media are important sources of this socialization. The map also attends to systemic, or structural, *control:* how ways of identifying, thinking, and acting keep gender hierarchy in place by generating conformity and compliance. Gender coding shapes and is shaped by dominant conceptual ordering systems that become institutionalized through favoring some practices over others. As individuals participate in these institutions, the power of gender coding and hierarchies tend to be reproduced, not least because doing so constitutes a path of least resistance. Moral and intellectual control is effected through privileging certain belief systems (masculinism, myth, religion, rationalism, science) so that gender becomes pervasive in social life. More direct social control is effected through job markets, laws, governance, and physical coercion, which tend to reproduce gendered hierarchies and sustain elite power at the expense of obscuring its costs to the majority or identifying alternative ways of thinking and acting.

We begin with the earliest socialization individuals encounter: their emergence into the world as an effect of biological reproduction. We rarely question the need to reproduce social members, but under what conditions, how many, and to what purpose are perennially vexing questions. Actual practices of biological reproduction are shaped by cultural norms, economic conditions, demographic dynamics, reproductive health and technologies, and disciplinary regimes in regard to sex/affective relations.[6] Patriarchal belief systems (that essentialize heterosexual families) and institutionalization of patriarchal ordering (positioning males as heads-of-households, as citizens, and as religious, military, and political authorities) have over millennia become normalized in virtually all social formations. Hence, heterosexism (belief in heterosexuality as the only "normal" mode of sexual orientation, family life, and social relations) is currently the hegemonic model worldwide. Heteronormative ideology assumes a binary construction of (hetero)sexual difference, some form of heterosexual union, and heterosexual patriarchal families as "givens." Critics challenge the adequacy of this assumption, which is increasingly belied by actual arrangements.[7] Sexual relations and family structures have taken diverse forms in the past, and contemporary sex/gender identities, sexual practices, and family forms are undergoing continuous change. The point here is that conventional representations of social reproduction are selective, projecting (hetero)sexual identities, heteronormative families, and (hetero)sexual reproduction as simply given and "natural." But they in fact are embedded in and (literally) embody particular sociocultural, economic, and political relations.

Procreation is a starting point for thinking about gender, but the reproductive choices, practices, and strategies in which procreation occurs are already embedded in social formations with their particular gender codes and patterned expectations. In this sense, socialization precedes and shapes the birth of individuals and how their arrival will be experienced: For many reasons, some are more welcomed than others. However welcomed, the arrival of infants launches socialization processes for that infant. Binary sex-differentiation is key: If newborns are not unambiguously male or female, this poses difficulties that may be variously addressed (depending on cultural contexts and prevailing practices) but will not go unnoticed. Establishing the "sex" of newborns constitutes a basis for responding to and socializing infants, which at the same time shapes the gender-differentiated subject formation processes that infants undergo. Gender identities that subsequently develop are cross-cut by other axes of difference, but our earliest sex-differentiated gender identifications constitute particularly defining elements of "who we are" throughout life. In this sense, the essentialized binary of sex difference (which appears across cultures) is both internalized as a defining "core" of individual identity, and materialized in the production of embodied, gendered individuals.[8] And in a larger sense, the subjective internalization of gender difference and historical normalization of gendered and heteronormative social ordering become deeply embedded, stabilized, institutionalized patterns in how we identify, think, and act.

From birth on, the way we are treated depends on our gender assignment, and we learn in multiple ways how to adopt gender-appropriate behaviors (as these are shaped by age, race, class, nationality, etc.). There are few occasions or interactions where our gender is truly irrelevant: our names, clothes, hairstyles, toys, games, rewards, threats and punishments, the attention we get, the activities we are encouraged to engage in, the roles we are expected to assume, the subjects we study, the knowledge claims we make, the jobs we work at, and the power we have are all profoundly shaped by gendered expectations. As individuals, we differ considerably in the extent to which we conform to cultural expectations. But none of us escapes gender socialization.

Everyone is born into a *culture*—a *set of shared ideas* about the nature of reality, the nature of right and wrong, *evaluation of what is good and desirable*, and the nature of the good and desirable versus the bad and nondesirable. As totally dependent infants we are *socialized*—taught the rules, roles and relationships of the social world. In the process we learn to think, act, and feel as we are "supposed to" (Richardson and Taylor 1983: 1, emphasis in original).

As noted earlier, political theorists recognize that the most effective way to maintain systems of rule is not through direct violence but through ideology: persuading those who are subordinated that inequalities and social hierarchy are natural, therefore inevitable, and even desirable. When people believe that differences in status and power are part of the "natural order of things," they are less likely to see or challenge how society is organized to benefit some more than others. Such people do not require constant external policing because they have internalized their own policing in terms of selective perceptions and lowered expectations. As a consequence, they internalize an acceptance of their own unequal positioning and status quo inequalities between groups. In short, our early socialization into hierarchically ordered systems plays a crucial role in reproducing inequalities and undercutting—though not precluding—resistance. The gender socialization we encounter in early childhood is reinforced by gendered stereotypes, dichotomies, and ordering systems that are present in all cultures. Gender stereotypes pervade the fairy tales, myths, and stories we tell children, the cultural representations they are exposed to (in schoolbooks, religious training, popular media), and the ubiquitous advertising that is now present worldwide. What these communications typically share is a message conveying categorical (essentialized) distinctions between boys and girls, men and women. In many of the world's cultures, dominant, idealized gender stereotypes depict men/masculinity as strong, independent, worldly, assertive, rational, tough, and "in control"; women/femininity are portrayed as the opposite: weak, dependent, naive, peaceful, emotional, gentle, and often unpredictable. This exemplifies the binary structure of gender: constructing man/masculinity and woman/femininity as two poles of a dichotomy—as mutually exclusive or oppositions—that define each other. Not all men (perhaps very few) will meet the normative standards of the hegemonic model of masculinity, but all reap a patriarchal dividend: "the advantage men in general gain from the overall subordination of women" (Connell 1995: 79).

In short, the heteronormative dichotomy or polarization of gender insists (1) that sex difference is ontologically binary, essentializing males and females as unambiguously distinguishable; (2) that there are different scripts (ways of identifying, acting, and knowing) for males and females; (3) that sex difference is important enough to shape diverse spheres of activity (leisure, work, governance); and (4) that persons deviating from sex-appropriate scripts are problematic (suspect as "unnatural" or "immoral"). Hence, heteronormativity insists on unambiguous distinctions between males/masculinity and females/femininity and cultivates *gendered* stereotypes, dichotomies, practices, and institutions in virtually all cultures. This gendering is structurally maintained not only through masculinist myths and narratives, but also through customs, policies, and legislation that impose heteronormative marriage and family arrangements, androcentric (male-as-norm) political institutions, masculinist security arrangements, and sex-differentiated labor markets.

Like dichotomized thinking more generally, putting so much weight on the differences between men/masculinity and women/femininity ensures that what we share is obscured and that any blurring of gender boundaries—and concomitant erosion of masculinism/heterosexism—feels uncomfortable or threatening (it is a path that encounters negativity/resistance) and is typically avoided. The gender dichotomy (and heteronormative denial of ambiguities) highlights distinctions between groups rather than differences within them or commonalities between them. For example, in reality not all males are engaged in "productive" labor, nor do all females bear children and no female bears them throughout her lifetime. But the dichotomy pitting men as performing productive labor (working for wages, creating ideas and products) against women as performing reproductive labor (maintaining the household, bearing and caring for children) masks this variation among females and commonality between males and many females.

Dichotomized thinking is both habitual and political: Its structure constitutes "man" as not simply a different category than "woman" (A and B) but in a relationship of hierarchical opposition (A and not-A); it thus reproduces either-or thinking and privileges some qualities and interests over others. Much is at stake, and it takes a great deal of power to maintain categorical boundaries between masculinity and femininity.[9] Gender stereotypes and dichotomies play a key role. Consider depictions of males and females in popular culture and media: How often is there a physically "rough" or politically powerful girl or woman, especially one who is likable? Or a boy or man who is nurturing and sensual as a constant way of being, not just in certain circumstances? Most telling, why are there so few media images of gender-neutral individuals—people whose gender status is not immediately and unequivocally apparent? Why are we so uncomfortable with gender ambiguities, virtually insisting that individuals be patently *either* men/masculine *or* women/feminine?

Our discomfort reflects two important points. First, gender ambiguity is uncomfortable because we simply do not know how to respond. That is, our expectations and behavior regarding gender are so taken for granted that when we are confronted with ambiguous gender signals, we become confused; we literally do not know how to act. When deeply programmed expectations of gender performance are disrupted—forcing us to think consciously about how to act or respond—we realize how much they (unconsciously) shape our habitual behavior. Second, and relatedly, we typically resent the discomfort and confusion. This reveals how significant our unacknowledged commitments to gender are. That is, when people confront us with gender ambiguity, we resent both not knowing how to act *and* the questions that our confusion raises. If gender identities are not reliable and stable, what does this mean for one's own identity? Because gender identification is so important for "knowing who we are" and how to act, and for securing self-esteem when we "do gender well," confusion about gender identification can feel very threatening.

In the context of masculinist/heteronormative culture, insecurity about one's gender identity is especially acute for males, and arguably a lifelong preoccupation. Because femininity is devalued and male expressions of femininity render their masculinity suspect, males face tremendous pressures to establish that they are "real men"; and being a "real man" requires that gender distinctions are unambiguous. Given the high stakes, it is not surprising that men consistently demonstrate greater discomfort with gender ambiguities than women do. For example, men are much more likely to express homophobia (the abhorrence of homosexuality), in part because homosexuality disrupts conventional gender distinctions and raises questions about what it means to be a "real man." Quite simply, in masculinist/heteronormative cultures, men are motivated to enhance and exaggerate their masculinity by denying any commonality between themselves and women or gay men.

The point to notice here is how completely fabricated—and thus ultimately fragile and unstable—gender is. It is constructed rather than natural, obvious, or unchanging, and men are never sufficiently masculine simply because they have the appropriate genitalia. Establishing one's masculinity is never a done deal: Males face relentless pressures to demonstrate they are "real men" by exhibiting unequivocally masculine qualities and distancing themselves from that which is defined as feminine (Kimmel 2008). This may involve avoidance of body decorations, bright colors, ballet, quiche, flowers, child care, gentleness, and asking directions. It may involve fear of acknowledging emotion, needs, vulnerabilities, and desires for affection/intimacy. It may involve exaggerating one's rationality, competitiveness, and power, or encouraging assertive, tough, and even violent behaviors. It may involve a preference for hard liquor, hard-hitting sports, heavy metal or rap music, militarized video games, or risk-taking exploits.

These examples suggest how cultural codes of gender come to pervade all aspects of social life because "appropriate" gender performance is not only expected but demanded by social ordering. We are thus deeply invested in gendered identities and performances because demonstrating that we are "real men" and "real women" matters emotionally and materially; there are a variety of costs—from mild to deadly—for not conforming to gender stereotypes. Because biological criteria alone do not establish our status as real men and real women, we must continuously "perform" (demonstrate, act out) gender attitudes and behaviors to "prove" our gender identification. Doing so makes all of social life a test of our performance: Gender comes to matter in what we wear, eat, and drink, how we talk, laugh, and gesticulate, what entertainment and activities we prefer, how we approach risk-taking and dependence, and how we measure intelligence, courage, and leadership.

In sum, the acting out of gender—and the importance we put on doing so appropriately—demonstrates (1) how gender is not biologically determined but socially constructed, expected, and performed throughout life; (2) how we become deeply invested in oppositional gendered identities and performing gender appropriately; and (3) how polarized gendered identities and their corollary performances then reproduce gender-differentiated identities, behaviors, and ultimately, inequalities. At the same time, the preceding points suggest the fragility of gender, how easily it can be disrupted and altered, how complex and differentiated our gendered lives actually are, and how much power it takes to sustain categorical gender distinctions and project the "superiority" of masculinity over femininity.

From yet another angle of vision, dichotomized gender is not only hierarchical (privileging the first term over the second) but also *androcentric* (assuming a male-as-norm point of view). This androcentrism has three interacting effects. First, because the primary term (A) is androcentric and privileged, it effectively elevates masculinist values over those of the secondary (not-A) term. Thus, reason, control, and culture are associated with maleness and are privileged over affect, uncertainty, and nature. Second and closely related, characteristics and activities associated with femaleness are deemed not only less important but also unworthy or undesirable because they appear to threaten the values represented by the primary term. Thus, emotion, relationality, reproduction, and caretaking are given less attention and often disparaged.[10] At the same time, reason, rationality, and rational agency are withheld from those feminized, reducing their thoughts, actions, and very beings to "instinctual" or "cultural" explanations. Moreover, rationality is reduced to only instrumental rationality put into the service of control.

Androcentrism has a third effect: It assumes that (elite) men are the most important actors and the substance of their lives the most important topic to know about. As long as the realities of women, nonelite men, and children are treated as secondary to the main story—as the background that is never important enough to warrant being spotlighted—we, as collective knowledge seekers, are made unaware of what the background actually is and what relationship it actually has to the main story. What we are unaware of we cannot understand or analyze. Nor can we understand to what extent and in what ways the main story depends on background that is made invisible or silenced by focusing illumination and attention elsewhere. Rendering the experiences or realities of "others" invisible tends to present the main story, which often rests upon unexamined or "naturalized" assumptions about "others," as real and authoritative, as if it was all that we needed to know to understand what is going on. In all three cases, assumptions of privilege and importance encourage an attitude of superiority and dismissal or fear of what constitutes the background. From the lofty heights, contrasting experiences and alternative perspectives are invisible and hence effectively excluded or silenced. Certain questions cannot even be asked, or concerns expressed. In IR, for example, a top-down preoccupation with elite governance, international militarism, and corporate profits renders everything that underpins and enables these activities—and their power—irrelevant.

This discussion begins to suggest how gender stereotypes interact with modernist, positivist lenses that rely on dichotomized thinking and tend toward acritical and typically conservative orientations. In Cynthia Epstein's words, "No aspect of social life—whether the gathering of crops, the ritual of religion, the formal dinner party, or the organization of government—is free from the dichotomous thinking that casts the world in categories of 'male' and 'female'" (1988: 232). Our earlier account noted how poststructuralists criticize binary logic for its role in sustaining status quo inequalities. But feminists go beyond that general critique to argue that dichotomized thinking cannot be adequately understood, critiqued, or effectively transformed without addressing how sex-differentiated gender "grounds," naturalizes, and reproduces binary thinking.

We have argued that newborns are assigned a gender identity on the basis of essentializing sex difference as "either male or female." Gendered subject formation ensues, we internalize oppositional gender coding at an early age, and "accept" both that males and females are fundamentally different and (because the dichotomy is hierarchical) that masculinity is more highly valued than femininity. Continual socialization operates by various means (gendered stereotypes, dichotomies, and ordering systems) to produce and enforce conformity to gender-differentiated ways of identifying, thinking, and acting. Deviating from gender norms is costly—and often severely punished. The desire for self-esteem and psychic coherence that conformity promises deepens our investment in performing gender appropriately, and as we do so throughout life, the hierarchical dichotomy of male/masculinity over female/femininity is reproduced—and further "naturalized."

We now add to this picture—and what we mean by the "power of gender"—by linking dichotomized gender and the status of dichotomized thinking in modernist, positivist orientations. The basic argument is that the essentialized binary of sex difference (that "grounds" and generates the dichotomy of gender differentiation) and the privileged status of dichotomies (that "grounds" rationality and objectivity claims) are *mutually reinforcing*. As a consequence, both are further naturalized (taken for granted), become constitutive elements of the power of gender, and operate systemically to shape conceptual and social orderings hierarchically.

On the one hand (as discussed earlier), poststructuralists and postcolonialists criticize the structure and status of dichotomized thinking that pervades modernist, positivist thought. They argue that dichotomies *structure* our thinking in ways that are stunted (reductionist), static (ahistorical), simplistic (decontextualized), and politically problematic (essentializing; disabling critical reflection). And the privileged *status* of modernist, positivist orientations sustains dichotomized thinking as a taken-for-granted and desirable outcome, obscures how dichotomies structure thought in extremely limited ways, and resists critical reflection on the politics of dichotomies and their divisive effects. As constitutive elements of ideological thinking, dichotomies essentialize particular group identities in oppositional, hierarchical terms, amplify and privilege the interests of elites at the expense of stereotyped "others," and obscure the commonalities and possible shared interests of larger collectivities and longer-term objectives.

On the other hand, feminists and other critics of heteronormativity have exposed the assumption of binary sex difference as stunted (reducing "sex" to paired opposites, precluding alternatives and commonalities), static (neglecting historical shifts in how "sex" is "seen" and responded to), simplistic (obscuring the complexity of "sex" and its relationship to gender), and politically problematic (unreflectively essentializing what is historically situated and socially constructed). Feminist research has additionally documented the deeply sedimented normalization of dichotomized gender (generated by essentializing sex as a binary) as a governing code valorizing that which is privileged as masculine, at the expense of that which is stigmatized as feminine. Gendered socialization and social control mechanisms amplify individual and collective internalization of, and investments in, reproducing gendered orderings. Here we argue that more adequate analyses of power require attending to and integrating the critical insights of poststructuralist, postcolonial, and feminist lenses. In particular, to comprehend the resilience of hierarchical thinking and its reproduction of divisions and inequalities requires making sense of the "power of gender" as a hegemonic and pernicious but typically unacknowledged worldview.

Stated simply and based on preceding arguments, the "naturalness" of sex difference becomes indistinguishable from the "naturalness" of dichotomized and hierarchical gender differentiation that we reproduce, consciously and unconsciously, as we "act out" gender in all areas of social life. Because of this interaction, gendered stereotypes have political significance far beyond their role in male-female relations. First, gender normalizes dichotomized thought as a deeply embedded practice reproduced throughout social orders. Second, the gender dichotomy is so taken as given that it lends authority to the binary logic that "naturally" divides terms and identity groups into polarized opposites. The "naturalness" of dichotomized gender then becomes indistinguishable from—and lends credibility and authority to—the "naturalness" of dichotomized thinking. Third, the normalization of dichotomized thinking not only reproduces gender hierarchy but other relations of inequality as dichotomies are taken for granted and effectively legitimate hierarchical ordering.

At the same time and as we argued earlier, the binary logic of positivist orientations normalizes and privileges thinking in dichotomies. The elevated status of this logic lends credibility and authority to the practice of essentializing categories as paired opposites, valuing one over the "other" term, and normalizing domination of whatever and whoever is "othered." In this sense, the normalization of dichotomies in modernist thought lends credibility and authority to the binary of sex and dichotomy of gender. Insofar as other familiar dichotomies have gendered connotations (culture-nature, reason-emotion, autonomy-dependency, public-private), when they are deployed in modernist thought, they buttress the stereotypes of masculine and feminine. Turn back to page 52 and take a moment to consider the dichotomies presented in Table 2.1 through a gender-sensitive lens. Consider how frequently and unconsciously we rely on these dichotomies when we think and communicate; how gender stereotypes infuse the terms in both columns, but with quite different valences: positive and privileged associations with masculinized qualities, negative and stigmatized associations with feminized qualities. Consider the political implications of relentlessly reproducing these patterns of hierarchical thought.

This is what we mean by mutually reinforcing: The dichotomy of gender gains its "naturalness" by being "grounded" in the "given" of essentialized sex difference; gendered orderings are "normalized" by being reproduced throughout social life; dichotomies gain their taken-for-granted and even desirable status by being privileged in modernist thought and acquiring credibility through the "reality" of pervasive gendered differentiation. The mutually reinforcing interplay of essentializing sex, dichotomizing gender, and the binary logic of positivism generates the constellation of dimensions we refer to as a meta-lens. Recognizing the power of these coding and filtering devices is crucial for improving our ability to "see beyond" essentialized identities and oppositional "wholes." There is yet one more aspect of the power of gender constellation that we need to clarify.

INTERSECTIONAL ANALYSIS AND "FEMINIZATION AS DEVALORIZATION"

We have argued that gendered coding and ideologies present in all social formations normalize and privilege masculinist ways of identifying, thinking, and acting. At the same time, stereotypes, dichotomies, and hierarchical ordering are present in all social formations, sustaining narratives of mutually exclusive, oppositional difference and legitimating the domination of some over "others." Although masculinism most obviously operates to devalue women and reproduce unequal positionings of men and women, it operates across hierarchies of ethnicity/race, class, nation, and sexuality as well. In this section we shift attention from men and women to ways in which ideological manipulation of gender coding and gendered differences produce and "justify" divisions and hierarchies.

The central point is that the symbolic, discursive, and cultural *privileging of masculinity does not privilege only men or all men*. Rather, privileging who and what is masculinized is inextricable from devaluing who and what is feminized. It is recognizing the interdependence of masculinity and femininity as oppositional but reciprocally defined terms— one "requires" the other—that provides analytical and political leverage. The claim is then that gender—with its lauded masculinity and denigrated femininity—pervades language and cultural codes, with systemic effects on how we take for granted (normalize and effectively depoliticize) the devalorization of all feminized statuses (e.g., "lazy migrants," "primitive natives," "effeminate gays"). Romanticizing femininity often appears to privilege it, but never empowers it. We argue instead that the more an individual or a social category is feminized, the more likely (not invariably) that their categorical difference and devaluation is assumed or presumed to be "explained." These claims advance intersectional analysis by enabling us to see how diverse hierarchies are linked and ideologically "naturalized" by feminizing individuals and social categories that are subordinated.

There are several interactive moves here that require closer inspection. In one sense, casting the subordinated as feminine devalorizes not only women but also sexually, racially, culturally, and economically marginalized men. Underpinning this claim is the observation that although structural hierarchies vary by reference to the "differences" emphasized and the disparate modalities of power involved, they typically share a common feature: their denigration of feminized qualities attributed to those who are subordinated (lacking reason, control, etc.). Because it is so taken for granted, invoking the "natural" inferiority of the feminine plays a powerful—though not exhaustive—role in "legitimating" these hierarchies. In a second sense, not only subjects (women and marginalized men) but also concepts, desires, tastes, styles, ways of knowing, cultural expressions (art, music), roles, practices, work, and nature can be feminized. This effectively reduces their legitimacy, status, and value and fuels stereotypical characterizations that can be deployed to depoliticize unequal valorizations. In both senses, devalorization powerfully normalizes—with the effect of "legitimating"—the subordination, exploitation of, and various forms of violence against feminized concepts, skills, activities and persons.

As intersectional analysts argue, oppressions differ, and so do attempts to explain and/or justify them. Feminization is then only one among a number of normalizing ideologies. To be clear: We are not arguing that gender hierarchy is the primary oppression or the most salient or powerful hierarchy in any particular context. As Yuval-Davis has noted, "in specific historical situations and in relation to specific people . . . some social divisions . . . are more important than others"; at the same time, some social divisions (e.g., age, gender, ethnicity/race, class) "tend to shape people's lives in most social locations," whereas other divisions (e.g., castes, status as indigenous or refugee persons) profoundly affect those subject to them but "tend to affect fewer people globally" (2006: 203). Nor is our objective to prioritize the subordination of women or deny the different organizing logics or modalities of power operating in racism, classism, nationalism, and so on. It is rather to note that even as social divisions have different ontological bases, they are not historically independent of each other, and gender is an important linkage among them, especially with reference to the political project of normalizing, hence depoliticizing, hierarchical valorizations.

The central point we make here emerges from earlier discussions to argue that what distinguishes feminization—and renders it so potent an aspect of the power of gender—is the unique extent to which it invokes the deeply embedded, internalized, and naturalized binary of sex difference and gender dichotomy. Ambiguities of sex and gender may be increasingly visible to some, but most people most of the time take "sex difference" completely for granted—as biologically "given," reproductively necessary, and psychosocially "obvious." We have argued, however, that sex difference is a (mistakenly) essentialized binary that (falsely) "grounds" gender as a system of difference construction and hierarchical dichotomy production. In this sense, the symbolic coding of gender differentiation and material manifestations of gendered hierarchies are mutually constituted and mutually reinforcing. To repeat: The naturalness of sex difference naturalizes dichotomized gender differentiations (pervading all of social life) and thinking in hierarchical, categorical oppositions more generally. Insofar as these naturalizations and masculinist (not necessarily male) privilege become common sense, their ideological power is then "available" (through cultural coding of reason, agency, governing and protecting, etc., as masculine; and irrationality, dependence, being governed and protected, etc., as feminine) for legitimating other forms of domination (e.g., racism, imperialism, militarism, homophobia, economic exploitation).

The power of gender produces a common sense of privileging the masculine and devaluing the feminine that is culturally and collectively internalized to such an extent that we are all variously complicit in its reproduction. It is also implicitly and explicitly manipulated to reproduce inequalities as if this were natural and inevitable, thus undercutting critique and resistance. In these ways, devalorizing the feminine produces even as it obscures vast inequalities of power, authority, and resource distribution. Exposing how this power operates must be one objective of a critical political agenda.

These points are crucial to the arguments of this text because the perpetuation of dichotomized thinking and its gendered normalizations reproduces hierarchical divisions and hence antagonistic relations between groups. What we referred to in Chapter 1 as re-masculinization of world politics involves reprivileging (elite) men as political and military leaders and media commentators, new forms of hegemonic masculinities, the manipulation of women's and feminist issues to support masculinist projects, and the manipulation of even the concept of gender equality to privilege some women over other women and some men over other men. The power of gender here operates to obscure intersectionality—how we have multiple identities carrying different forms and degrees of privilege that operate within as well as across groups. When the power of gender focuses attention on essentialized notions of gender—masculinity and femininity—we fail to see these as constructed and cross-cutting dimensions operating within any particular group and across groups. Similarly, when essentialized notions of group identities erase the differentiations within them, we fail to see the complexity of social orders and how inequalities are often sustained by pitting subordinated groups against each other. In the process, we lose sight of the potential for coalitions and more comprehensive resistances to unjust social and world political orders. Deploying intersectional analysis facilitates a more comprehensive notion of gender equality that is indivisible from racial, class, and sexual equality, and equality among nations. It encourages us to ask not just "Where are the women?" but also "Which women?" and "Where are the men?"

FEMINIST IR LENSES

More than three decades of feminist scholarship have re-positioned gender on the agenda of academic disciplines. Both within and outside of IR, feminist critiques have altered disciplinary givens, challenged conventional explanations, and expanded the reach of intellectual inquiry.

As noted earlier, feminists share a commitment to investigating gendered inequalities and to improving the conditions of women's lives. But neither feminists nor women constitute a homogeneous category, and there is no single meaning of feminism. Like theoretical lenses or perspectives in IR, feminist approaches vary and have been characterized in a number of ways.[11] Most important, endless mixing is the rule, not the exception, so assuming lenses constitute discrete "boxes" misrepresents the diversity, the range, and especially the extensive overlap among many perspectives. Individuals make assumptions that may be common to various lenses, they may make different assumptions when focusing on different substantive topics or normative issues, and how assumptions are mixed is an effect of learning, objectives, experience, and context. With these thoughts in mind, we present in this section a very brief introduction to feminist lenses and especially those developed in the context of IR work, though transgressing the boundaries of it.

Compared with other fields of inquiry, for a variety of reasons feminist interventions in the disciplines of IR (and economics) emerged only in the late 1980s and hence in the midst of debates throughout the academy regarding the nature and politics of knowledge claims. Their critiques of rationalism as masculinist positioned feminists as some of the earliest and most telling critics of modernist, positivist epistemologies. In IR, the "problems and pitfalls of positivism" featured in what has been called the discipline's "fourth debate" (Steans 2006: 22). As noted earlier, positivism is criticized for its dichotomizing assumptions (separating subject from object, fact from value), its essentializing (ahistorical and reductionist) tendencies, and how these generate an unreflective (acritical) attitude and hence conservative effects.

Feminist IR scholars adopt a wide range of positions and research orientations, but most identify with postpositivist—or at least constructivist (a distinction we drew earlier in this chapter)—epistemologies, in part because these permit a wider range of questions and afford more space for critical reflection on world-politics-as-usual. Like feminists in other disciplines, early efforts tended to focus on revealing how masculinist bias operated in, and hence distorted, the discipline's knowledge claims. This involved exposing androcentrism in fundamental categories, empirical studies, and theoretical perspectives; asking "Where are the women?" and making them visible; documenting mainstream constructions of abstract "woman" as deviant from or deficient in respect to male-as-norm criteria; and incorporating women's activities, experience, and understanding into the study of world politics. These inquiries tended to rely on gender as an empirical category—in effect, as a reference to embodied sex difference—that permitted researchers to "add women" to existing scholarship (our "position of women" in earlier editions of this book). They also tended to reflect existing feminist lenses that we briefly characterize here.

Liberal feminisms gained formal expression in the context of Europe's bourgeois revolutions that advocated equality but limited its application to (propertied) males. Built upon Enlightenment claims and shaped by its historical context, liberal feminisms tend toward positivist inclinations, decrying the exclusion of women from, and promoting their "addition to," male-dominated activities and power structures. Socialist feminisms draw on Marxist traditions to foreground economic inequalities between women and men. They link capitalism and patriarchy to expose how gender hierarchy operates in the workplace *and* the home, and thus challenge categorical boundaries between public and private spheres. Radical feminisms problematize the cultural denigration of femininity and link this to masculinist violence across all levels of analysis. They expose how experiences and activities associated with women and female bodies are devalued, how sexual violence is a form of social control of women, and how heterosexism reproduces the objectification of and violence against women (and feminized men).

Asking initially "Where are the women?" and subsequently "adding women"—and comparing their positions to those of men—were and remain productive orientations. They make embodied women (and men) visible in our picture of world politics, illuminate how women and men are differently engaged with and affected by international politics, and reveal women as agents and activists, as well as victims of sociocultural, economic, and political oppressions. But adding women to existing paradigms also raised deeper questions by exposing how the conceptual structures themselves presuppose masculine experience and perspective. For example, women/femininity cannot simply be "added" to constructions that are *constituted* as masculine: the public sphere, rationality, political identity, objectivity, "economic man." Either women as feminine cannot be added (i.e., women must become like men), or the constructions themselves are transformed (i.e., adding women as feminine alters the masculine premise of the constructions and changes their meaning). In this sense, the exclusions of femininity are not accidental or coincidental but *required* for the analytical consistency of reigning explanatory frameworks.

The lesson that emerges from these studies is that we cannot systemically "add women" without rethinking gender—recognizing it not only as an empirical category or variable but as an *analytical* category and governing code. Doing so requires acknowledging the constitutive power of language, which is most effectively addressed through a poststructuralist lens. This redirects our attention from adding women and deploying sex as a variable, to analyzing gender as a category of mental ordering that produces masculinity and femininity as hierarchical power relations. In effect, examining the "woman question" leads us to examine the "man question," which in this text we argue leads us to examine the "race," "class," "sexuality," and "nationality" questions as well. Doing so requires acknowledging intersectionality, derived from antiracist and postcolonial feminist thought, as a necessary analytic, which is also further illuminated through poststructuralist lenses. As used in this text, poststructuralist lenses in general reject essentialized categories, unitary meanings, sovereign claims, universalizing solutions, and presumptions of (foundational) objectivity associated with positivist and modernist commitments. Moreover, feminist poststructuralists criticize the residual essentialism that haunts references to "women" and other "identity-based" groups, rendering them homogeneous, undifferentiated wholes and erasing hierarchies within as well as across all groups.

As in other disciplines, we have seen that diversity among women has forced feminists in IR to reflect critically (and uncomfortably) on the meaning of feminism, definitions of "woman," the politics of representation, and the dangers of universalizing claims. "Sisterhood" aspirations have always been in tension with differences of ethnicity, race, class, age, physical ability, sexuality, and nationality, and are especially fraught in a global context marked by stark inequalities *among* women. Intersectionality approaches attempt to address these issues by rejecting ahistorical and essentialist identities and recognizing "complex or hybrid subjects" (Grewal and Kaplan 2001, 669). These lenses owe much to "women of color" in the North, women of the global South, and postcolonial critics.

Postcolonial feminists criticize the presumption and privilege of Western feminists and insist on the importance of local and "Third World" agency in identifying problems and negotiating remedies (Mohanty 2003; Chowdhry and Nair 2002). They expose how the ideologies of racism and imperialism continue to reproduce the subjugation and exploitation of "women of color" worldwide. They draw attention to the economic, political, and sociocultural forces of contemporary recolonizations and to nationalist and/or religious fundamentalisms that are dominated by men and deployed to discipline women. Through a postcolonial feminist lens, globalization is both a continuation of colonizing practices that span centuries and, through neoliberal capitalism, an intensification of the exploitation of women in the global South (which includes poor and migrant women in the North). Postcolonial critics challenge the binary "othering" that Eurocentric discourse invokes as a perpetual explanation for and justification of hierarchical power in world politics. They put into sharp relief how gender, race, class, nationalist, and imperialist hierarchies are interwoven in ways that particularly undermine the lives of women (and men) in the global South—physically, politically, economically, and culturally.

As feminist IR lenses have shifted, combined, and recombined through a greater multiplicity of theoretical voices and orientations—creating their own productive tensions—subjects of feminist IR inquiry have also shifted. Tickner (2006) expressed this in generational terms: First-generation feminist IR scholars tended to focus on deconstructing key concepts in IR—sovereignty, the state, security, development, and the economy—exposing or unpacking their masculinist bias and underpinnings. Through these openings that put gender inquiry on the IR map, second-generation scholars have applied gender analysis—often in more intersectional ways—to a range of world politics topics: both familiar (alliance constructions, state militaries, peacekeeping, peace agreements, trade agreements, UN conventions) and unfamiliar (sex tourism and sex work, homework and domestic service, migration, social movements, and even world art and the cruise industry).[12] In doing so, they have not only greatly expanded what world politics inquiry entails but also have rethought earlier approaches to gender theorizing in IR. At the same time, they have multiplied the methodologies used in world politics inquiry in order to get at the multiple ways in which world politics is gendered. In contrast to conventional positivist IR research, feminist IR scholars (and other transnational feminist scholars who engage with and contribute to feminist IR thought) have often utilized such qualitative approaches as ethnographic fieldwork learning about the lives of the nonelite, social action research through participant observation of social movements, and discourse analysis of classic IR texts, world leaders' pronouncements, (inter)governmental policies and documents, NGO campaigns, and local group articulations of social problems. They also plumb cultural sources, such as popular-culture images on the airwaves and the Internet and even literature, art, and poetry to find expressions over time and space of resistance to world-politics-as-usual in unusual places (Ackerly, Stern, and True 2006).

Such practices seek to reveal the underside of world politics, simultaneously exposing the gendered dynamics that underlie and infect the thought, language, structures, and practices of it, and privileging dissident and alternative voices about how it might be rethought, rearticulated, and rearranged. These practices also require reflexivity about the power relations between the researcher and the researched. In cases of "studying down"—such as working with nonelite actors—feminist IR scholars aim to be cognizant of their privilege, and thus their responsibility to allow such actors to represent themselves in their own ways so as not to impose Eurocentric/Orientalist, heteronormative, or classist interpretations on the motivations, nature, and outcomes of their struggles. When "studying up"—or dealing with elite or more privileged actors—feminist IR scholars aim to be cognizant of how such actors limit access to researchers engaged in critical scholarship and mystify their power through bureaucratic language. Discourse analysis is thus especially productive when studying up, because it enables reading between the lines and catching how the powerful consistently represent themselves and how they consistently represent "others" to justify their policies and actions. In these ways, feminist IR scholarship itself seeks to counter the crisis of representation both in the field of IR, in which the study of people and especially nonelite people has historically been absent, and in world politics, which has historically operated as if people and especially nonelite people did not matter.

In sum, as we move across the array of feminist IR lenses and the array of actors and subjects they reveal as operative in world politics, attention focuses less on "women" as an empirical variable and more on gender as an analytical category and the power of gender as a meta-lens that (re)produces positivist presumptions and systemic difference construction. Critiques of gender inequality emerge from positivist, constructivist, postpositivist, and poststructuralist orientations. As we noted earlier in relation to nonfeminist world politics lenses, postpositivists vary significantly in how and to what extent they politicize language and acknowledge the politics of knowledge claims. We argued that constructivist lenses prevailing in IR remain insufficiently critical of how power operates through symbols, codes, lenses, and analytical frameworks. With reference to developments in Britain, Squires and Weldes (2007) distinguish "gender and IR" (GIR) from "feminist IR" and argue that the former—which includes positivist, constructivist, and explicitly non-feminist approaches—avoids the self-marginalization that haunts the latter. Whether and in what ways narrowly constructivist and explicitly noncritical approaches leave world-politics-as-usual problematically in place is an ongoing debate.

In subsequent chapters we employ a range of feminist IR lenses to examine re-positionings of women and men and the power of gender in world politics, drawing from the extensive and variant feminist IR and transnational feminist literature that now exists. The very extent and diversity of contemporary feminist IR work reveals that it is not engaged in static, monological, or universalizing analyses that deflect debate. Due to our explicitly critical and intersectional commitments, in this text poststructural and especially postcolonial orientations inform our analysis. These feminist lenses share a critique of positivism's essentialized and homogeneous categories, oppositional dichotomies, and universalizing narratives. But postcolonial lenses emphasize as well how earlier and continuing imperialist practices produce the racialization of "others," the marginalization, devalorization, and even elimination of alternative visions and voices, and the presumption of Eurocentric superiority in moral, political, military, and economic terms. In Chapter 6 we return to these issues as we imagine de-gendering as a transformative response to global crises of representation, security, and sustainability.

GLOBAL GENDERED, RACIALIZED, AND SEXUALIZED DIVISIONS OF POWER, VIOLENCE, AND LABOR AND RESOURCES

In this section we introduce the issue areas examined in the subsequent chapters and begin to expose—bring into focus—how the power of gender operates to shape conventional accounts of IR and produces and reproduces crises of representation, insecurity, and sustainability.

Politics and Power

Masculinism pervades politics. Wendy Brown wrote: "More than any other kind of human activity, politics has historically borne an explicitly masculine identity. It has been more exclusively limited to men than any other realm of endeavor and has been more intensely, self-consciously masculine than most other social practices" (1988: 4).

In IR, as in political science, power is usually defined as "power-over," specifically, the ability to get someone to do what you want. It is usually measured by control of resources, especially those supporting physical coercion. The appropriate analogy might be power understood as tools: if you have them, you can use them to get certain things done if and when you choose, and some have more of these tools than others. This definition assumes measurable capacities, privileges instrumental rationality, and emphasizes separation and competition: Those who have power use it (or its threat) to keep others from securing enough to threaten them. The emphasis on material resources and coercive ability deflects attention from the fact that power reckoning is embedded in dominant conceptual orders, value systems, disciplinary practices, and institutional dynamics.

In IR the concept of "political actor"—the legitimate wielder of society's power—is derived from classical political theory. Common to constructions of "political man"—from Plato and Aristotle to Hobbes, Locke, and Rousseau—is the privileging of man's capacity for reason. Rationality ostensibly distinguishes man from other animals and explains his pursuit of freedom—from nature and "necessity" as well as from tyranny. Feminist scholarship has exposed how models of human nature presupposed in constructions of "political man" are not in fact gender-neutral but androcentric, based on exclusively male (especially elite male) experience and perspective. "Political man" also presupposed "civilizational" status: Early Greek texts excluded "barbarians" and Persians; premodern European texts excluded "primitives" and racialized "others" within Europe and outside of it as colonization proceeded.

With reference to gender divisions of power, "woman" is excluded conceptually from political power by denying her the rationality that marks "man" as the highest animal. Substantively, women have historically been excluded from political power by states' limiting citizenship to those who perform military duty and/or are property owners. Under these conditions, most women are structurally excluded from formal politics, even though individual women, in exceptional circumstances, have wielded considerable political power. Women worldwide have largely won the battle for the vote, though definitions of citizenship continue to limit women's access to public power, and their political power is circumscribed by a variety of indirect means (discussed elsewhere in this text). Most obvious are the continued effects of the dichotomy of public-private that privileges men's productive and "political" activities over women's reproductive and "personal/familial" activities.

With reference to gender*ed* divisions of power, historically men and women of various "othered" groups have been excluded from political power by various means: barred on the basis of property claims, denied leadership in their own lands by colonial domination, displaced to other lands and denied power through slavery and debt bondage, and more generally, excluded from citizenship rights based on criteria related to birth location, "appropriate" documentation, or "economic" status. Today most people have a "right" to political participation, but the most powerful decision-makers in world politics are those occupying positions of power in national and international governmental institutions and transnational corporations. Occupants of these positions continue to reflect privileged statuses, especially of national and economic power, which are also marked by ethnicity/race, gender, and sexuality.

These conventional constructions—of power, "political man," citizenship, public-private, and so on—reproduce masculinist, androcentric, and heteronormative assumptions. For example, sovereign man and sovereign states are defined not by connection or relationships but by (masculinist) autonomy in decision-making and putative freedom from interdependence and collective responsibilities. Security is understood not in terms of producing and sustaining life but acquiring sufficient power to protect "one's own" and keep "others" at bay. The androcentrism of Hobbesian claims is revealed when we ask how helpless infants ever become adults if human nature is universally competitive and hostile. Through a lens on child-rearing practices—necessary for life everywhere—it makes more sense to argue that humans are naturally cooperative, for without the cooperation that is required to nurture children, there would be no men or women. And although Aristotle acknowledged that the public sphere depends upon the (re)production of life's necessities in the private sphere, he denied the interdependence that this implies when articulating political theory. In the modern era, colonialism racialized and sexualized divisions of power, justifying the conquest of "others" by coding Europeans as uniquely moral and "respectable" as well as racially superior.

Divisions of power in today's world politics suggest a crisis of representation and equity. "Democracy" is strategically promoted while its radical promise is undermined by fraudulent elections, political machinations, and imperial impositions. As we address in greater detail in Chapter 3, "global governance" sounds good and is presumably desirable in some form, but its current form obscures the predominantly nondemocratic and unaccountable forms of international rule. Behind this friendly face, the diffuse power of neoliberal governmentality effectively disciplines us all by securing our consent to disciplining ourselves and—through acquiescence to surveillance, fear, and oppositional politics—each other.

In these senses, analyzing divisions of power requires greater attention to political, economic, and sociocultural forces below and above the level of the state, thereby revealing the greater complexity of global politics, which cannot be reduced to the actions of state elites and their international organizations or the top-down "problem-solving" orientation they advocate. Such a lens would highlight the diffusion of disciplinary techniques and how their micropolitical effects individualize responsibility and undermine collective solidarities. It would reveal inequalities as a source of conflict in world politics and illuminate divisions within groups—as well as linkages among groups—not only along national lines but also gender, race, class, sexuality, and culture lines. The corollary of this is that many people are resisting world-politics-as-usual by finding common cause with each other across national boundaries and "identity politics" and thus creating a different kind of international relations, or world politics, from that of elite policymakers.

Given their interest in stability, elite power-wielders in world politics (and many who study them) act to maintain current divisions of power and their corollary forms of (nondemocratic) political representation. Nonelites around the world (and most who study them) focus on divisions of power that are created in the name of stability but undermine democracy and accountability and compromise the security of the global majority. People around the world struggling against the tyrannies of sexism, homophobia, racism, classism, militarism, and/or imperialism seek justice, which requires upsetting the status quo. The danger is that even in struggle, the power of gender prevents seeing beyond particular interests and oppositional politics to the collective interests of all planetary inhabitants and the complex politics of social justice. It thus (re)produces a crisis of representation by (re)producing global gendered, racialized, and sexualized divisions of power.

Security and Violence

Essentializing claims about men's superior strength are favored justifications for gender hierarchy. But such claims are misleading. On the one hand, men's strength varies cross-culturally and within cultures, and a considerable number of women are in fact stronger than men. On the other hand, why do we consider men's upper-body muscular strength more significant than women's burden-carrying strength and greater endurance? Decades ago Ashley Montagu undertook a comprehensive review of scientific literature and concluded that "the female is *constitutionally* stronger than the male": She has greater stamina, lives longer, fights disease better, and endures "all sorts of devitalizing conditions better than men: starvation, exposure, fatigue, shock, illness and the like" (1974: 61–62).

Historically, the upper-body strength of (some) males was presumably an important factor when the success of hunting large game or the outcome of conflicts depended on this particular strength. Modern technologies, however, have dramatically altered the relationship of muscular strength to success in battle or in the workplace. Yet a cultural preoccupation with power and strength defined in masculine terms endures.

With reference to sports, Mariah Nelson (1994) has acknowledged that typical men's and women's bodies differ in terms of athletic qualities (oxygen-carrying capacity, muscle mass, flexibility, etc.), and the advantages of each depend on what sporting event is featured. Dominant media worldwide, however, overwhelmingly privilege sports that favor male bodies, thus reproducing the invisibility of women's particular strengths and sustaining the illusion of men's "supremacy."[13]

With reference to gender divisions of violence, stereotypes of superior male strength are inextricable from hegemonic constructions of masculinity that cultivate male arrogance and overweening power. Most models of masculinity, historically and today, include elements of courage, competition, assertiveness, and ambition that are difficult to disassociate from physical aggression and even violence, especially when males are systematically placed in situations where proving their manhood involves aggressive behavior. Willingness to engage in violence is then easily mobilized, whether against feminized intimates (lovers, wives) or feminized "others" (opponents, enemies). As one effect, across national contexts men (especially of particular ages) engage in violent behaviors more frequently and with more systemically destructive effect than do women.

With reference to gender*ed* divisions of imperialist violence, Europeans manipulated ideologies of superior (masculinist) "strength" to justify colonial wars and obscure their racist, economic, and heteronormative dynamics.[14] What surfaces repeatedly are characterizations of the colonized as feminine: weak, passive, irrational, disorderly, unpredictable, and lacking self-control. This afforded European power-wielders (not only men or all men) a justification for military interventions by casting themselves in favorable masculinist terms: as uniquely rational, sexually and morally respectable, and more advanced economically and politically. In colonial wars and geopolitical "othering," civilization became a code word for European heteronormative masculine superiority. Through this lens, imperial violence was perhaps a regrettable but nonetheless a necessary component of "enlightening" and "civilizing" primitive, unruly, feminine "others." As Eisenstein observed, although Europeans extolled the virtues of reason as a progressive force, they positioned rationality "against savagery (natives), emotionality (women), and sexuality (racialized others)" (2004: 75).

At the same time—and complicating simplistic models of gender—
the development of European nationalisms and normalization of bourgeois respectability produced an idealized model of (bourgeois)
femininity: passive, pure, dutiful, maternal. This superficial valorization
of femininity did less to empower women than render them perpetual
dependents, as feminine virtue and morality were best assured by confining these qualities and "good women" to a private sphere of domesticity and assigning men the public-sphere responsibility of defending
and protecting feminized dependents. The patronizing and protection-
ist logic of bourgeois norms provided imperial governments a moral—
as well as rational—justification for militarized colonization: The
barbarity of "other" men was proven by their (allegedly) oppressive treatment of women, and this *called for* the rescue of victimized females by
honorable, civilized men. In short, the defense of idealized femininity—
to paraphrase Gayatri Spivak's (1988) apt analysis—justified wars by
white men to "save" brown women from brown men.[15] This protec-
tionist and crusading rhetoric obscured exploitative agendas and appeared to legitimate militarized violence. As we discuss in Chapter 4, it
resurfaces—with particular vengeance and new complexities—in contemporary global security practices, including militarization—the extension of military thinking and practices into civilian life—and
imperialist projects.

The U.S.-led "war on terror" exemplifies gendered divisions of violence
and how a crisis of (in)security escalates when masculinist arrogance
spurs imperial strategies. Some argue that Bush's "forceful" response to
the 9/11 bombings involved not only his outrage and claim to military
leadership but his desire to establish a hypermasculine image—of himself *and* the United States.[16] For many, U.S. identity and power had been
feminized by its defeat in Vietnam, made more humiliating by losing to a
people stereotyped as ethnically/racially inferior. Feminization anxiety
was also fueled by the increasing visibility of women in politics and
the workplace and the growing strength of LGBTQ social movements in
the United States. Given these conditions, a yearning to remasculinize the
nation (Jeffords 1989) was easily tapped by Bush and his neoconservative advisers.

Like earlier imperial powers, Bush used the gendered logic of crusading protectionism to justify his warring agenda, claiming instead to be

liberating women of Afghanistan and Iraq. Silencing any alternative interpretation, the war story he broadcast featured monstrous terrorists inexplicably committed to destroying freedom and democracy by extremes of violence; enemies this irrational and unpredictable could only be defeated by drawing an absolute line between good and evil and eliminating the latter. The power of gender operates here to vilify (feminized) enemies as so categorically different from and absolutely opposed to "us" that the only viable strategy is their annihilation. In a parallel move, those who were skeptical, fearful, or actively opposed these strategies were rendered unequivocally suspect—as unpatriotic, anti-American, naively (irrationally) out-of-touch, or quite simply *unmanly* (lacking the guts to do what must be done) (Peterson 2007). Feminization here vilifies dissenters and denies absolutely the rationality of any critique. Dissenters are simply and irredeemably discredited: unwilling to stand up for their country, ungratefully abandoning the United States and freeloading on its military power, and/or failing to grasp real-world politics. In the former president's imperial words: "Those who are not with us are against us." And as enemies, those who are against us lose any claim to inclusion, respect, or (apparently) rights.

Today's crisis of insecurity is also revealed when we look beyond direct to indirect or structural violence, exemplified by increased health risks to families and the poorest when war-making undermines access to safe water, food, and medical attention. Neoliberal globalization erodes state authority, welfare provisioning and employment security, whereas global militarization increases violence and amplifies the need for legitimate and stable authority, social welfare programs, and survival resources. Structural violence disproportionately affects women and groups subordinated by cultural markers and economic inequalities, and when we ignore this fact, we ignore the (in)security of the planet's majority.

The power of gender produces a crisis of violence and global insecurity. It constructs a world shaped by hostile forces and naturalizes war against all who are feminized. In a self-perpetuating cycle, threats (real or fictive) increase preparations for defense and/or retaliation that are inextricable from conditions of structural violence. An essentializing, oppositional lens magnifies and legitimates self-other, us-them, aggressive-passive, soldier-victim, masculine-feminine, and protector-protected dichotomies. These exemplify how the binary terms are interdependent and "call forth" each other problematically: Assuming the "other" is threatening justifies preemptive or confrontational behavior; assuming women are weak (or victims) justifies pumping up real men who "must" protect them. Neoliberal capitalism and global militarization merge in today's Empire, as inequalities between groups provide motives for conflict and fuel militarization, and wars provide profit-making opportunities for some that delay the resolution of conflicts and deepen the crisis of insecurity for all.

Labor and Resources

Divisions of labor and resources within households and the global workforce are shaped by masculinist and capitalist ideologies, both of which entail relations of inequality and exploitative dynamics. Gender divisions of labor are particularly visible through a lens on how "work" is defined and "counted," what kinds of work are most valued, who does what work, and how much—if anything—they are paid. Stereotypes of women and femininity here interact powerfully with dichotomies of public-private, productive-reproductive, and mental-manual to generate quite rigid labor patterns between men and women, rich and poor individuals, "skilled" and "unskilled" workers, and nations of the global North and South. Just as the public is seen as (politically) more important than the private, (ostensibly less skilled) reproductive and manual labor is monetarily devalued, accorded less status, and rendered less visible, even though it constitutes the structural underpinning of what "more important" workers—especially elite men—do.

As we examine in greater detail in Chapter 5, for the past several decades, geopolitical elites have promoted neoliberal policies that effectively restructured production and financial arrangements worldwide. Deregulation has favored private capital at the expense of public provisioning and shifted risks and responsibilities from the collective to the individual. Increasing "flexibilization" of work arrangements has dramatically re-positioned men and women in relation to paid, safe and secure ("formal," long-term, with benefits) forms of employment. With reference to gender*ed* divisions of labor, male workers in general face increasing un- and underemployment (work "below" their skill level), and the poorest workers in the global North and South face declining prospects for any "meaningful" work or income sufficient to escape poverty. Greater numbers of men and women are on the move globally in search of work, and these racialized flows alter "identity politics" and heighten immigration "issues." Women virtually everywhere are increasingly entering the workforce, but for the vast majority, they find work only in low-status and poorly paid jobs.

The power of gender operates here to (re)position women primarily in services, and especially in taking care of the emotional (counseling, nursing), "entertainment" (performing arts, sex industries), production (word processing, assembly-line jobs), and maintenance (cleaning, clerical, child care) needs of men as individuals and the masculinist social system generally. Second, it operates as well to continue the concentration of jobs that assume low technologies and minimal skills—and/or are physically demanding, unsafe, and risky—in poorer and racially marked groups and in the nations of the global South. And it operates in a pervasive sense to devalorize all jobs—and the men as well as women doing them—associated with or sharing the stereotypical characteristics of "women's work": unskilled, informal, reproductive. This devalorization is manifested conceptually (affecting self-esteem and status) and materially (affecting wages and physical well-being). In these senses, the feminization of work raises a host of issues regarding gendered divisions of labor and potential foreclosure of traditional masculinities. The "feminization" and flexibilization of employment does favor some women and some workers, but this is most often at the expense of "decent" or "secure" employment more generally, and entails a deterioration in working conditions and real wages for most of the world's workers.

Although women often seek paid work because males in the household are un- or underemployed, the division of labor in the household is rarely transformed when women (re)position themselves in the workplace. Rather, studies worldwide confirm that women who work for pay rarely do less unpaid work at home because even when men are unemployed, they resist doing "women's work" in the home. One effect is a global trend of women doing more work than ever: still carrying the primary responsibility for child care, the emotional and physical well-being of family members, and everyday household maintenance, but now also earning income for the family and often being called upon to nurture community survival networks in the face of worsening socioeconomic conditions.

The power of gender operates here to perpetuate categorical distinctions between what "real men" and "real women" do, which encourages men to avoid feminized activities even when participating would benefit loved ones. And it operates to sustain expectations that women, consistent with the stereotype of femininity and ideology of patriarchal households, work to serve others—both at home and in the workplace. In this sense, women are seen to work "for love" or as secondary income earners to sustain families, rather than primarily for income or status as most cultures expect men to do. When economic conditions deteriorate, women are expected to take up the slack—working in whatever capacity to keep the family/household going no matter what sacrifices of self are necessary. Of course, the trade-offs for women who do this work vary tremendously. Nor do *all* men seek or benefit equally from the exploitation of women's labor. But as a generalization, men in the aggregate do benefit in various ways from the systemic masculinism that treats women's energies, lives, skills, intellects, demands, and needs as secondary to those of men.

The larger problem, however, is not simply a failure of men to "do their share" but the structural contradictions of neoliberal capitalism and crisis of social reproduction they constitute. In the context of deteriorating economic conditions and reduced public support, there are ultimately limits to how far and how long women can "stretch" their energy and labor to meet survival needs and ensure the daily reproduction of social life. Bakker and Gill have referred to "a global contradiction between the extended power of capital (and its protection by the state) and not only sustainable but also progressive forms of social reproduction for the majority of the world's population" (2003: 4). In short, neoliberal restructuring is undermining the viability of social reproduction, upon which all productive processes, indeed human life, depend. The crisis of social reproduction in daily life and the household is thus inextricable from a crisis of sustainability borne of gendered divisions of resources and environmental degradation.

That a crisis of social reproduction and its implications remain largely invisible in mainstream accounts of economics and world politics reflects the power of gender as well. Quite simply, "women's work" and economics within the family/household are deemed unimportant compared with "men's work," formal, productive economic activities, and male-dominated financial arrangements. Economic vision is further compromised by adopting methods of inquiry that discount subjective, qualitative, and cultural dimensions of social life. Mainstream IR scholars draw on neoclassical economic theory both as a methodological preference and to study the global economy. Most endorse neoliberalism as the optimal strategy not only for pursuing economic growth and prosperity but also for promoting "democracy" worldwide. Until the recent financial crisis, neoliberal commitments to deregulation and liberalization were assumed to be the most efficient and therefore most desirable approach to national and international economic relations. Through this lens, an expanding world economy would provide an ever-larger pie and, through a process of "trickle down," ever-bigger pies would translate into larger slices, theoretically, even for those with few initial resources. Even before the current economic crisis, cumulative data indicated that resource inequalities within and between nations had not declined but become more polarized under neoliberal policies. Tragically, the crisis in social reproduction and environmental sustainability that feminists have long foreseen is now merging with the crisis of financial destruction that critical economists also foresaw but that its perpetrators still find "surprising."

On the face of it, advocates of traditional approaches tend to reproduce rather than challenge the status quo because the questions they frame result in answers that confirm the assumptions upon which the questions are based. The power of gender is presupposed in the dichotomies favored by economic analysis: paid-unpaid work, formal-informal, providers-dependents, production-reproduction, and "autonomy" in the marketplace versus interdependence. Just as women are deemed feminine by their dependence within the family, "less developed" nations and their people are "unmanned" by their position of dependence in the global economy. Finally, trickle-down theories tend to benefit those who control the most resources by promoting the continued growth that delivers the biggest pieces of pie to those in power. Many argue that not only do the poorest never see trickle-down benefits but even if they get marginally larger pieces, the proportional distribution of the pie does not improve—in fact, the proportion going to a very small elite has increased. And not least, today's ecological crises (which hurt the poorest the most) challenge the entire premise of ever-expanding growth.

Through conventional lenses, IR scholars distinguish the "high" politics of state-centric security from the "low" politics of economic relations, and effectively discredit environmental concerns as "soft politics." More recently, the seriousness of environmental degradation, an emerging consensus on global warming, and the deadly politics of oil have prompted a shift in focus, though not a transformation in this paradigm (explored more fully in Chapter 5). Taking environmental issues seriously would entail a critical analysis of how resources are used, distributed, and controlled, and this exercise would reveal the disproportionate and, to a large extent, irresponsible consumption of resources on the part of the global minority/North that so exacerbates resource depletion.

Ecological irresponsibility is spurred by multiple factors: inflated desires, ill-conceived projects, short-range planning, greedy consumerism and profit-seeking, unrealistic expectations, and unintended consequences. The "success" of industrialization fueled "growth-is-always-good" and "technology-can-fix-it" mentalities and exploitative, wasteful practices. Poor and nonindustrialized peoples rarely have the luxury of operating on a throw-away mentality, and without the illusion of constant growth, many live in a symbiotic relationship with their environment. Population expansion in environments often made resource-poor through colonization, war, and the like, however, increasingly forces people to secure their everyday subsistence by depleting the very resources they depend upon. Water, food, and fuel for domestic use are essential for life, but the acquisition and consumption of these goods in the short term often conflict with long-term ecological planning and resources. Many economic development policies (securing foreign currency through the sale of timber, building an industrial base with fossil-fuel-driven factories) have costly ecological consequences. The choices for developing (or underdeveloped) countries are especially stark, but many overdeveloped nations deny their historical role in creating these stark choices and decry the desire of "others" to industrialize in ways that exacerbate environmental degradation.

Gender divisions of ecological resources are problematically revealed when we consider how women are assigned primary responsibility for social reproduction, which requires basic resources, but they have little control over how local and global resources are used, distributed, and controlled. Gender*d* divisions are institutionalized with the growth of science and industrial technologies in service to capitalist and colonial projects. At core, the modernist, Eurocentric ideology of limitless growth presupposes a belief in (white, Western) "man's" dominion over nature (promoted, for example, in Christian and capitalist belief systems) and the desirability of (white, Western) "man's" exploiting nature to further his own ends. Conquering nature, digging out "her" treasure and secrets, proving (white, Western) man's superiority through control over and manipulation of nature—these are familiar and currently deadly refrains. The identification of nature as female is not an accident but a historical development that is visible in justifications by elites for territorial and intellectual expansion. Exploitation is most readily legitimated by objectifying who or what is exploited. Understanding people or nature as "objects" denies them agency, purpose, feelings, intelligence, a right to exist and/or to warrant respect. Through the lens of (white, Western) man's dominion, it is taken for granted that natural resources are there for humans to exploit and control: no questions asked, they are "there for the taking." In various ways throughout history, aboriginal peoples, women, colonies, and the earth's bounty have all been treated as such natural resources (Mies, Bennholdt-Thomsen, and von Werlhof 1988). The gendered dichotomies of culture-nature, mind-body, subject-object, control-uncertainty, exploiter-exploited, and dominator-dominated variously shape how we think about and hence treat that which is objectified. But we are learning at great cost that (white, Western) "man's dominion/domination" over feminized (and racialized) nature is neither morally acceptable nor environmentally sustainable.

Gendered divisions are revealed in terms of who has access to what resources, who controls resources and to what ends, who suffers most from environmental degradation, and how masculinist lenses normalize irresponsible resource use. Worldwide, but particularly in the global South, females are more dramatically affected by environmental degradation than are males. As food providers, women find their workload increases when water, food, and fuel resources deteriorate; as last and least fed, they suffer most from starvation and malnutrition; and as caretakers, they have to work harder when economic, health, and environmental conditions deteriorate and when families and communities are victims of environmental disasters. Economically and ethnically marginalized populations are also more directly affected and more starkly than elites. As the poorest, they lack resources and power, and they are least able to quit jobs, acquire adequate health care, purchase safer products, move away from toxic environments, or prevail against those who seek to dispose of toxic waste in "their backyard." As the most politically marginalized and devalorized groups, they are less visible when they protest, are silenced (or seen as "overreacting") in what debates do take place, their neighborhood and community claims are disregarded, and they are subject to being seen as "disposable" themselves.

In these multiple senses, divisions of labor and resources—and the inequalities and crises they generate—expose starkly who and what is valued and who and what is not. The power of gender operates to privilege and (over)valorize skills, workers, and "production" associated with hegemonically masculine identities and activities; and these identities and activities presuppose (white) man's dominion over females and nature, as well as capitalist commitments to growth. In complex ways, these patterns of devalorization determine the world's winners and losers and, specifically, those consigned to what Agamben (1998) has characterized as "bare life": an exceptionally abject and materially precarious condition.

We suggest here how the gendered divisions of power, violence, and labor and resources constitute crises of representation and equity, insecurity and violence, social reproduction and environmental sustainability. We argue throughout this text, and document in subsequent chapters, how the power of gender is not simply an aspect of these crises but productive of them. Consider how the premise of "disposability" is built into currently dominant ways of thinking and acting in world politics: top-down governance by elites and experts, imperial violence as how to settle differences, commodification as a cultural logic, and growth as a capitalist imperative. These lenses variously *presuppose* that inequalities of authority, power, and resources are inevitable, and therefore some individuals, peoples, and natural resources will necessarily (though perhaps regrettably) be "wasted." Once disposability is built into expectations and operating rules, it raises the question of who shall be disposed. The power of gender operates both to produce the necessity of the question and to provide (or at least guide) the answer. On the one hand, it underpins these lenses by normalizing masculinist, objectivist, and modernist modes of instrumental rationality and Eurocentric moralizing, which assume superiority and categorically preclude alternative visions or even alternative questions. On the other hand, the power of gender "answers" the question by normalizing categorical and hierarchical oppositions, essentialized "othering," and devalorization of the feminine, which operate simultaneously to identify who is most disposable and to justify that disposal.

Crises produced by gendered divisions of power, violence, and labor and resources, and the power of gender that sustains them, cannot be addressed without de-gendering world politics, the topic of our concluding chapter.

Notes

1. In the interests of brevity and accessibility, we often rely on this oversimplified contrast between positivist and postpositivist orientations in this text. Later in this chapter, we further specify the "conventional constructivism" that prevails in IR and argue that its retention of narrow rationalism renders it problematically positivist. Later still, we clarify our preference for a more explicitly poststructuralist (or postmodernist; we do not distinguish between these) and postcolonial orientation in this text.

2. English-language training exacerbates this tendency by teaching word meanings as opposites. Learning antonyms forces us to think in apparently unchanging oppositions: right-wrong, hot-cold, friend-foe, boy-girl, night-day, us-them. Dichotomized or dualistic thinking is criticized from diverse perspectives, but especially from those identified as postpositivist, poststructuralist, or postmodernist.

3. References to ideology do not always emphasize their role in justifying inequalities, but that is our focus here.

4. See Martha McCaughey (2008) for an accessible critique of how evolutionary theory is today increasingly used to render stereotypes of male desire, sexuality, and violence—the caveman mystique—as "natural."

5. As we noted earlier, many feminists have shifted from seeing "sex" as an essentialized, biological binary of embodied female and male difference to understanding even that binary is socially constructed, thus blurring any categorical distinction between (biological) sex and (social) gender. "Gender is not a synonym for women" is Terrell Carver's (1996) book title.

6. "The conceptual category sex/affective production is a way of understanding the social organization of labor and the exchange of services that occur between men and women in the production of children, affection, and sexuality" (Ferguson 1984: 154; also 1989). In the present book, sex/affective relations include exchanges between men and between women as well as heteronormative couples. Links to the state include marriage and family law, antihomosexuality legislation, sex and reproductive education, maternal health and parental support policies, domestic and international politics of reproductive health, and population politics.

7. While heterosexual intercourse was—until recently—a necessary condition of biological reproduction, this biological demand did not require the normalization of heterosexist/patriarchal families as the exclusive basis of intimacy and group reproduction.

8. Some cultures afford space for more than two genders, or more complex constructions of gender. See for example Nanda 1998; Roscoe 2000; Fausto-Sterling 2000.

9. Enloe's (1989) early treatment starkly exposed how much power it takes to keep gender in place in world politics and keep world politics gendered. This remains an eye-opening and especially teachable text.

10. Consider how mainstream media and academic studies highlight issues and activities that are masculinist or male-dominated: competitive sports, sexual pursuits and conquests, male bonding, crime and espionage, fighting and killing, war-making, risk-taking, public figures and events, making money, national and international politics. In comparison, media and academic studies, except those that have been impacted by feminist perspectives, rarely focus on issues and activities associated with women's lives: cooperative and care-taking activities; building interpersonal and community relations; poverty and physical victimization (assault, rape, homicide); reproducing everyday life and activities—in the home, family, workplace—and, especially, reproductive issues involving women's mental and physical health and when, whether, and under what circumstances to bear children.

11. For feminist lenses in IR, see, for example, Tickner 2001; Steans 2006; Squires and Weldes 2007.

12. See multiple issues of *International Feminist Journal of Politics*, the journal devoted to feminist IR scholarship and emerging from the Feminist Theory and Gender Studies Section of the International Studies Association.

13. The title of Nelson's (1994) book contends that "the stronger women get, the more men love football." As women gain some measure of equality and erode men's athletic claims to superior bodies, men become more ardent fans of those sports—gridiron football, baseball, basketball, ice hockey—that appear to sustain the illusion of unequivocally male superiority.

14. Key works include Said 1979, 1993; Spivak 1987; McClintock 1995; Eisenstein 2004.

15. Cultural generalizations of enemy groups or nations typically feminized them and European notions of ethnic/racial hierarchies permitted selective valorization of men identified with "martial races" and "warrior" cultures. Without conceding any sense of their military superiority, imperial governments selectively allied with soldiers of particular cultural identities to advance colonial interests. The British, for example, recruited Nepali Ghurkas to fight their wars, and now recruit Fijian men. In the "war on terror," the Bush administration selectively allied with ethnically and religiously differentiated groups—without exception extremely masculinist—that best served their short-term military objectives, with little attention to the hierarchies—especially of gender and sexuality—these exacerbate.

16. Zine captured succinctly the political work this war story does: "the archetypal image of the deprived and debased Muslim woman was resurrected to perform her

duty as a signifier of the abject difference of Muslims; the barbarity and anti-modernism of Islam and its essential repression of women; and most importantly as camouflage for US military interventions" (2006: 34). Many feminists criticized these wars (Hawthorne and Winter 2002; Joseph and Sharma 2003; Eisenstein 2004; Hunt and Rygiel 2006; Alexander and Hawkesworth 2008) and Bush's co-optation of feminist discourse, especially given his history of antifeminist policies (e.g., indifference to Taliban practices preinvasion; cutting domestic programs that benefit women; restricting access to contraception at home and globally).

3

◄○►

Gender and
Global Governance

How does the power of gender affect "who rules the world?" What do gendered divisions of power tell us about how the world is ordered and for what purposes? How are women and men positioned and re-positioned in and by global power structures and with what effects? In this chapter, we look at the relationship between gendered inequalities and global governance. Although there is no world government, and much conventional IR thinking continues to see states as the central actors in world politics, in recent years the term "global governance" has come to refer to a constellation of global actors including states; IGOs such as the UN bodies and agencies, the World Bank, the International Monetary Fund (IMF), and the World Trade Organization (WTO); regional governments such as the European Union (EU) and regional IGOs such as organizations of African, American, and Asian states and free-trade regimes like the North American Free Trade Agreement (NAFTA); global market actors such as transnational corporations (TNCs) and transnational NGOs (Rai 2008: 22). States make up IGOs, and the wealthiest and most militarily powerful states hold primacy in them. At the same time, states are variously subordinated to IGO rules made by state representatives (with increasing input by NGO actors), which range from international laws and regulations to agreed-upon norms. Thus, although we especially focus on the power of gender to shape the meaning of state power in world politics and the relative positionings of women and men as state actors in world politics, we also look at other gendered institutions at the global level and the new gender rules that are emanating from some of them and that are having impacts on states and the re-positionings of women and men. We conclude, however, that these new rules associated with the new global politics of gender equality do not necessarily disrupt gendered divisions of power and leave intact the power of gender.

Before examining the gender distribution of global power, we begin with the gendered nature of the idea of "power" itself. The definition of power conventionally favored in IR, as in political science generally, is one of "power-over." Power-over is captured in Robert Dahl's (1961) classic definition: the ability of A to get B to do something that B would not otherwise do. Defining power in this way emphasizes control of material—especially military—resources and a willingness to use them in order to enforce one's preferences. It is power-over in the sense of being top-down (those on top, where the most resources are concentrated, are determined to have the most power) and coercive (the ability to force compliance is presumed to be the surest sign of power). When we use only this narrow definition of power to study world politics, however, we neglect investigating how other dimensions of social reality—moral commitments, religious beliefs, ethnic allegiances, disciplinary practices, sociopolitical ideologies—shape how power works and who rules the world. Finally, and singularly relevant to our thesis, this definition of power is masculinist to the extent that it presupposes androcentric notions of strength, competition, aggression, and coercion, and because it focuses on power understood only in terms of public-sphere activities that are dominated by elite men who embody these traits and exercise these power-over strategies that are assumed, particularly in realist thinking, as endemic to states.

One aim in this chapter is to examine where women are positioned relative to men as political elites in formal global power structures. In doing so, we address the following questions: Where are the women who wield power in global governance? Why have women and gender issues been so underrepresented in global power structures, how may this be changing, why, and with what effects? This chapter further demonstrates how the power of gender remains systematically at work by engaging an apparent paradox. On the one hand, women gaining positions of power challenges gender stereotypes that portray women as uninterested in or unfit for political leadership, and greater attention to gender equality in global governance could be read as a success story. On the other hand, gains in women's power positions in global governance do not eradicate gender stereotypes, and gender-oriented policies are more an effect of neoliberal restructuring and governmentality than of commitments to gender justice. These realities preclude fundamental change in the conduct of world politics and its priorities. The gendered concept of power as power-over—accompanied by the co-optive power of neoliberalism—maintains gender, race, class, sexual, and national hierarchical dichotomies (gendered divisions of power) that continue to be productive of world crises even as more women are represented in, and gender equality gets on the agenda of, global power structures.

As intimated in the last chapter, these *gendered divisions of power* include dichotomies of political-apolitical, reason-emotion, public-private, leaders-followers, active-passive, and freedom-necessity. Those feminized—including most women and many men—are generally denied the status of independent and rational agency and leadership qualities in the public sphere and are reduced to the ground upon which real men act, thus enabling political man to be released from and unmindful of the necessities of everyday life. At the same time, these divisions narrowly define rationality as instrumentalism in the service of power-over and control, disregard the intertwining of private life with public life and domestic politics with international politics, and mistake acting together (or interdependent action) and refraining from harmful actions as signs of weakness, passivity, and lack of autonomy. Autonomy (or reactionary individualism devoid of affective relationships and concern) becomes privileged as the "true" meaning of freedom, which sets in motion a zero-sum game. The overall effect is a *crisis of representation* whereby large numbers of people, peoples, identities, and perspectives remain un- or underrepresented in formal and informal positions of power, and those who supposedly speak for "others" misrepresent them, their issues, and their aspirations in service to the priorities and desires of the few at the top of whatever hierarchical structure. This crisis of representation, in turn, feeds crises of insecurity and sustainability that, in turn, silence or marginalize alternative or dissident voices, all of which sustains the crisis of representation. This vicious cycle sets up the dynamic of reducing responses to bureaucratic "problem-solving" rather than efforts toward transformation of the cycle itself. Thus, the power of gender remains relatively undisturbed even as there are some shifts in the gendered divisions of power.

FEMINIST APPROACHES TO POLITICS

Prior to the rise of feminist IR, feminist interventions had been made in a host of disciplines primarily in the humanities and social sciences since at least the 1960s. The general trajectory of these interventions was also to initially ask, "Where are the women?" The women first identified as missing were "women worthies" (Harding 1986), or those women whose outstanding contributions to literature, art, history, and social, political, and economic thought were overlooked or hidden because they were produced by women in patriarchal societies that could not imagine women as capable of great things. In political science more generally, this meant recovering histories of women political thinkers and leaders (Smith and Carroll 2000) to make the case that women have always been fit for politics and have generated significant and original political thought, despite ideologies to the contrary. This was an important insight, but it still did not yield significant change in women's representation in political office or significantly increase women's access to and participation in formal politics more generally. Such a focus on "women worthies" also limited feminist interventions to getting relatively few women into the relatively few positions of formal power. This led feminist political theorists to question the very definition of politics and the standards by which political behavior is judged.[1] That public-sphere, formal politics is only one form of politics was revealed by showing how the private sphere and everyday life are shot through with power relations and negotiations ("the personal is political"). This drew attention as well to ways in which women engaged in nonformal political action to turn practices assumed to be natural and unchangeable (such as rape and domestic violence) into "political" (and thus changeable) "issues." Feminist political theorizing also revealed that formal politics was defined and political behavior judged on the basis of (hegemonic) male norms that privileged notions of politics as winner-take-all affairs, effectively necessitating individualist and aggressive traits to be successful in such politics. This problem is magnified in the case of international politics, which could be defined as hypermasculinist when compared with masculinist domestic politics, and which feminists have also shown are not separate from international politics ("the personal is international").

These points suggest how this shift in analysis, in turn, shifted strategies: from "adding women" to formal power structures to valorizing feminine traits in order to redefine politics from power-over to power-to (or power-with or enabling power) and change the standards of political behavior in favor of interdependence and cooperation. Still, this left intact a lingering and limiting referent to "women" that did not dehomogenize the category to recognize power differentials among women and the power some women hold over some men. It also left intact the association of embodied women with feminine values, which led, on the one hand, to essentialist assumptions about women as cure-alls for social (and global) ills; and on the other hand, positioned certain embodied men (largely non-Western, non-white, and/or lower-class) as the villains of the piece. In the process, attention is deflected from the complicity of both women and men—particularly those with the most power and privilege—in contributing to global ills. It also misrepresents feminist politics as exclusively about women rather than about resisting gender and gendered hierarchies and the ills they cause globally. This is not to say that raising the status of women and other subjugated people—in politics and other facets of life—is not necessary to increase formal representation and better equalize voice, but to note that it is insufficient if there is no attendant ideological shift away from politics as power-over to politics that enables resistance to and transformation of world-politics-as-usual, which the power of gender sustains.

In this chapter we follow the general trajectory of "adding women," to disturbing gender and gendered assumptions, to complicating gender, and, finally, to expanding feminist politics beyond the issue of women in politics. This brings us to the matter of resisting the contemporary world political force of neoliberal governmentality, which has the capacity to manage or depoliticize feminist critiques and resistances. As we conclude, the antidote to this is repoliticizing such demands for change.

WOMEN ACTORS IN GLOBAL GOVERNANCE

State and National Leaders

Heads of states and/or governments are among the world's most powerful political actors, and a number of women have held these powerful positions over the past century and into the current one (ERGD 2009).

Heads of state are key executive decision-makers and policy-implementers within the nations they lead. At the same time, their power within the state has external, international consequences to the extent that the military, political, economic, and cultural priorities they establish extend beyond territorial borders. Additionally, heads of government "represent" their states culturally as well as politically: In varying ways they come to symbolize the values of the country they represent. Female heads of state and government are no exception.

Individual elite women have, throughout history, wielded considerable political power and influence. Consider such legendary hereditary rulers as Cleopatra, Queen Elizabeth I, and Catherine the Great, and such well-known twentieth-century leaders as Indira Ghandi, Golda Meir, and Margaret Thatcher. However, they have so far proved to be more the exception than the rule when we recognize that only about 58 women have been appointed or elected as prime minister, president, or chancellor in 45 countries, with an additional 11 serving as acting heads of state or government in the twentieth and twenty-first centuries (ERGD 2009; Hoogensen and Solheim 2006: 15). It is notable, however, that at the time of this writing women are leading thirteen countries (including Germany, Ireland, Finland, Chile, New Zealand, Philippines, Liberia, Mozambique, India, Argentina, Ukraine, Moldova, and Iceland) on five continents (ERGD 2009), and the United States has had its first competitive woman contender for president. This suggests that increasingly women can achieve such power across a range of political systems and cultures. However, as Gunhild Hoogensen and Bruce Solheim have noted, certain patterns do persist—namely, the continued importance of dynastic political family ties that enable women to play on their names to downplay their gender, the continued paucity of women leaders at the top in most of the most powerful countries in the West and the global North compared with the global South, and the contemporary trend of more women coming to power in conflict or postconflict areas of the global South (with the exception of much of the Middle East) where women leaders "might be perceived as being less corruptible, mother figures, and often tap into the power of martyred husbands and fathers" (2006: 16, 128–132, 129).

This latter trend can particularly be seen in parliamentary statistics on women (Inter-Parliamentary Union 2006). As of 2006, postconflict

Rwanda topped the world in the percentage of women elected to parliament, standing at 48.8 percent women members of parliament (MPs) then, and in 2008 their representation reached over 50 percent. This makes it the first country in the world with more women than men in a national legislative body. The Welsh Assembly reached male-female parity in 2002 (Hoogensen and Solheim 2006: 16), while Sweden's parliament is close to parity. By 2006, most other Western European, and particularly Nordic, countries had reached or transcended the minimal threshold of 30 percent women in national legislatures that was called for in the 1995 Beijing Platform for Action (BPA). But so too had Costa Rica, Cuba, Argentina, Mozambique, South Africa, New Zealand, Burundi, and Tanzania, putting all of these in the top 20 of countries with the highest representation of women legislators (compared with the U.S. rank of 67 with only 15 percent women) as of 2006. According to UNIFEM's Progress of the World's Women Report 2008/2009, "the proportion of women in national assemblies has accelerated over the past decade from 11.6 percent in 1995 to 18.4 percent as of May 2008," compared with only a one percentage point gain between 1975 and 1995 (2008: 21). UNIFEM accounts for this relatively dramatic rise by pointing to primarily the increased use of legally required or voluntary quota systems and proportional representation (PR) electoral systems, practices which in some cases were stimulated by gender equality advocates working at international and national levels who have used the BPA for leverage and by the adoption in 2000 of the United Nations Millennium Development Goals (MDGs),[2] which include Goal 3 that promotes gender equality and women's empowerment (UNIFEM 2008: 20). (These advances are discussed in more detail later in this chapter.)

In the 46 countries with constitutional or electoral law quotas, women's representation averages 21.9 percent compared with a 15.3 percent average for the rest of the world regardless of political system (UNIFEM 2008: 22). Almost all countries with 30 percent or more women represented use some form of legal or voluntary quota system (UNIFEM 2008: 22). Moreover, those countries with PR systems in which "seats are assigned in proportion to the percentage of votes won by parties"—as opposed to simple majority or winner-take-all systems— allow more women to compete, resulting in on average 20.7 percent of the seats held by women compared with 13.3 percent on average in non-PR states (UNIFEM 2008: 21).

Hoogensen and Solheim note one other particularly significant feature shared by those countries with the highest proportions of women in national legislatures: a strong separation between church and state (2006: 17). According to UNIFEM, other strategies that appear to promote women's numerical representation in national public office-holding include (1) seeking parity in executive positions in political parties (such as in the rare case of Costa Rica); (2) further developing women's parties that have existed in such countries as Iceland, Sweden, the Philippines, and now Afghanistan and that circumvent mainstream parties to bring gender equality issues to the fore; (3) campaign finance reform that provides equitable public financing and is tied to developing or sustaining party quota systems; (4) more women's political action committees that raise money for women candidates; and (5) combating sexism in media coverage of women candidates (2008: 23–26). UNIFEM, however, cautions that these still-minimal gains overall are in jeopardy should there be any letup in efforts on any of these scores. Moreover, the gendered divisions of power that portray—and internalize in women—the sense that women are unfit for politics, the masculinist construction of power as aggression and confrontation, and the separation between public and private that leaves women leaders (most of whom are mothers) responsible for the family on top of political responsibilities remain strong countervailing forces (UNIFEM 2008: 22). These and other barriers to women's representation are discussed more fully later.

Gains have also been seen in the percentage of women in national cabinets, rising from 8.7 percent in 1999 to 15.2 percent in 2007 (WEDO 2007b). By that time, Finland (at 55 percent women cabinet ministers) topped the list of 18 countries in Western Europe, Latin America, Sub-Saharan Africa, and the Caribbean that had reached approximately 30 percent or more. Regions with among the lowest percentages included Eastern Europe (10 percent), Asia and Pacific (7 percent), and North Africa (4 percent), with North America coming in at about 22 percent (WEDO 2007b). As pointed out by the U.S.-based transnational Women's Environment and Development Organization (WEDO), which leads a 50/50 campaign to gain gender equality in government positions worldwide, cabinet ministers are appointed and thus not subject to quota systems for parliamentarians that some countries have adopted. Instead, increases in this area must rely on enlightened heads of state and government backed up by gender equality advocates within and outside government. Despite some notable gains in this area (including three female U.S. secretaries of state since the 1990s, one of whom was African American), cabinet appointments that go to women tend to be clustered in domestic-focused social welfare agencies, while men far more routinely head foreign affairs, military defense, and finance ministries that have far more influence internationally (Hoogensen and Solheim 2006: 17).

UN and Other IGO Officials

As IGOs have become more significant actors in global governance, more attention has been given to women's representation in these bodies. In 1995, the UN committed itself to increasing the number of women on its professional staff to 30 percent by 1990, which it achieved in 1991. In 1998, the General Assembly further committed to the 50/50 goal of gender parity in all posts in the UN system (UN 2000: 167), but this is far from being achieved. According to UNIFEM, as of 2006, women remain concentrated in the lowest levels of the UN professional staff (2008: 104), and it is primarily UN agencies with social welfare portfolios and/or that have been headed by women (such as UNITAR, UNFPA, UNESCO, FAO, UNHCR, UNAIDS, and UNDP) that have reached the "parity zone'" of 40 percent women on professional staffs (UNIFEM 2008: 105). Moreover, although the UN has a "gender architecture," which includes the Office of the Special Adviser on Gender Issues (OSAGI), the United Nations Development Fund for Women (UNIFEM), the United Nations Division for the Advancement of Women (UNDAW), and the International Institute for Research and Training of Women (UN-INSTRAW) along with gender units within many UN agencies, these tend to be comparatively weak in terms of staff and resources. For example, in 2003, UNIFEM had only 47 core staff compared with UNICEF with 2,794 (UNIFEM 2008: 104).

Member state performance with respect to women's representation at the UN has been no better considering that as of 2001, only 26 women were serving as ambassadors to the UN in New York or Geneva (UNIFEM 2008: 16). At the same time, although 37 member states had 50 percent or more women working in the UN Secretariat, 44 had none (Focal Point for Women in the Secretariat 2001). Many more women have served as ambassadors to other countries, practicing the art of diplomacy that is well recognized as a dimension of effective international relations. However, because women's numbers still remain comparatively small in diplomatic and foreign policy circles, women have organized lobbying and policy groups (such as the Associates of the American Foreign Service Worldwide and Women in International Security or WIIS) that both expose and influence gender dynamics in ministries, departments, and committees dealing with foreign affairs.

What remains most problematic is the relative lack of women in IGOs that have real enforcement power. As of 2005, only one woman had ever served as a judge on the International Court of Justice (ICJ) (NCRW 2006: 42). A few more women, however, have been appointed as judges to the more recently formed International Criminal Court (ICC), which tries individuals for crimes against humanity, including genocide and war crimes such as sexual assault, when national courts fail to do so (UNIFEM 2008: 79). Just as disconcerting is the paucity of women at the top of international financial institutions (IFIs), which have much say in the workings of the global economy. As of 2002, three women served on the 175-member Board of Governors of the IMF, none on the IMF's 24-member Board of Directors, 10 on the World Bank's 171-member Board of Governors, and 4 on the World Bank's 22-member Board of Directors (NCRW 2006: 24).

Global Market and NGO Actors

Many observers of the global political economy see global market actors such as TNCs as rivaling state power on the world stage, particularly since the 1990s. But just as women are heavily underrepresented in economic decision-making within state and IGO bodies, so too are they poorly represented in the top echelons of global business entities. As of 2008, women's share of senior management positions in the world's corporations ranged from 3 percent in South Asia to 12 percent in Latin America and the Caribbean (UNIFEM 2008: 65). In 2005, there were only 19 women chief executive officers (CEOs) at the helm of the Fortune 1000 companies and only 9 of those were CEOs of Fortune 500 companies (NCRW 2006: 65). These kinds of statistics prompted Norway to pass legislation that required Norwegian corporations by 2008 "to have at least 40 per cent female membership on their management boards" or risk closure (UNIFEM 2008: 64). Women now constitute 38 percent of board seats of Norwegian corporations, up from 7 percent in 2002 and well over the 9 percent average in Europe and the 15 percent average in the United States among the Fortune 500 (UNIFEM 2008: 64). While such radical action does not appear in the offing elsewhere, this demonstration project might have some persuasive effect on corporations to adopt their own quotas, particularly as they come under greater scrutiny, experience managerial shake-ups, and engage in internal soul-searching in the midst of the current world financial crisis and economic recession.

At the other end of the spectrum of women's representation in global governance are transnational NGOs. Few formal statistics exist on women's participation in NGOs, but it is estimated that women constitute the majority of members of NGOs, particularly at the local, grassroots level, but also through the transnational level given that they have much more access to and voice in them when compared with their prospects for participating in formal political office-holding and decision-making. Although women constitute the majority of rank-and-file members of most NGOs, particularly those concerned with human rights, labor, social justice, and environmental causes but also more conservative issues, women exercise the most NGO leadership in women's NGOs. Although women's transnational NGOs have a long history (consider, for example, women from warring countries gathering at The Hague during World War I to form the still-extant Women's International League for Peace and Freedom), most contemporary women's transnational NGOs, sometimes referred to as transnational feminist networks (TFNs), began forming during the UN Decade for Women and proliferated particularly in the 1990s. Margaret Keck and Karen Sikkink (1998) have hypothesized that such TFNs are part of a generalized rise of transnational social networks (TSNs) that emerged in response to their causes being blocked at the state level and the political opportunity structures the UN provided (through conferences, consultations, and so on) that enabled them to air their issues at the international level to pressure states to act. Valentine Moghadam (2005) divided up TFNs that have been most active and influential in international forums and policymaking contexts into five issue areas: women's human rights; peace, antimilitarism, and conflict resolution; ending violence against women; reproductive health and rights; and economic critique and justice. We would also add environmental protection and sustainability. TFNs also tend to interconnect these issue areas (discussed in subsequent chapters). But our main point here is that women participate most in global governance through these channels, albeit exercising little masculinist "power-over" but significant "power-with," a feminist conception of power that stresses shared, collective, bottom-up empowerment.

BARRIERS TO WOMEN'S PARTICIPATION IN GLOBAL GOVERNANCE

As can be seen from this brief review of women's contemporary numerical representation in global governance, women's recent, highly uneven, and fragile gains in this area have been largely due to the institutionalization of particular gender equality measures at international and national levels advocated primarily by TFNs and national women's movements. Such measures as gender quotas were advocated to address persistent and otherwise intractable barriers to women's political participation at almost all levels, but particularly the highest, and in all arenas of government and governance. Researchers have extensively studied gender differences in political participation—in particular, the low percentage of women in high political office. Two conclusions emerged repeatedly from this research. First, women do not lack interest in or motivation for political action: Studies of women's participation in grass-roots organizing, community politics, election campaigns, and political organizations suggest that "women are as likely (if not more likely) to work for political causes or candidates as are men" (Lips 1991: 91). Second, a point related to the first, women's underrepresentation in political office and leadership positions is linked to gender-differentiated patterns still pervasive in today's world. Gender socialization, situational constraints, structural obstacles, and institutional impediments interact in favoring men and discriminating against women as formal political actors (Randall 1987: 83–94).

Gender Socialization

Early studies tended to focus on the effects of sex-role stereotyping—that is, on the enduring consequences of childhood socialization of girls and boys into mutually exclusive gender roles. Presumably, socialization into appropriate "feminine" behavior makes women less likely than men to pursue traditionally defined political activities. For example, feminine identity formation is inextricable from cultural expectations that motherhood is the primary role of women, that women's domestic role is antithetical to public-sphere activities, and that traits associated with political efficacy (ambition, aggression, competitiveness, authority) are distinctly unfeminine. To the extent that women internalize these stereotypical norms, then, they are less likely to perceive themselves as political actors or aspire to public office.

As a corollary, socialization into appropriate "masculine" behavior makes men more likely than women to identify with political activities. Just as important, gender stereotypes, because they are held by men and women, create a climate that encourages male participation while discouraging female participation in politics. Thus, individual women who seek leadership positions must struggle not only with their own internalized stereotypes but also with the fact that gender stereotyping in general fuels resistance to women as political actors. Finally, for women who do achieve positions of power, expectations of appropriately "feminine" behavior are often in conflict with qualities required for successful leadership. In short, gender stereotypes suggest that appropriately feminine women (passive, dependent, domestic; engaged in meeting private, familial needs) are by definition inappropriate political agents (active, autonomous, public-oriented; engaged in meeting collective, not personal needs).

This picture is further complicated by men's and women's positions in relation to race/ethnicity, religion, sexual orientation, ability, age, and so on. Masculinities and femininities vary along these dimensions, and not all men are socialized to desire or expect political participation or leadership. These variations matter significantly in terms of who actually enters and/or succeeds in politics. But despite hierarchies among men, the consistency of gender stereotypes is so strong that within particular groups, more men than women will be associated with public-sphere activities, political participation, and corporate power.

Situational Constraints

Gender socialization produces different male and female orientations toward political participation. Also, gender stereotyping produces behavioral patterns that result in different concrete living situations for women and men that also constrain women's participation. Hence, we are better able to explain gendered political participation if we look at the *interaction* of stereotypes (for example, how women are assigned domestic and mothering responsibilities) and gender-differentiated living situations (for example, how the gendered division of labor limits women's involvement in traditional or formal politics). In masculinist societies, it is women who confront the time and energy demands of having primary responsibility for family and home care. Family care includes child-rearing and/or care of the elderly or infirm as well as the emotional maintenance work required to sustain intimate and extended family relationships—responsibilities that disproportionately fall on women regardless of their sexuality or the family form in which they live. Worldwide, home care involves ensuring that food is secured and prepared for all and that the household is physically maintained. For millions of women, the latter entails arduous efforts to secure water and fuel. For most women, it means responsibility for cleaning, laundry, upkeep, and seeing that the household functions adequately. Even for affluent women, it means a great deal of shopping, scheduling, and transporting family members. Not surprisingly, because these demands are placed on women more than men, women are constrained in terms of how much time and energy they have for political participation, especially the pursuit of political office. When this reproductive work is coupled with productive work for an income that most women in most of the world perform, whether in formal or informal sectors, women's energy and time are further constrained. It is not simply the double workload of reproductive and productive labor that inhibits women's participation in politics; it is also women's lack of control over when they will be available and whether (or how) family obligations will interfere with political pursuits (Randall 1987: 125).

Men are typically not forced to make these choices because their political activities are considered separate from their domestic relations. Women, in contrast, are so closely identified with the domestic sphere that when they take on political activities it is considered in combination with, not separable from, their role in the family. It is also important to note that globalization or global economic restructuring (see Chapter 5) for the most part exacerbates this gender imbalance. Men increasingly confront un- and underemployment. But this change in their workday still rarely translates into their making greater contributions to family and home care. At the same time, withdrawal of social and welfare services by the state disproportionally hurts women, who (in their role of family and home caretakers) are assigned responsibility for "taking up the slack."

> Decreased public spending on education, health, and food subsidies means that increased costs must be borne by women, who work longer hours, look for less expensive food, spend more resources on basic health care, make difficult choices about which children will get an education and which will work to sustain the family economy, and face lower wages or fewer job opportunities as the wages in female-dominated industries decline or as the returns to agricultural labor are not sustained (Chowdhury and Nelson, et al. 1994: 6).

Hence, insofar as political participation requires time, resources, and control over them, capitalist and masculinist conditions make women's participation exceedingly difficult. For women of nondominant race/ethnicity and of subordinate classes, the obstacles are multiplied.

Structural Obstacles

Clearly, stereotypes and situational constraints shape the gender of political activism, but the recurring differences in women's and men's participation must also be examined in relation to large-scale, interacting, and enduring social structures. Here we refer broadly to sets of power relations and/or social-cultural institutions that determine the boundaries of individual behavior. Understanding why so few women hold political power requires understanding how social structures and their interaction make it much more difficult for most women (than for most men) to seek and secure political office. Although primary gender socialization occurs in childhood, the hierarchical dichotomy of masculine-feminine is enforced throughout our lives. The gender dimensions of multiple social structures interact and, in effect, "discipline" individual behavior to conform to stereotypes.

For example, traditional religious belief systems and institutions play an important role in perpetuating images of women that deny them leadership positions. All too frequently, women are portrayed as either the source of evil (the uncontrollably sexual whore) or the model of saintliness (the self-sacrificing virgin). Neither is an appropriate identity for political leadership. In addition, the vast majority of religious institutions themselves exclude women from top leadership roles. No matter how this exclusionary practice is legitimized, it in fact sends a clear and unequivocal message that reinforces gender stereotypes: that women are not equal to men and that they cannot be trusted with or lack the qualifications for positions of authority and power.

Religious beliefs interact with and may reinforce other cultural sources of gender stereotyping. This is generally the case in regard to identifying the home/family as woman's sphere and the public/politics as man's sphere. It can also be quite explicit, as in the seclusion of women (*purdah*) practiced in many Islamic countries or in Western ones where neoconservative policies (sometimes inspired by Christian fundamentalism) seek to return women to the home and reconstructed patriarchal and heteronormative families. The point is that the structural separation of public and private has gendered consequences. Religious, educational, and judicial institutions tend to reproduce the ideological—and gendered—division of public and private. And both informal and formal public-private separations affect women's political participation negatively by identifying women exclusively with the private sphere.

Thus, our expectations of different behaviors for men (appropriate for politics) and for women (inappropriate for politics) make it difficult, first, for women to see themselves comfortably in conventionally defined political roles and, second, for men and women generally to see and accept women as political agents. In the latter case, negative attitudes toward women's political participation are often expressed as lack of confidence in and support for female candidates and politicians (UN-DAW 1989: 6). In sum, to the extent that we perpetuate the stereotype of "a woman's place is in the home" (or in the bedroom), we ensure that women will be seen as "out of place" in political office.

The horizontal and vertical segregation of both men and women in the workforce affects women's access to political power. Horizontally, women are concentrated in fewer occupations than men and in jobs where women are the majority of workers—clerical work, elementary teaching, domestic maintenance, daycare, nursing, waitressing. Moreover, these are not occupations from which political candidates are traditionally recruited. In general, the work women do for pay is an extension of the feminine role assigned to women (and feminized others) and replicates work that women, according to both gender and heterosexual norms, are expected to do as mothers and wives: caring for dependents, serving the needs of others, providing social and physical necessities, and being docile, flexible, emotionally supportive, and sexually attractive (Macdonald and Sirianni 1996). Not only are women (and feminized others) clustered in certain jobs, but they are also expected to be "feminine" in whatever job they hold.

The workplace is also segregated vertically, with women concentrated in pink-collar jobs (men in blue-collar), in domestic services (men in protective services), and in light industry (men in heavy industry) (Sapiro 1983). Vertical gender segregation (the higher, the fewer) occurs both within and across industries: Women generally are concentrated in part-time, temporary, nonorganized, lower-status, lower-paying, and less-powerful positions. As a result, women earn less money, have less-secure jobs, and rarely climb into powerful executive ranks. Race, ethnicity, and class discrimination interact with gender discrimination to exacerbate the self-perpetuating cycle of elite males holding onto power at the expense of all other groups.

Gendered divisions of labor affect women's political participation in multiple ways. Most obviously, women's structural disadvantage in the labor market translates into their having fewer resources, less status, and less experience wielding power when competing with men for political office. And when it comes to recruiting and promoting people for political office, educational and occupational structures interact to exacerbate women's disadvantage. Women receive not only a different education from what men get but also, in most of the world, a good deal less education than men. Because education is so closely related to occupational opportunities, lack of educational training fuels the gender segregation of the workforce and its negative consequences for women. Moreover, certain professions have historically been associated with or appear particularly compatible with achieving and maintaining political power: law, military, career civil service, big business. It remains the case that women are underrepresented in these occupational areas and are especially absent at the top levels from which political leaders are often recruited.

Other obstacles to women's political participation are direct and indirect legal barriers. It is only in the past century that most women secured the rights to vote and to hold political office, which are prerequisites to seeking formal power. Women in some of the Arab world as well as some women (and men) elsewhere continue to be denied these rights, either due to their gender, race or ethnicity, or sexuality. Military experience has also been a traditional path to power not only in authoritarian states but also in democracies such as the United States. To the degree that women remain small percentages of state militaries, are legally prevented from holding combat roles, and/or are excluded from being in such militaries because of their sexuality or ethnicity, this avenue is effectively blocked. Moreover, as long as military experience is perceived as a requisite criterion of manliness for high political office, women may be pressured to "out-macho" their male counterparts and sublimate any "feminine" concerns that they might bring to high office.

For women who do gain power as the result of family connections and, specifically, the death of a father or husband who is in office or in the midst or wake of a conflict situation where symbols of unity, compromise, or conciliation are sought, being a woman and expressing traditional femininity can be an advantage. But when women act "like women," even though they are at the helm of national governments, the traditional picture of gender is not disturbed. Similarly, when women assume national leadership as a result of their success in grass-roots activism, their association with "soft issues" (the environment, peace, feminism) can reinforce the traditional disassociation of women with "hard issues" (national security, economic competition) and the masculine traits assumed necessary for dealing with them (fearlessness, calculative reason).

It is not surprising, then, that women who achieve national-level leadership positions "on their own" are often identified as especially masculine. Some research suggests that women aspiring to or holding political office play down feminine qualities in order to appear more appropriate for statesmanship" (Randall 1987: 51). The overall picture remains one of continued gender dichotomies: Women succeed through their identification as "traditional" (feminine) women facilitating male-defined projects, as trivialized "soft leaders," or as manlike by playing down any association with feminine "weakness." It appears that being seen as politically powerful in the traditional sense requires that women become "like men." As long as female political actors are perceived either as traditional women or "invisible women" (because they are acting "like men"), hierarchical gender expectations are not really disrupted. Paradoxically, even when women wield the highest state power, by continuing to behave in gender-stereotypical ways they often reinforce rather than challenge the politics of gender. Even though the power of gender is at work here (shaping pathways to and the exercise of power), it remains "invisible" to observers of world politics. In other words, by appearing as traditional women or honorary men, female politicians do not challenge the categorical distinction between femininity and masculinity and do not politicize this gender dichotomy. Their conformity to traditional gender stereotypes in fact works to reproduce them.

The pervasive bias of androcentrism in political science and international relations operates to produce this no-win situation. One effect of this bias is the assumption that political actors are men. Another is the narrow definition of politics as exclusively public-sphere or governmental activities. Yet a third effect is the narrow definition of power as the capacity to enforce one's will ("power-over" in contrast to an alternative feminist conceptualization of power, namely empowerment or "power-to").

These effects are not simply an academic concern, because the definitions they take for granted are promoted outside of academic disciplines as well. Consider the focus of television news on "spectacular" (rather than everyday) events: wars, weapons, violence, crises, men as leaders/ legislators/protectors, and women as dependents/victims. The leaders we see tend to be heads of government of countries that are geopolitically powerful or of foreign policy significance. Otherwise, international news is almost exclusively viewed through the lens of various crises: seemingly hopeless extremities of governmental, military, economic, refugee, population, health, food, water, fuel, and/or ecological breakdown, all seemingly emanating from the global South. Such images sustain gender, race, class, and nationality stereotypes, denying political agency to women and people of the global South and the roles of men and the global North in precipitating such crises. (The exception is international sports, which foster instead nationalist "ownership" of outstanding performances of individuals and teams—still heavily men except during the Olympics.)

In these accounts, gender operates but remains invisible in various ways. Attention to wars and spectacles is at the expense of everyday maintenance activities that in fact are a precondition of the world's continuing to function. The latter are largely ignored, yet they are the activities occupying women's—most people's—lives. To the extent that women appear in depictions of politics, they tend to be acting "like men" (Margaret Thatcher) or in supporting roles to the main/male actors (for instance, as wives, secretaries). In depictions of crises, women (or what Cynthia Enloe (1990) has termed "womenandchildren") are the ever-present victims in need of protection by men or through male-defined programs. Not inconsistent with the crisis picture, women occasionally appear as saints and crusaders (Mother Theresa, Princess Diana), whose model of sacrifice and commitment spurs men on to greater feats of protection (or competitive performance), thereby strengthening male roles.

Again, not only are women and their activities depicted as secondary to (or merely in support of) men's public-sphere pursuits, but also the way in which women make an appearance tends to reinforce rather than challenge conventional gender stereotypes. From manner of dress and demeanor to lifestyle and sexual orientation, we rarely observe any blurring of rigid gender boundaries in the mainstream media. Left in place are androcentric accounts that obscure women as powerful actors and leaders across a spectrum of political activities, that deny the politics and societal importance of ostensibly private-sphere activities, and that mystify the role of masculinism (ideologically and structurally) in the continued subordination of women and perpetuation of multiple social hierarchies. In short, the gender dynamics of politics—especially international politics—remain in place yet invisible as long as women "appear" only when they adopt masculine principles or epitomize feminine ones.

Institutional Impediments

From another angle of vision, political institutions themselves can be seen to impede women's participation. Vicky Randall has identified three institutional barriers in her discussion of political recruitment and promotion (1987: 92–94). First, at each level, political advancement requires "appropriate" political, leadership, educational, and/or occupational experience: As already noted, these criteria discriminate against women who are structurally likely to have different and fewer resources and/or who start later in their pursuit of office.

Second, the institutions associated with politics and power and the norms and practices of these institutions are those of "a man's world." Exclusively male until recently and still dominated by men, they are hegemonically masculinist in the following senses: Behavior traits deemed suitable, sometimes essential, for political success are stereotypically masculine (ambition, leadership, rationality, competitiveness, authority, toughness); meeting times and locations as well as socializing (networking) activities are, in practice, convenient for men's (not women's) schedules and geographical mobility; and issues of central importance are not those most immediately relevant to most women's lives ("women's issues" have been treated as peripheral to conventional politics until very recently) (Randall 1987: 93).

Randall identified a third institutional barrier in the direct expression of male prejudice: outright discrimination against women (1987: 132). Forms of discrimination in the workplace vary, but the presence of gender hierarchy and sexism (complicated further by racism and/or heterosexism for women in racial and sexual minorities) creates a less favorable environment for women, who must then struggle harder than their male counterparts to be successful. As long as the workplace and political office are identified as "male terrain," women constantly confront and must deal with resentment of their unwanted presence. Women are most frequently reminded of their outsider status when they are viewed not as colleagues but in terms of their gender and sexuality. Subtle and not-so-subtle references to women and sexuality produce an atmosphere of male dominance in which women must either become "like men" or become invisible. These are not trivial aspects of power. The pervasiveness of masculinist assumptions, of androcentric worldviews, and of sexist and heterosexist humor poses formidable obstacles. Because we are so saturated with gendered assumptions, these obstacles typically go unrecognized or are not taken seriously as the pillars holding up male privilege and power—at the expense of women's participation.

In sum, long-entrenched gender stereotypes and the *interaction* of situational constraints, domestic responsibilities, and religious, educational, economic, legal, and military structures, and institutional impediments have so discriminated against women's political participation and, especially, their access to high political office and global power structures that feminists have long concluded that major policy interventions must be launched even to hope to level the playing field.

INSTITUTIONALIZING GLOBAL GENDER EQUALITY

As indicated earlier, the 1995 BPA arising out of the fourth UN world women's conference, which was unanimously supported by UN member states, provided a major impetus for the widespread adoption of a range of gender equality policies and measures at national and international levels. These include not only gender quotas, but also the institution of women's policy agencies, the practice of gender mainstreaming, the inclusion of women's empowerment in the MDGs, and the creation of two global measurement systems to track gender (in)equality and rank states on the basis of it—the Gender-related Development Index (GDI) and the Gender Empowerment Measure (GEM). Prior to these instruments was the adoption of the Convention on the Elimination of All Forms of Discrimination Against Women (CEDAW), which is binding on states that have ratified it (with the notable exception of the United States and a handful of states in the global South, such as Iran, Qatar, Somalia, Sudan, and Tonga, as of this writing). CEDAW's objective is, among other things, to ensure that gender equality, as defined by CEDAW, is enshrined in and enforced through state constitutions and laws to achieve equality outcomes. Far fewer countries have signed onto the CEDAW Optional Protocol that makes them liable for complaints made to the CEDAW committee (of which there have so far been very few formal ones), and many countries ratified CEDAW with reservations that reduce its intent and enforceability (UNIFEM 2008: 74–75). However, CEDAW has also been the basis of an international women's human rights movement that has added to the definition of human rights certain previously unrecognized rights, such as reproductive rights, sexual rights, and rights to be free from domestic and sexual violence. Although such women's human rights are unevenly accepted by states, they are reflected in the BPA as a norm-setting document.

These are significant developments that bear testimony to the success of the "power-with" strategies of national women's movements and TFNs working in concert with UN women's agencies to hold the international community accountable for gender equality. However, as we address in our review of these measures, institutionalization carries not only rewards but also risks in terms of uneven implementation, co-optation, and deepening divisions among women. It can also maintain the power of gender by institutionalizing gender difference while depoliticizing it, shifting attention away from a broader feminist critique of gendered power relations that uphold world-politics-as-usual in favor of simply increasing women's (and only certain women's) participation in those politics.

Gender Quotas

A quota is typically seen as an affirmative action measure designed to redress to some degree (ranging from setting minimum numbers or thresholds to creating representative balance) the political underrepresentation of a particular group, which can include women, ethnic minorities, indigenous peoples, and even geographical groups. Dahlerup has distinguished among three major types of quota systems currently in use that target an increase in women's political participation: quotas that enlarge the candidate pool usually determined voluntarily by political parties; candidate quotas for party lists, which may be voluntary party quotas or legal or constitutional quotas that mandate all parties to comply; and reserved seats quotas that require by law, the constitution, or ruler edict that a certain number of seats must be occupied by the target group. There are also so-called "soft" quotas that involve recommended targets set by political parties and governments (Dahlerup 2006b: 19–21). Party quotas were first adopted in the Nordic countries of Western Europe by leftist political parties in the late 1970s and early 1980s, but only after women had secured between 20 to 30 percent of parliamentary seats, in part due to robust feminist movements, political cultures oriented to social welfare values, and PR systems. These party quota systems have remained voluntary and representative of what is called an "incrementalist" approach to women's empowerment (Friedenwall, Dahlerup, and Skjeie 2006: 49–50). Even though Nordic countries have not used legal or constitutional quotas to reach consistently high numbers of women in political office, the Scandinavian case has been cited as an example of what can be achieved with some form of quota system, and especially a more "fast-track" one that is legally or constitutionally mandated. This is particularly the case in those countries where women's share of political power has been persistently low and incrementalist change is unlikely to change that any time soon.

Feminists have long made the argument that getting more women into political office is not only a matter of fairness but also crucial for having any true democracy. The quota argument gained significant traction in the 1990s when a range of countries were undergoing transitions to some form of democracy and entering into the rising global capitalist economy. This was the same period in which UN agencies and international financial institution (IFIs) began to take up the argument that gender equality was necessary both for democratization and as a feature of a modern market economy and good governance. The conflation by IGO actors of gender equality with not only democratization, but also mature market-based economies, accelerated the top-down institution of legal or constitutional gender quota systems, particularly in the South. The assumption was that such commitments to gender equality would help to legitimize the countries that adopted them as modern, democratic, and market-oriented (Matland 2006: 277; Squires 2007: 29). At the same time, most older democratic nations have tended to resist legal quotas on the assumption that they have already achieved democracy, regardless of the current statistics on women's representation.

Thus, of the 90 or so countries with some kind of party or legal gender quota system as of 2006, most of the 40 with legal quotas (heavily concentrated in Latin America and sub-Saharan Africa but also including countries like Afghanistan, Iraq, and Nepal) are not part of the Organization for Economic Cooperation and Development (OECD) to which mostly Western democracies belong. Moreover, most legal quotas (including reserved seats systems that can be found in parts of the Middle East, Africa, and Asia) were adopted after the Beijing women's conference in 1995 or in the wake of the institution of MDGs in 2000. In contrast, voluntary party quotas are more typical in OECD countries with parliamentary systems that include social democratic or other left-leaning parties. The United States has remained hostile to quotas (with the exception of their use by the Democratic Party in the early 1970s), although the two major political parties are mindful of the need for some women's (and racial minority) representation and thus exercise informal or "soft" quotas (Squires 2007: 26–28). Democratizing Eastern and Central European countries have been more resistant to gender quotas that are seen as smacking of old forms of central control (Dahlerup 2006a: 197–198); thus, there has been little recovery from the post-Communist downward plunge in women's relatively high formal political representation (albeit not in the most powerful echelons) during the Communist period.

Women's Policy Agencies

It was following the first UN Decade for Women conference in Mexico City in 1975, which called for the adoption of state machineries to advance the status of women, that the first women's policy agencies were instituted. Since that time, as a result of continued TFN lobbying using CEDAW and UN women's conference documents as leverage coupled with pressure from UN women's agencies, 165 countries had created some form of national women's policy agency by 2004 (Squires 2007: 33). These range from "stand-alone government ministries" and "offices within the head of state's department" to "quasi-autonomous state agencies such as national commissions or divisions for gender equality within ministries for labour, social welfare or national development, parliamentary commissions and delegations" (Squires 2007: 34). Although they vary considerably in terms of resources and functions (ranging from policy formation or input to mere reporting) and thus influence, they have been productive of what is termed "state feminism," with insider "femocrats" working to advance women's representation and issues not only in elective arenas, but also in bureaucratic ones (Squires 2007: 33).

In the midst of the initially laudable and rapid institutionalization of women's policy agencies, feminist "outsiders" have questioned to whom femocrats are really accountable (typically governments rather than women's movements), how they can effectively represent diverse women (as they are largely elite women), and what women's issues they tend to advocate (typically those that are digestible by a government in power, leaving more radical demands by the wayside) (Squires 2007: 119).

Moreover, since the mid-1990s, they have been charged with the advocacy of gender mainstreaming, which shifts attention away from women, women's movements, and women's issues. Instead, their focus is on what is seen as a more expert-based, bureaucratic exercise that has been adopted, like gender quotas and women's policy agencies, less because of any commitment to gender equality and more because of states' desires to appear more modern and market-oriented.

Gender Mainstreaming

Although the BPA calls upon governments to engage in gender mainstreaming, it is largely a creation of IGOs. Conceptually developed by the World Bank and the UN Development Program (UNDP) in the early 1990s, it has been globalized through its adoption by the UN, the OECD, Northern development agencies (which also disseminate it to the South), and especially the EU since 1995 (Squires 2007: 41–42). Somewhat differing UN and EU definitions of gender mainstreaming share the following in common: the goal of integrating the experiences, needs, and concerns of both women and men into the design, planning, implementation, monitoring, and evaluation of all policies (economic, political, and social) with the aim of achieving gender equality (Squires 2007: 39–40).

At first blush, gender mainstreaming constitutes a significant improvement in how to bring about gender equality in that it attempts to decenter the male norm upon which policymaking has rested and within which women have to fit. Moreover, it represents a more thoroughgoing application of gender equality norms into all spheres of policymaking and makes all government agencies accountable for this application. It need not await parity in women's political representation that is still a long way off, nor is it the sole responsibility of typically underresourced and more lowly women's policy agencies. Plus, its focus on gender moves away from constructing "women" as the problem toward tackling the problems that have arisen as a result of gender inequalities, such as poverty and violence. Thus, TFNs and femocrats in state and UN agencies have supported it.

However, studies have found that its rapid adoption by states and IGOs appears to be yet another attempt to conform to "favoured international norms such as modernization and good governance" rather than a desire for "gender justice" (Squires 2007: 48). As a result, not only is it quite unevenly enforced where it has been adopted, but also it is most often engaged in through an "expert-bureaucratic model" rather than a "participative-democratic model," thereby cutting out consultations with and accountability to social movements and relying on femocrats (Squires 2007: 41). It has also had the effect of pulling back commitments to women's policy agencies on the assumption they are less needed under this diffused approach, and reducing a transformational political struggle for gender equality to a management technique whereby gender audits and assessments are performed through largely quantitative approaches that are seen to adhere to the social science ideals of objective truth and rationality (which are also most associated with masculinity and masculinist commitments to positivism) (Squires 2007: 143). Those social movements and NGOs who do not present their claims through such language and filters are dismissed, This has spawned cadres of NGO gender experts, typically at the transnational level, who can speak in the language of gender mainstreaming bureaucracies at the cost of being further separated from the struggles of the movements they claim to represent (Squires 2007: 145–154).

Gender Equality Indices

Beginning in 1995, the annual UNDP's *Human Development Report* began issuing GDI and GEM statistics by country. The GDI is an adjustment of how countries rank on the Human Development Index (HDI) based on gender differentials in life expectancy, adult literacy, and primary, secondary and tertiary education. Whereas the HDI measures general quality of life, the GDI represents statistical penalties or rewards depending upon whether or not that quality of life is shared by both men and women in terms of the above measures. Not surprisingly, in the period 2007–2008, most Western European nations as well as Canada, Japan, the United States, and New Zealand were in the top 20 of the HDI. However, the following countries received GDI demerits: Norway (−1), Ireland (−10), Switzerland (−2), Japan (−5), United States (−4), Austria (−4), and Luxembourg (−5). Others received GDI upward adjustments ranging from +1 to +6, including Australia, Sweden, the Netherlands, France, Finland, Spain, the UK, Belgium, and Italy. GDI demerits were highest for Oman and Saudi Arabia (both −13) even though they ranked 58 and 61, respectively, in the HDI. For those mostly African states at the bottom of the HDI, GDIs ranged only between −3 to +3 (UNDP 2007a: 326–329).

The GDI measures capabilities relative to gender, whereas the GEM measures opportunities by gender based on relative numbers of women in parliament, official and managerial positions, and professional and technical work, as well as women's earned income relative to men's. Far fewer countries are ranked in this index for lack of data. Of the top 20 countries according to HDI rankings, a few dropped below the top 20 in the GEM rankings. For example, HDI number seven, Switzerland, ranked 27 on the GEM measure, and Japan fell to 54 under GEM compared to 8 on the HDI. Not surprisingly, the Nordic countries ranked higher on the GEM than on the HDI as did a number of Latin American countries with gender quotas. Those that ranked the lowest on the GEM relative to their HDI standings were largely in the Arab world (UNDP 2007b: 330–333).

On the one hand, the gathering of such data on the relative "female-friendliness" of states and the seriousness with which it is now taken by forming these global indices is welcome. On the other hand, such measurements are representative of the kind of quantitative policy world to which gender equality politics has been reduced. Similarly, while these indices have no doubt facilitated the contagion of states institutionalizing gender quotas, women's agencies, and gender mainstreaming, they also tend to set up gender equality as a feature of modern progress and development rather than a matter of gender justice. Finally, although such statistical rankings are helpful to social movement and NGO actors seeking leverage to advance gender equality, they can also be used by powerful states and IFIs to punish less powerful states, through, for example, decreased aid or trade on the basis of their gender equality failings. At the same time, more powerful Western states that underperform on gender measures relative to expectations and resources (like the United States) are not subject to such "discipline." These latter two concerns also relate to the MDGs that constitute "the new aid agenda" (Antrobus 2006: 39).

Millennium Development Goals

The UN General Assembly approved the UN Millennium Declaration in 2000 that sets out eight MDGs as the basis of the international development agenda ideally to be achieved for the most part by 2015. These goals include (1) eradicate extreme poverty and hunger; (2) achieve universal primary education; (3) promote gender equality and empower women: (4) reduce child mortality; (5) improve maternal health; (6) combat HIV/AIDS, malaria, and other diseases; (7) ensure environmental sustainability; and (8) create a global partnership for development (UNIFEM 2008: 118). So central are these seen to women's well-being that UNIFEM devoted an entire section of its 2008/2009 report on the progress of the world's women to progress made on MDGs.

Progress on these goals is measured and monitored by the UN (based on statistics provided by states) in relation to particular quantitative targets set over time within each of the goals, such as cutting in half by 2015 the proportion of people with incomes of less than one dollar per day and suffering from hunger, as well as the more recent target of achieving full employment in decent work for all people by that date to reach Goal 1 (UNIFEM 2008: 118). Various indicators are used and periodically added to measure these targets, such as the proportions of the population living on one dollar per day, dietary consumption rates of the poor, and numbers of underweight children, as well as newer indicators, which address new targets and further refine data, including, for example, the proportion of employed people making below one dollar per day, the amounts of "own-account" workers and "contributing family workers," and the relationship between gross domestic product (GDP) growth and employment (UNIFEM 2008: 119). Not all of such data is sex-disaggregated, but of the data that is in relation to Goal 1, UNIFEM reports that women's "vulnerable employment," which is greater than men's and concentrated most in Sub-Saharan Africa and Asia, "has decreased globally by only three percentage points since 1997" (UNIFEM 2008: 118). Moreover, whereas "60 to 80 per cent of all men" are employed, only "20 to 65 per cent of women" are, with South Asia, the Middle East, and, interestingly, North America coming in at the lower ends of this and thus using the least "productive potential" of women (UNIFEM 2008: 119). Based on available data related to Goal 1, UNIFEM concludes that "women are still more likely than men to be poor and at risk of hunger because of the systematic discrimination they face in access to education, healthcare and control of assets" (2008: 119). Other data on MDG goals are discussed in later chapters, but here we turn to Goal 3 as it is most focused on the issue of women's political representation.

Goal 3 is the one goal that specifically targets women in general (not just mothers as in the case of maternal health) and promotes gender equality even though all the other goals, as we can see from the preceding description, relate to the multiple conditions that (dis)empower women. As UNIFEM points out, the particular weakness of Goal 3 is that it has only one target—ending educational disparities between females and males in all levels of education by 2015. It does, however, use indicators not only focused on women's educational attainment relative to men's, but also on women's share of wage labor (in nonagricultural work) and women's representation in national parliaments. The good news is that gender parity in primary education has already been reached in most regions, with the exception of Sub-Saharan Africa, South Asia, and the Middle East and North Africa, which are all close. In terms of secondary education, only Latin America and the Caribbean have more women than men in school, and only "developed regions" (excluding the countries of the former Eastern bloc) as well as East Asia and the Pacific region have reached gender parity, although among those regions that have not, the gender gap is not huge and is closing. "Tertiary education—essential for women's leadership roles in politics, the economy, and administration—presents a different picture" (UNIFEM 2008: 124) and a far worse one in the cases of Sub-Saharan Africa and South Asia. However, women are outpacing men in higher education in aggregate in the "developed regions," the former Eastern bloc, and Latin America and the Caribbean, and have reached parity in the Middle East and North Africa (UNIFEM 2008: 124).

The attainment of these educational targets in many cases does not tell us anything about the quality of education enjoyed (or not enjoyed) by women relative to men, nor do they address fields of study pursued (or tracked into) that can also divide women from men and account for continuing occupational segregation, if, indeed, there are even jobs for women who complete higher education. According to UNIFEM, professional women from developing regions are increasingly having to leave these areas to find professional work (2008: 124), and women's nonagricultural wage labor worldwide has increased by only 3 percent since 1990 (2008: 123). Meanwhile, some quota system approach, as we have seen, is the highest predictor of women getting into national office, although educational attainment relates to increasing the pipeline of women eligible for national office. Still, despite the fact that the pipeline has grown to the point that more women than men are gaining higher education in several regions, women's political representation still lags considerably behind in most cases.

Aside from the weaknesses of Goal 3 in terms of its singular target and relatively few indicators as well as the problematics in general of quantitative indicators as reductionist tools that fail to capture the richness and complexity of social reality, the MDGs do represent a seeming shift in global priorities. As we discuss in Chapter 5, the dominant approach to development since World War II and through most of the twentieth century was one focused on economic development to the exclusion of social or human development. Large scale, capital-intensive, and high-technology projects that privileged male actors, from decision-makers to workers, were systematically promoted and funded by the World Bank to "modernize" (read, Westernize) the infrastructure and economies of the so-called developing countries. GDP—a measurement of the output of domestic goods and services by a nation—does not measure human well-being and in fact externalizes (or does not take into account) the costs of human misery and environmental destruction, yet it became the central indicator of "growth," and economic growth was to be pursued at any human and environmental cost.

Beginning in the 1970s, feminists focusing on development began pointing out that women were being left out of and even harmed by these modernizing ventures, leading to, first, a Women in Development (WID) model that was unevenly taken up by some Northern development aid agencies to "integrate" women into development. The insufficiencies of this model, which saw women integrated only at the margins of economic development through separate, small-scale "income-generating projects" and the like, gave way to the gender and development approach (GAD) in the 1980s. GAD not only focused on attending to gender relations that needed to be shifted for women to have a say in concert with men on what forms of development would most benefit them and their communities, but it also focused attention more generally on development "with a human face." Various economic shocks occurred from the 1970s through 1990s that particularly hit the global South, ranging from the debt crisis and IMF-imposed structural adjustment programs (SAPs) to the "transition" to liberal capitalist democracy undergone primarily by Eastern bloc and Latin American countries (which was often referred to at the time as going through "shock therapy"). At the same time, the rise of globalization was shifting production from North to South in search of cheap labor and reducing social welfare commitments by states. In the process, human immiseration was becoming increasingly evident and tied in with the very economic development policies of the World Bank and the IMF. By the mid-1990s, the World Bank underwent an "ideological shift" that "entailed the increased acceptance of policy intervention to temper market excesses and heightened emphasis on participation, empowerment, and poverty alleviation" (Squires 2007: 45). Not coincidentally, this occurred at the same time as the Beijing women's conference that called for similar priorities in the BPA arising from it. This brief history and the BPA are also the backdrop for the MDGs, but as Peggy Antrobus has argued, the BPA is much more comprehensive than the MDGs, has much more legitimacy among women's movements that worked on it, is far more political than "technical," and is less captured by the "neoliberalism, religious fundamentalism, and male backlash" (2006: 48–49) that served to limit what the MDGs entail and what they measured when they were generated in 2000. Although Antrobus recognizes the MDGs are here to stay and can still be used as leverage, she recommends that "when others talk MDG, we must think BPA" (Antrobus 2006: 48–49).

It is particularly essential to think BPA because the MDGs imagine development, albeit far better conceived than in the recent past, as separate from security issues, whereas the BPA includes the effects of armed conflict on women and human development. As we discuss in the next chapter, the very resources that are needed even to hope to reach the far more modest MDG goals by the end of this century (as all concede the 2015 date is utopian) are steadily eaten up by military expenditures, and militarized violence continues to produce human degradation and environmental destruction. Human development continues to be feminized and deprioritized as "low" or "soft" politics in relation to the masculinized "high" and "hard" politics of state security. At the same time, masculinist neoliberal constructions of and commitments to the global capitalist economy have loosened little in the wake of the MDGs, which do not call for a transformation of global economic structures controlled primarily by the North, and particularly the West. Under such circumstances, MDGs, which are ideally goals that all countries should work to achieve through cooperation and a massive redistribution of resources not just within but across countries, can also be used as "conditionalities" to withhold the distribution of aid more in the interests of power politics than in social justice. Relatedly, as we discuss next, gender equality itself can be used as a pawn of power politics, sustaining both neoliberalism (covered in the next section) and neocolonialism or (neo)imperialism (covered in the next chapter).

NEOLIBERAL GOVERNMENTALITY AND THE NEW GLOBAL POLITICS OF GENDER EQUALITY

As indicated by the preceding analysis, the recent gains made in women's representation in global governance and global governance attention to gender equality have been cause for some celebration but also significant suspicion among feminists. Postcolonial feminists in particular have pointed to these advances as the "neoliberal governmentalization" of gender equality. This refers not just to the co-optation (and attendant depoliticization) of gender equality by global governance bodies, but more significantly to the way in which gender equality (and more generally women's human rights) has been made coterminous with neoliberalism. In this view, it is no accident that gender equality becomes (at least a rhetorical) priority in global governance precisely at the time that neoliberal ideology is globalized.

This critique stems from another conceptualization of power put forth by Michel Foucault (1991), who coined the term "governmentality" to refer to how individuals and populations "could now be controlled, administered, empowered, or disciplined through certain governmental techniques" (Woehl 2008: 69). Governmentality pertains not only to state and suprastate bureaucratic apparatuses and policies but also to civil society institutions (including NGOs) that enable governing on the basis of rational, scientific, and statistical calculations and produce subjectivities that are amenable to being "managed" or "regulated" and even participate in self-management or self-regulation in conformance with rationalized approaches to "problem-solving" (Woehl 2008: 65–66), now associated with "good governance." Power in this sense is more diffuse and both repressive and enabling, but rests upon "hegemony," or the inculcation of "the right order" that brooks no deviation. Neoliberal governmentality refers to the ascendance of the global capitalist economy and "economic rationality" as "the sole criteria for governance" (Woehl 2008: 69). Under neoliberal governmentality, the state is reduced primarily to the promotion of the "free market," leading to the privatization of social welfare and the "marketization" of political and social life, whereby populations are to be "free, self-managing, and self-enterprising individuals in different spheres of life—health, education, bureaucracy, the professions, and so on. The neoliberal subject is therefore not a citizen with claims on the state but a self-enterprising citizen-subject who is obligated to become an 'entrepreneur of himself or herself,'" (Ong 2006: 14). In this scenario, gender equality becomes the technique to "free" women to be these free market actors, taking care of their own needs without resort to the state for their welfare. The male (and class-based) norm of "free market" actors, devoid of dependents and interdependencies, and an androcentric construction of states as not responsible for the welfare of their citizenries are strengthened by this reduction of gender equality to the production of "economic woman" in the form of "economic man."

Thus, the traction that gender equality has gained in the context of global governance can be read more critically and most cynically as just a neoliberal strategy, with NGOs, TFNs, and femocrats being turned into agents of neoliberal governmentality. Indeed, the very proliferation of these NGOs and TFNs can be seen as a feature of neoliberal governmentality, taking on roles of states to "manage" (depoliticize) populations and their problems and even providing services, albeit in far more underresourced ways, that states used to provide. This has implications as well for women gaining public office in states, for if the reigning ideology is that states are to withhold public service in favor of privatization that makes individuals solely responsible for their own welfare, then it is difficult to mount more expansive public commitments and garner more public resources for changing negative conditions for women (as well as children, nonelite men, and even the planet).

There is little question that IGOs and especially IFIs frame gender equality as a matter of modern economic efficiency. States have been most responsive to this framing, and TFNs have often made their own arguments in relation to it. However, it is also the case that local, grass-roots, and national women's movements have drawn on these instruments of neoliberal governmentality to make claims on states, although NGOs, TFNs, and state feminists, to varying degrees, continue to critique the insufficiencies of governmental responses. Thus, there are contradictions in this process that open up opportunities for resistance to neoliberal governmentality and for more radical demands than it typically allows (which we note next and address more in Chapter 6). However, just as neoliberal governmentality circumscribes how (global) gender issues are framed, the presence of women in global governance is no guarantee that they will be acted upon or reframed in social justice terms.

WOMEN IN POLITICS VERSUS FEMINIST POLITICS

There is no one-to-one relationship between the presence of women in politics and the extent of feminist politics. Women cut across the political spectrum and can just as easily hold antifeminist views or very narrow feminist commitments that justify the opening of doors for women like themselves to be in power but do not translate into supporting policies that improve conditions for all women or "other" women. Nevertheless, in its 2008/2009 report on the progress of the world's women, UNIFEM reports on several international and national studies finding that women in public office (1) tend to raise and give priority to "women's issues," (2) tend to encourage women in civil society to engage more in the political process, and (3) have some relationship to diminishing political corruption (2008: 26–27). These trends and their relative strengths, however, are also predicated on the numbers of women in a particular governing body (the BPA calls for at least 30 percent), the presence and resourcing of women's caucuses and machineries within government, and the transparency of the governing body within which they serve (UNIFEM 2008: 27–28). Other studies show that unless women in government are tied strongly to women's movements, whatever women-centered policies they raise will not be successful (Lovenduski 2005). Moreover, a recent study on the effects of the much-heralded women's majority in the Rwandan parliament shows that although they have put such issues as HIV/AIDS and women's property rights on the political agenda, have built some solidarity among themselves (and with men) through collaborative work, maintained some contact with grass-roots women's groups, and created a more "normalized" environment for women in politics, they have had no real success as of yet in the area of policy outcomes (Devlin and Elgie 2008). Thus, states and governments, as masculinist (and increasingly neoliberal) formations, continue to be resistant to substantive change on so-called "women's issues" despite advocates, and even large numbers of them, on the inside.

At the same time, feminists themselves have begun to question the very notion of some universalist construction of "women's issues" or "women's interests" or even women's human rights, especially in light of the co-optation of such concepts by neoliberal governmentality (Chappell and Hill 2006; Hesford and Kozol 2005). Jennifer Chan-Tiberghien (2004) expresses this as the tension between the "gender boom" in transnational feminist organizing and "gender skepticism" in postmodern or poststructural feminist thought. The latter sees dangers in "essentialist" assumptions about the nature and very category of "women." Negative and even valorized constructions of "women" as some kind of undifferentiated group seen only in relation to the undifferentiated category of "men" sustain a "gender hegemony" or meta-lens (that we refer to as the power of gender) that entraps, conforms, excludes, and manipulates human subjectivities and actions. The key to resisting this is to resist rigid categorizations of "women" and "gender" altogether, seeing them rather as fluid and unstable signifiers that cannot be pinned down and thus not subject to control. From another angle, as we have repeatedly pointed out, postcolonial feminists argue that universalist categorizations of "women" and "gender" obscure differences, and more importantly, power relations among women who are differentiated by race, class, sexuality, nationality, physical ability, age, and so on (which are productive of what we call gendered divisions not only between women and men but also among women and men) and fail to recognize that women (and men), in fact, have a range of "genders" as a result of these other infinitely varied combinations of social locations and identities. When these multiple genders go unrecognized, policies made in the name of women or gender tend to be based on a particular hegemonic construction of women (e.g., racially privileged, Western, heterosexual, middle-class, able-bodied, and so on) and their interests. At the same time, "other" women are lumped together (often statistically) under various "victim-categories" within which women constitute the majority—such as the poor, the diseased, refugees, the hungry, and the raped and battered in war and peace—and targeted as problems to be solved through outside intervention and rescue (whether by Western-dominated IGOs or NGOs), thereby not according women in these categories agency themselves. These are important critiques, but gender skepticism carries the danger of undercutting political claims made by and for women, whether by movements, NGOs, or state feminists, even though such claims are necessarily based on a fluid and unstable category.

As Chan-Tiberghien has observed, one effect of not seeing women as a highly diverse category at the level of global governance is that the 1965 International Convention on the Elimination of Racial Discrimination (ICERD) has long been seen as separate from CEDAW (2004: 465), as if racial discrimination had nothing to do with gender discrimination. This has been changing since the 2001 UN World Conference Against Racism (WCAR) where UNIFEM and women's NGOs made this link in official ways, getting reference to gender into "forty-one paragraphs of the NGO outcome documents and sixteen in the IGO documents" as well as additional references to "multiple forms of discrimination" and even "intersectionality" in these documents (Chan-Tiberghien 2004: 468–469). "Sexual orientation," even though also prominent in NGO documents, was excised in IGO documents (Chan-Tiberghien 2004: 469).

While IGOs in general continued to prefer "adding 'women'" and to resist more radical and complex notions of gender beyond a male-female sex binary, what emerged especially from the Women's Caucus in the NGO Forum held alongside the WCAR was an insistence that "women's issues" be expanded to include "globalization, colonialism, slavery, foreign occupation, caste, HIV/AIDS, etc., in addition to the theme of intersectionality of gender, sexuality, and race" (Chan-Tiberghien 2004: 468). Yet states and IGOs continue to be silent on most of these because they consider them improper women's issues (Chan-Tiberghien 2004: 467). This "gender in intersectionality approach," as Chan-Tiberghein termed it, has also affected how women's NGOs and TFNs are using CEDAW to highlight the conditions of ethnic minority women (including undocumented migrants) who are typically left outside of narrow gender policymaking (Chan-Tiberghien 2004: 477–778). Squires also reported that at least within the EU there is now some attention being given to "diversity mainstreaming" to address race and disability as well as gender discrimination (2007: 163–164). However, little progress has been made on this, and the additive approach of IGOs continues to pit gender inequality against race inequality in terms of which should get priority and resources, as if many women did not experience both (Squires 2007: 165). Meanwhile, class inequalities remain unaddressed in state and IGO constructs of diversity under neoliberal governmentality, and continue to divide women not only on the ground but also in global governance insofar as only the most privileged from North and South can participate most directly in it (Chan-Tiberghien 2004: 468), albeit still in numerically fewer, more marginal, and subordinated ways.

More recently, in December 2008, 66 member states of the UN supported a nonbinding UN declaration to decriminalize homosexuality, which is outlawed in nearly 80 countries and punishable by death in at least six countries (Macfarquhar 2008). This was broadly supported by the entire EU, a number of other Northern states, and many Latin American states, but it was condemned by the Vatican and the Organization of the Islamic Conference. Continuing its resistance to global equality norm-setting declarations and conventions, the United States, under the Bush administration, also refused to support this declaration (Macfarquhar 2008). With the Obama administration and a Democratic majority, there is considerable hope that the United States will sign on to such declarations and ratify the many conventions it has failed to thus far, including CEDAW. The very election of an African American man, who is multinational, multicultural, and liberal or progressive (and liberal feminist) in U.S. political terms, is no small feat and speaks to the continued enormous symbolic and material importance of working to diversify political leadership in terms of race/ethnicity, gender, class, culture, and nationality, and most important, ideology—particularly in the most powerful states—to bring about political change. It is also notable that Johanna Sigurdardottir has just been appointed as the first openly lesbian prime minister of Iceland, making her the first openly lesbian head of government worldwide. However, the actual illegalization of nonnormative sexual identities bars many more women, men, and other sexes/genders from public power and can even cost them their lives.

Thus, the meta-lens of the power of gender continues to operate in terms of sorely limiting whether women, and which women (and men and others), can gain power in global governance, and in what contexts do "women's" or "gender" issues get attention and why, how such issues are framed and through what mechanisms, and how they are acted upon (if at all). Despite recent progress of the type we have detailed here—mostly as a result of considerable "insider" and "outsider" feminist organizing—the continued power of gender largely keeps gendered divisions of power intact, which, as discussed in subsequent chapters, also leaves relatively undisturbed gendered divisions of violence, and labor and resources. These all contribute to the crisis of representation that un-, under-, and misrepresents citizens, but also noncitizens, meaning those defined as stateless, estimated by the UN High Commission on Refugees to be up to 12 million people (UNHCR 2009a). The power of gender also ensures that when formal representation is achieved, it is circumscribed and co-opted by neoliberal governmentality. Nevertheless, these processes are being countered through feminist struggles to deepen democratization within global civil society upon which democratization of formal politics depends. This includes democratizing feminist movements through the hard work of forging shared interests through politics, or an open process for debate and the expression of differences and dissent through which shared and conflicting interests can be declared, worked through, and aggregated to make change (Vickers 2006: 32–33). As Mary Ann Tetreault and Ronnie Lipschutz (2005) remind us, politics, understood in this way, is the opposite of and the foil to neoliberal governmentality. As they put it,

> "Too political" is code for the creation of a space of appearance in which people can engage in politics and practice. People experience what is possible in these spaces, and they learn that action is a form of productive power . . . politics challenges the very basis of governmentality. It

challenges exactly those principles, practices, and policies that seek to "manage" the problem by managing populations in a way that keeps people out of the process. Speech and action offer a different way to build a life, one that grows out of association, coming together to engage in common enterprise (Tetreault and Lipschutz 2005: 184, 185).

As we argue throughout the text, but particularly in the conclusion, re-politicization is key to resisting the crisis of representation and its related crises.

Notes

1. For examples of early and influential contemporary challenges by feminist political theorists to conventional constructions of politics and political actors, see, for example, Okin 1979; Jagger 1983; Benhabib and Cornell 1987; Pateman 1988; Brown, W. 1988; and Phillips 1991.

2. See Web Resources listed at the end of this text for the online location of the full text of the UN Millennium Development Goals (MDGs).

4

—◄○►—

Gender and Global Security

What is security and how is it obtained? Whose security are we talking about? At what expense and whose expense are national and global security pursued? Can security be disarmed? Chapter 3 examined how gendered divisions of power marginalize women's (and other feminized people's) status in conventionally defined politics as well as how the power of gender sustains the crisis of representation even in the face of recent gender policies aimed at increasing women's formal representation and attention to gender inequality as a source of world political problems. This chapter examines how *gendered divisions of violence (security)* and the power of gender that produces them construct and reproduce massive insecurities, or the *crisis of insecurity*. To organize the discussion, we identify three interacting components: (1) the gendered security ideology at work (its underlying assumptions and expectations); (2) the differential effects of this ideology on differing men and women (the roles they are assigned in relation particularly to militaries); and (3) the systemic consequences of these intersectional gender dichotomies (exacerbating global insecurities). The patterns we identify through the examples we offer (which are, by no means, exhaustive) paint an overwhelmingly negative picture of the gendered effects of violence pursued in the name of security; however, it is necessary to understand the full impact of the gendered divisions of violence in relation to the gendered divisions of labor and resources that we cover in Chapter 5 and to appreciate the varied struggles against these interrelated processes that we document in Chapter 6.

To review, what we mean by the gendered divisions of violence are the hierarchical dichotomies of self-other, us-them, aggressive-passive,

143

soldier-victim, and protector-protected that divide the world into masculinized offenders and defenders and feminized populations over which
they fight and seek to conquer or defend. This has long been the main
story of IR, although only recently has this been understood in gender
terms within IR. Moreover, although IR was founded ostensibly to address
how to end war, its masculinist bias and imperialist commitments—born
of its creation initially by elite, Eurocentric men who made it a useful
tool for elite, Eurocentric statesmen—have made it less about ending
war and more about controlling it and using it more effectively in the interests of those in power. Given the masculinist construction of politics
as aggressive and combative power-over practices, it was an easy leap to
argue, as Clausewitz (2004) did in the nineteenth century, that war is the
extension of politics by other means. However, if, as we argued in the last
chapter, politics is seen as enabling power, than politics is the opposite of
war, which shuts down debate in the face of the raw power of might
makes right. Similarly, for war to be contemplated and waged "effectively," those against whom it is waged must be dehumanized (typically
through feminization and racialization) in order for aggressors to feel
superior and righteous in their actions. At the same time, both offenders
and defenders need to justify their actions by waging war in the name of
those who cannot fight and, thus, are in need of and worthy of protection (typically one's "own womenandchildren"). Such rationales for war
are disturbed by the realities that "womenandchildren" are now rarely
protected from direct violence in most contemporary wars and that the
structural violence of homelessness, hunger, disease, and so on visited by
war, particularly in the global South, and war spending affects especially
civilian populations the world over. These inconvenient truths also redirect attention to the most historically frequent reasons for war and conquest, namely the colonizing practices of the extraction of wealth and
resources through the brutalization of populations in order to destroy
communities and thus the will to resist such extraction. But the power of
gender covers up this inconvenient (and currently politically unpalat-
able) truth and sets up the dynamics, in the forms of the gendered divisions of violence, which justify war and other forms of violence with
which it is connected.

There have long been critiques of and resistances to war by women for
the harm it does—ranging from the (male-authored) fifth-century BCE

fictional play *Lysistrata*, which (comically) portrays women withholding sexual servicing from men until they stopped fighting, to such an actual action by Iroquois women in the seventeenth century that opened the way for the long peace of the Iroquois Federation, to the writings of pacifist women (such as Christine de Pizan, Bertha von Suttner, and Virginia Woolf), from the times of medieval Europe through the world wars (and to the present day). But it was only in the past few centuries that there has been organized resistance to war in the form of peace movements. We argue, however, that the association of peace with the (hyper)feminine and the association of war with the (hyper)masculine have disadvantaged and marginalized calls for and analyses of how to bring about peace, not only as the absence of war and other forms of direct violence but also as the end of structural violence. Only by addressing both direct and structural violence can the crisis of insecurity be reversed.

FEMINIST APPROACHES TO SECURITY

Feminist IR approaches to war and violence and peace and security have their roots especially in the thinking of nineteenth- and early-twentieth-century women peace theorists and activists. Many of these early thinkers and activists based their arguments against war on women's maternalist desires to protect their children from the ravages of war, neither wanting their sons to become cannon fodder nor their daughters to suffer from the destruction of families and communities (Pierson 1987). For those who were steeped in the biological determinism characteristic of nineteenth- and early-twentieth-century thought, these maternalist desires were seen as innate, making women "natural" peace supporters and peacemakers. Maternalist arguments continued through the Cold War, when women's peace organizations sought to protect future generations from the threat of nuclear war, and into the present day, but more contemporary feminist peace researchers and activists have argued that maternalism is not innate but rather the result of women being made largely responsible for "maternalist practices" or caring work, whether or not they have children (Ruddick 1984). This makes them more likely to have empathy for "others" and the world's children and to be against war and its destructive power.

Other contemporary feminists, however, have pointed out that women have historically supported wars (both imperialist wars and wars of national liberation) and fought in them, often in the name of maternalism. Sending sons and daughters to war can be seen as a patriotic motherly duty, and fighting in wars can be seen as a form of motherly protection of the homeland (Elshtain 1987). At the same time, many women have become soldiers out of economic necessity or sought gender equality in soldiering as a ticket to full citizenship and a path to public power for women. Thus, the idea that women are either naturally or socially geared for peace has been put in question and even seen as an impediment to women seeking gender equality because it bars them from or marginalizes them in militaries that control significant resources and are particularly valorized in the stories of nations and the fabric of national life. This produces a "gendered nationalism" in which only men who forged a nation in blood get to define what that nation is, regardless of whether women spilled blood for it or on its altar as (fewer) combatants or (many) noncombatants, and regardless of the many other contributions that women make to (re)producing and sustaining the life of a nation (Enloe 1989: 63). When women are seen only as the symbols and the reproducers of the nation and not seen as agents in its narratives, then they become subject to an array of controls over their bodies and their beings by men of the nation (Kaufman and Williams 2007: 16–18; Yuval-Davis 1997).

Nevertheless, still other contemporary feminists have shown that there is a relationship between international violence and domestic violence, which gives women particular interests in resisting warfare and war preparedness because it produces men who do not visit violence only on the "enemy" but also on their own wives, partners, and children. But men, too, feminists have argued, can develop interests in resisting war because of the harm it does to their bodies and psyches, leading to the destruction of their loved ones and self-destruction. What keeps more men—particularly those in subordinate positions in militaries whose bodies are most on the line—from developing such interests is the valorization of war as the penultimate masculine activity through which men can prove they are "real men" (Whitworth 2008). As we have pointed out, heteronormative masculinity is an extraordinarily fragile and unstable construct and identity that leaves men having to prove repeatedly that they have "it." They are put in constant fear and anxiety that they will be dubbed less than "real men" and, therefore, be demoted down the gender hierarchy and be subject to greater violence by other, higher men.

But while there are high costs for subordinated men both to participate in and to resist war, feminists have particularly focused on the fact that women pay high prices for its valorization and conduct. Militarized violence makes them more subject to gender violence (whether they are combatants or noncombatants) in the forms of militarized domestic violence, rape, and prostitution and more subject to the structural violence of dislocation, poverty, and disease that war leaves in its wake. Military spending also extracts resources needed for social welfare, shredding social safety nets, which leads to the violence of desperation. But even beyond this, postcolonial feminists in particular point to the costs of women's and subordinated men's support of imperial warfare and violence, typically in the name of national security and increasingly global security (Eisenstein 2007). As long as wars of extraction, most typically waged on the soil of the South, are cloaked as "civilizing," "pacifying," and "liberating" missions to protect national and global security, women and subordinated men in states with imperialist ambitions can be drawn in to support them and do the work of violence associated with them. This is at the expense of forming solidarities among women and less privileged men across North and South to resist war and violence that most harms them. Such solidarities can be built on the recognition that exclusivist and violent ethnic nationalisms (whether of the imperialist or anti-imperialist variety) are "'integral' to globalizing processes," with "opportunistic" nationalist movements "seeking statehood in some instances" while not being able to legitimately provide for the welfare of citizens under globalization and others "sustaining their power through the market economy" (Giles and Hyndman 2004: 18).

We argue in this chapter that the power of gender obscures and mitigates against the potential alliances between women and men and among them across borders to resist war and other forms of violence. In the process, we problematize dominant constructions of security, examine the strategy of "adding women" to security structures and policies, destabilize assumptions undergirding the gendered divisions of violence, and take on the question of Empire, which keeps the world enthralled in violence but which still can be resisted. We are critical of "solutions" that

put peacemaking and peacebuilding solely on the backs of poorly resourced and marginalized women and vilify only certain men to deflect
attention away from elites (including some women) who promote militarism and war in the name of security. But we also see some value in
what has been called "strategic essentialism" (Spivak 1987), which constitutes a political strategy for women to articulate interests in and paths
to peace and act together (with supportive men) to bring about disarmed security.

GENDERED SECURITY

War—its causes and effects—animated and has long dominated the
study of IR. Since the Cold War period, war has been studied in IR under
the rubric of "security" studies. In (neo)realist security studies, the
maintenance of security is understood as controlling and containing,
but not eliminating, direct violence between state militaries through bal-
ances of military power and nuclear terror as well as collective security
measures that rely on sustaining both credible threats to use force and
the actual use of force. Ironically and problematically, this ensures the
continued growth of militaries and the continuation of war to promote
security—but only the security of the state, not necessarily of people
within or across states and certainly not of the planet.

The early post–Cold War period of the 1990s brought more interest
within the discipline in wider definitions of security, ranging from economic to human, environmental, and even food security. These redefini-
tions occurred in the face of new "threats" to state security (such as
globalization and global warming, discussed in the next chapter), but
also newly recognized notions of security, arising from critical perspectives (including feminist ones) entering the field, which pointed out that
state security often compromised the welfare of people and the planet.
Nevertheless, conventional security studies have enjoyed somewhat of a
resurgence in the post-9/11 period because decisions to engage in interstate and intrastate conflict and the globalized "war on terror" have once
again spiked militarized violence. The resurgent interest in direct violence has once again been at the expense of attending to structural violence and the insecurities generated by structural inequalities. We must

be mindful that direct and indirect (structural) violence are not separate but interdependent. The inequalities of the latter shape the expression of the former. As dire as are the effects of direct violence, indirect violence shapes the lives of all of us all of the time—and especially injures women and other subordinated and marginalized people.

Hence, feminists argue that to understand violence and insecurities we must look not only within particular "levels" but also at the linkages among them. In Ann Tickner's words:

> Feminist perspectives on security would assume that violence, whether it be in the international, national, or family realm, is interconnected. Family violence must be seen in the context of wider power relations; it occurs within a gendered society in which male power dominates at all levels. . . . Any feminist definition of security must therefore include the elimination of all types of violence, including violence produced by gender relations of domination and subordination (Tickner 1993: 58).

We would add that gender in combination with racialized, sexualized, and class violence also reveals the interconnections between relations of domination and subordination that are present across all levels and constitute the conditions (structural violence) and goads for war (direct violence) as well as the effects of war or militarized conflict. Unless these are taken seriously, even rival notions of (nondisaggregated) human security to state security will fail to recognize all the sources of insecurity (bred of the injustices of structural violence) and their differential effects.

At the same time, we share the more poststructural feminist view that security is always "elusive and partial" (Tickner 2001: 62) because the quest for absolute security is in itself productive of violence, for it relies on the eradication of all threats, real or imagined, and thus sets up a never-ending defensive and offensive posture. Such a posture is emblematic of the "sovereign man" (Ashley 1989), who, like the sovereign state that is fashioned upon this construct of hegemonic masculinity, thwarts connection and interdependence in fear of engagement with difference that might break down walls between the sovereign "self" and the "other" on whom is projected all that one denies in oneself (Eisenstein 2007: 13).

On this point, Susan Faludi's *The Terror Dream* (2007) is quite instructive. Not only does this work document the U.S. resurgence of state security discourse proffered across the airwaves, almost exclusively by military men (to the almost absolute exclusion of female and particularly feminist voices representing alternative views) in the post-9/11 period, but it also analyzes the resurgence of older sexist and racist mythologies from America's past called up to cover up the chink in the sovereign man's armor. Whether it was the lionizing of male rescue workers at "ground zero" (and the attendant silencing of female rescue workers long discriminated against, as well as widows who questioned the U.S. military response, because neither conformed with adulating male protection and security at any cost), the ersatz "rescue" of U.S. soldier Jessica Lynch supposedly from rapacious Iraqi captors (who turned out to be caring medical personnel), or overblown (and in most cases untrue) claims about women opting out of the workplace to return home to raise babies and become "security moms" in support of war, Faludi has argued that these convenient "fictions" have roots in earlier frontier stories, captivity narratives, and Cold War hysterias. These get trotted out whenever there are fears of "masculine insufficiency" because hegemonic masculinity cannot countenance "vulnerability" (Faludi 2007: 280).

When we look more closely at the events behind these earlier narratives, we find that white male frontiersmen (such as Daniel Boone) were in fact undistinguished as providers or protectors and more often relied on the provisioning and protective skills of their wives, children, and indigenous peoples to survive (Faludi 2007: 256–262), and the majority of white women taken captive by indigenous peoples either preferred to stay with their newfound families into which they were adopted or won their release from their captors on their own (Faludi 2007: 212). Nevertheless, Faludi argues, insecure times in patriarchal cultures summon up the need for elaborate mythologies that "measure national male strength by female peril," requiring that "women be saved from more and more gruesome violation to prove their saviors' valor" (2007: 262). In U.S. white patriarchal cultural imagination, that peril is limited to concerns for white women and symbolized most by racialized men, whether they be indigenous "captors" of old, or the new Iraqi ones, the "yellow" and "Hun" hordes of World War II, or the "red" Communist threat of the

Cold War. In each case, fears of "alien" invasion required the "securing of American domesticity" that conjured images of (white) women (re)confined to the home front, obsessions with "women's sexuality purity" supposedly at risk from racialized men, and a summoning of "John Wayne and his avenging brethren" (Faludi 2007: 282–283, 286). As Faludi concludes, the constant replaying of this "security myth" (currently evoked by obsessions with "homeland security") disables an alternative response that "involves learning to live with insecurity, finding accommodation with—even drawing strength from—an awareness of vulnerability" (2007: 286) in order not to create sacrificial altars, but instead to create space for multiple voices and ways of acting and being.

The too easy devolution of security into continuous justifications for violence also makes us wary of new processes of "securitization" associated with a widening security agenda. On the one hand, the application of the term "security" to an issue elevates it to a matter of "high politics," as security (matters of war and peace) has traditionally held pride of place in IR theory and practice. Thus, relatively new conceptions of human security and environmental security, and even more recently, food, water, energy, and health security, have brought welcome international attention to sources of structural violence that undermine the well-being of people and the planet. On the other hand, there is also a tendency to reduce these once again to state security matters to be handled not through more collective and more nonviolent means, but more typically through war, or some approximation of it. Resource wars, wars on terror, wars on AIDS, wars on drugs, and so on all follow a similar logic. As Zillah Eisenstein argues, the logic of war of any kind is "opposition, differentiation, and the othering of peoples" (2007: 25). Thus, gendering, racialization, classing, and sexualizing go on unabated (and become even more pronounced) in order to affix blame and control, contain, and quarantine these "new" threats. For example, racial profiling becomes a weapon in the war on terror, targeting sexual minorities and sex workers becomes the focus of the war on AIDS, and peasant farmers become the main casualties of the war on drugs.

The logic of war also entails resort to military means and as more and more issues are securitized, more and more of daily life is militarized. As Cynthia Enloe (2007) points out, anyone, any group or institution, and anything can be militarized. In her words, "To be militarized is to adopt militaristic values (e.g., a belief in hierarchy, obedience, and the use of force) and priorities as one's own, to see military solutions as particularly effective, to see the world as a dangerous place best approached with militaristic attitudes" (Enloe 2007: 4). Thus, militaries are only a small part of the actual "security" apparatus. They rely on wider civilian cultures to enact militarized values, whether in the form of wearing "fashionable" camouflage clothing, joining militaries, working for defense industries, supporting national security over civil liberties, calling for closed borders and more prisons, and so on (Enloe 2007: 4–5). As a result, although "security," perhaps more than any other activity, has been constructed as "men's" business, its logic and enactment must be shared widely to shore up the elevation of militaries as the pinnacle of masculine endeavor. As we shall see in the following sections, the price of this elevation is too high for both women and men and the planet.

WOMEN, MILITARIES, AND POLITICAL VIOLENCE

Although it is often assumed that women serving in militaries is a relatively recent, "modern" phenomenon, throughout history women have fought in wars. In *Women Warriors: A History*, David Jones has provided an account "of the female martial tradition in a pan-historical and global perspective" (1997: xiv). He documents how women warriors have had an important presence across cultures and throughout history. They have led armies, constituted women's battalions, passed themselves off as male soldiers, rallied the troops as symbolic leaders, defended family and community structures in the absence of men, and exhibited the same courage, loyalty, steadfastness, heroism, and even bloodthirstiness that we associate with male warriors. Jones argues that "from the beginning women shared the qualitative experience of the warrior; everything men have ever done in warfare, women have also done, and, in many instances, they have done it better" (1997: xiii). Despite such evidence and the fact that even in the United States it is increasingly more commonplace to hear references to "men and women" in the armed forces and the gender-neutral term of "troops," there is still discomfort with—and even a desire to reject—the image and, indeed, the reality of *women war-*

riors. Still lingering and still powerful gendered divisions of violence account for this.

Gendered Divisions of Violence at Work

With modern state-making, gendered divisions became codified in particular ways. Liberalism in political theory favored divisions of power into public-private, government-household, whereas capitalism in economic theory favored divisions of labor into paid-unpaid, productive-reproductive. Interacting with these developments, modern state-making promoted particular divisions of violence. Masculinity involved not only heading the household and earning a "family wage" but also being prepared to defend "home and country." As Jean Bethke Elshtain has noted: "War is the means to attain recognition, to pass, in a sense, the definitive test of political manhood. . . . The man becomes what he in some sense is meant to be by being absorbed in the larger stream of life: war and the state" (1992: 143). Femininity involved not only bearing and rearing children and maintaining the home front, but also serving, symbolically and literally, as that which required protection. Whereas men served their country in combat, as "life-takers," women served their country as mothers, as "life-givers" (Elshtain 1987).

In recent centuries, most male-dominated societies have constructed elaborate sanctions and even taboos against women as warriors, and especially against women bearing arms and initiating violence. As a result, men have gained almost exclusive control over the means of destruction worldwide, often in the name of protecting women (and children), who are either discouraged from or not allowed to take up arms to protect themselves or to be warriors protecting others. It is therefore not surprising that war—which remains the centerpiece of IR—is seen as *men's* deadly business. We argue, however, that war has always involved women as well as the power of gender to promote masculine characteristics—typically, as we already noted, at the expense of cooperation, interdependence, and conflict resolution (Grant 1994). Moreover, the identification of war with men and peace with women completely unravels in the face of war practices over the past century and into the current one in which civilians have been increasingly subject to direct violence and even more to structural violence.

As life-givers, women are not only prevented from engaging in combat but are also expected to restore "life" after a death-dealing war is over. Women are expected to mourn dutifully the loved ones who fell in war and then to produce new lives for the nation to replace its lost members. Thus, after the devastation, they must "pick up the pieces" and create the conditions for repopulating society. These conditions include creating more men, who too often serve as soldiers, and more women, who too often bear sons only to lose them through war. The work of men as life-takers thus creates perpetual work for women as life-givers.

In this sense, women are not separate from either the production or the consequences of war, even though they are often prevented from engaging in direct combat. Yet in spite of their participation, women remain associated with war's opposite—peace. By denying the historical construction of gender stereotypes, the characterization of "woman" as passive and submissive is often translated into the idea that women are pacifist by nature. This reinforces the stereotype of women as life-givers and portrays them as insufficiently fit or motivated to be life-takers. The assumption that women have a natural revulsion against war also makes them undesirable partners in combat: How can women be trusted on the battleground if they are unwilling to fight and kill? Men, in contrast, are stereotyped as naturally aggressive and competitive, which presumably prepares them to kill or be killed. In addition, through heteronormative lenses, it is assumed that the presence of women on the battlefield will distract men from fighting successfully, perhaps by turning their aggressions away from fighting and toward sexual conquest or by tying them down to protect "weaker" female comrades, thereby endangering the pursuit of body counts. In this view, men might lose the war by pursuing or protecting women on the battlefield rather than fighting successfully to protect their women at home.

After the battle, women are expected to take care of returning soldiers, salving their wounds and psyches as well as meeting needs—for food, clothing, and shelter—previously met by the military. When the "boys come home," women are expected to serve them, and to do so with gratitude for those who fought and took life on behalf of their women and their nation. If women fail in these duties, then male protectors are often given tacit approval for "disciplining" their women, through physical violence if necessary. Such physical violence is learned on the playground when boys "play" war in preparation for their adult roles as potential soldiers. The role is honed when men are actually trained by militaries and participate in "real" wars. Life-takers have no responsibility for "unlearning" these skills when they leave the war front; global statistics on domestic violence suggest that men may use these skills against the women and children they protected in wartime if the latter do not please them in the home. Thus, those who are denied access to the means of destruction to protect themselves during wartime also have little protection against the wartime protectors who may turn violent in the home (Sharoni 1995: 127; Nikolic-Ristanovic 1996).

As Faludi's (2007) study of the continuation of the security myth previously discussed shows, gender dichotomies such as the following are still powerfully at work in reproducing the gendered division of violence: soldiers-mothers, protectors-protected, aggressive-passive, battle-front–home front, batterers-victims. However, it is becoming harder to sustain these dichotomies in the face of women's greater visibility in armed forces and as perpetrators of political violence (that is, sanctioned or extralegal violence against or in the name of the state) in recent years. These still constitute in relative terms what Elshtain (1987) refers to as the "ferocious few," but they nevertheless challenge the old story to a degree.

Military Women

Just as conforming to rising UN-sponsored gender equality norms (at least in terms of rhetoric and formal policy if not in terms of actual enforcement and results) is motivated by states' desires to appear modern, the presence of women in a state's armed forces is increasingly seen as another mark of modernity. By 1994 there were more than 500,000 female soldiers serving in regular and irregular armed forces (Smith 1997: 64), but women still typically made up less than 10 percent of state militaries as a whole, with many militaries still excluding them altogether. There have been some increases, however, since then in those countries, with the highest percentages in the mid-1990s. By 2005, the United States went from 12 to 15 percent; Canada from 12 to 16.3, and New Zealand from 14 to 15, with others holding relatively steady, such as Australia at 13 percent and Russia at 11 percent. Israel, Latvia, and South Africa have the highest percentages of women in the military, at 37, 23, and 22 percent respectively (Enloe 2007: 70; Seager 2009: 103). The vast majority of countries (including the United States) disallow or significantly limit women in combat. Also, other than most Western European countries as well as Canada, Australia, South Africa, and Israel, most countries ban lesbians and gays from their militaries (including the United States at this writing through its "Don't ask, don't tell" policy, which, however, is under review by the Obama administration). In addition to the still relatively low rates of female participation in state militaries worldwide that speak to the continuing masculinization of military jobs, Enloe (2007) reminds us that increases in women's soldiering must be analyzed very carefully. On the surface, they may appear to be the product of "'postsexist' enlightenment" (Enloe 2007: 73) and modernity, but underneath there are different stories. The unprecedented South African case represents the results of a postapartheid debate (that included feminists) about the need to create more democratic armed forces in terms of both race and gender, but the Israeli case reveals a more cynical approach that relies on conscripting Israeli women to make them complicit in the occupation of Palestine while portraying Israeli female solders as sexual appendages to and assigning them more domestic duties in the army to keep them in their place (Enloe 2007: 73, 75).

Most often it is for such unenlightened reasons that women are included in state militaries. For example, Francine D'Amico has argued that because of the shift to an all-volunteer U.S. army, women (and people of color) were recruited to address the *man*power shortages, not to promote equality (1997: 199). But this led to fears of the feminization (and racialization) of the armed forces. Thus, during the pre-9/11 period of force reductions—referred to as "the drawdown," which entailed a one-third cut in military personnel—the U.S. military was more interested in controlling its composition along racial and gender lines than in creating a truly representational force (D'Amico 1997: 199). Black women in particular were targeted for reduction to deal with the perceived "overrepresentation" of women and African Americans in the military (D'Amico 1997: 220). Indeed, by 2005, despite post-9/11 increases in U.S. armed forces numbers, African American women dropped from 48 percent of women under arms in the late 1990s to 38 percent in 2005 (Enloe 2007: 69). Moreover, between 1998 and 2004, 6,000 soldiers were discharged for being gay (Eisenstein 2007: 6) with lesbians accounting for 31 percent of those discharged for sexual orientation up to 2002 (Seager 2009: 102). Far from yielding to feminist and other demands for democratization, the U.S. military continues to seek to preserve "its racist, androcentric, and heterocentric foundations" (D'Amico 1997: 200).

These foundations are responsible for other forms of discrimination against women in the military. Despite the fact that women have "routinely been assigned to combat operations" (Enloe 2007: 66) in the U.S. wars in Afghanistan and Iraq where 99,467 women soldiers and 37,925 women reservists and National Guard members had been deployed by the United States by 2006 (Enloe 2007: 89), formal combat exclusions disable most women from claiming the combat experience that has often served as a prerequisite or a test of leadership skills for those seeking high political office. Moreover, when we consider that as of 2008, worldwide military spending reached $1.473 trillion with the United States accounting for almost half of this at $711 trillion, followed by Europe at $289 trillion (Center for Arms Control and Non-Proliferation 2008), the considerable resources devoted to war-making end up in overwhelmingly male (and Western) hands. These huge political and material consequences for women of men dominating the means of destruction are sustained through not only keeping women's numbers down in militaries, but also creating elaborate prohibitions on and punishments of women who do get into militaries.

Although women enter militaries for many of the same reasons as men (including out of patriotism or nationalism), in the United States they report most often that it is for education, jobs, and career training (Eisenstein 2007: 21). However, because militaries are first and foremost about maintaining masculine (typically along with racial majority and class) privilege, women must enter them on certain terms—those that conform to "gender differentiation" (Eisenstein 2007: 6) while at the same time adopting masculinist militarist values. While the film version of *GI Jane* had her become a "man" to fit into the culture of an elite commando unit and thereby end the sexual harassment she was subjected to by her comrades-in-arms, the more typical reality for women soldiers is they are expected to remain "women" and put up and shut up about sexual harassment and assault, which has reached "epidemic" proportions today (Enloe 2007: 85), despite revelations about it over the past two decades that supposedly were being addressed by military hierarchies.

Since the 1991 Tailhook Convention, where women officers of the U.S. Navy were subjected to intense sexual harassment and abuse by male naval officers, widespread cases of sexual harassment and rape in the armed services continue to come to light. A year before the 1996 U.S. Army Aberdeen Proving Ground scandal in which two dozen female recruits charged that they were repeatedly sexually harassed and abused by training officers, the Pentagon surveyed 90,000 female soldiers, sailors, and pilots and found that "nearly 1 in 10 Army women reported being sexually assaulted, and 6 in 10 said they had experienced some form of sexual harassment" by military men, totaling tens of thousands of incidents (Weiner 1996: A1, A16). To add insult to injury, an investigative report in 1997 revealed that "since 1990 the Army prosecuted 1,329 soldiers for rape and other sexual assaults. Of the 870 convicted, 135—about one in six—got 90 days or less. Ninety-three got no jail time at all" (Carollo, Nesmith, and Jaspin 1997: A1). A more recent study by the British military found that one-half of 4,000 British women soldiers surveyed named sexual harassment as a serious problem, whereas British male soldier respondents did not see it as a problem (Enloe 2007: 87). As of 2005, 2,375 rape cases had been reported to the U.S. Department of Defense by military women, but it has also been found that 75 percent of military women do not report this crime against them by their fellow soldiers and officers above them (Whitworth 2008: 120). In 2007 alone, U.S. military women serving in Iraq reported 2,688 incidents of sexual assault by other U.S. military personnel (Seager 2009: 103), but this, too, could be an underestimation given the trend of underreporting. Thus, while military officialdom primarily in the West periodically tracks sexual crimes—typically after some highly visible incident—there is little real response for fear of undermining male soldier morale (and recruiting) by reducing the sexual privileges that male soldiers expect to go along with the job. At the same time, women are discouraged from reporting such incidents because they are rarely acted on, but also in the name of protecting (male) military morale to which they are expected to kowtow. Thus, sexual assaults, harassment, and even murder[1] of sister soldiers by their brethren continue unabated and are on the increase.

In addition to suffering physical violence at the hands of their own comrades-in-arms, women in the U.S. military are discriminated against in a host of other ways that, in the United States, are tracked by the

Women's Research and Education Institute (WREI), which also gathers data on discrimination against women in other Western militaries. The litany remains the same year after year: "exclusion from combat jobs, sexual harassment, antilesbian 'witchhunts,' discrimination in promotion evaluations, and neglect of employment and health needs of the growing number of women veterans" (Enloe 2007: 86). Such circumstances mirror the experiences of civilian women in other male-dominated occupations, but there are deadlier twists in the case of the military, which is a far more captive and dangerous environment for military women, who are at more risk from their own militaries than from foreign ones, even as female casualties mount on the battlefield.

Feminists who question whether it is possible to democratize the military tend also to question democratizing moves by the military insofar as an increased presence of women serves to legitimize the institution by giving it a facade of egalitarianism. When women accept the "warrior mystique," they soften the image of the military as an agent of coercion/destruction and help promote the image of the military as a democratic institution, an "equal opportunity employer" like any other, without reference to its essential purpose. In this sense, they serve as what Zillah Eisenstein (2007) has referred to as "sexual" or "gender decoys" (and in the case of women of color, "race" as well as gender decoys). Such decoys "camouflage" and distract attention from any actual evaluation of the efficacy of militaries and the consequences of militarist values. If the symbol of modernity is the equal participation of women in acts of torture, such as those perpetrated at the Abu Ghraib prison in Iraq by U.S. women soldiers, then gender equality based on women conforming to masculinist and racist norms becomes not a significant source for reducing structural and direct violence but rather a basis for furthering it.

Women's Political Violence

Despite the seemingly more commonplace event of seeing women in militaries, the image of them as actual killers and purveyors of other forms of direct violence, rather than simply "support" personnel who happen to carry weapons, still remains unsettling under the gendered division of violence. It is particularly unsettling when that violence is "proscribed violence," or violence that violates laws within and between states, including torture, genocide, and terrorism. As Laura Sjoberg and

Caron Gentry (2007) have argued, women who commit such violence are reduced to mothers, monsters, or whores (or all three) to explain their behaviors because they are not accorded political motivations for their crimes. The association of aberrant violence with aberrant womanhood has a long pedigree. As Kelly Oliver points out, motherhood is constructed as Janus-faced in patriarchal culture—at one and the same time the source of life-giving and the source of death (through the power of withholding nourishment from infants and the symbol of mother earth to which the dead return) (2007: 21). Female sexuality is also constructed as intoxicating, beguiling, and more treacherous than anything men can deploy, and women's bodies themselves are seen as sources of concealment and dangerous fluids (Oliver 2007: 31, 38). Thus, it is a fine line in these imaginings between women's natural passivity and womanhood gone mad if not properly restrained. This supposed dual nature of women is used not only to justify their control but also to explain their behavior. But as Oliver also chronicles, this mythology has been "rationally" deployed in calculated ways to make women's bodies weapons in the current "war on terror." Detainees at Guantánamo Bay were smeared with (fake) menstrual blood by U.S. interrogators, and all-female teams of interrogators practiced "sexual lechery" on the most "troublesome" inmates to break them (Oliver 2007: 28–29). Thus, in an age of terror, women are constituted as the most terrorizing when unleashed. This then accounts for the particular horror many found in the images of U.S. women soldiers sexually terrorizing inmates at Abu Ghraib because it evoked deep patriarchal (and heteronormative) fears (Peterson 2007). These acts were also dismaying to those feminists who held out some faith in women as being more peaceful and potentially tempering of military excesses. But in the uproar over the (un)naturalness of women torturers, attention was deflected from what we now know was state-sponsored torture and terrorism, not just the work of a few bad girls and boys.

As Sjoberg and Gentry further chronicle, the demonization of the so-called "Black Widows" of Chechnya and the sensationalization of Palestinian women suicide bombers have also deflected attention from the political causes of and motivations for their actions. Since the nineteenth century, Russia has engaged in many massacres of the Chechen people, but the Chechen conflicts, from 1993–1996 and 1999–present, to stop

Chechen separatism from Russia have killed at least 20 percent of the Chechen population, produced at least 250,000 refugees, and legitimated wholesale rapes, beatings, torture, and disappearances (Sjoberg and Gentry 2007: 90–91). The conditions became so severe that some Chechen women became suicide bombers starting in 2003. They have been portrayed, however, not as rational actors responding to the political crisis in the few ways open to them, but as vengeful mothers, brainwashed dupes of Islam, and monsters born out of desperation. The very moniker of "Black Widow" both racializes and genders them to evoke no sympathy for them and to justify ever greater attacks on Chechen women by Russia, which constructs its actions as part of the "war on terror" rather than owning up to the savage civil war it is conducting (Sjoberg and Gentry 2007: 89). Similarly, Palestinian women suicide bombers' actions are most commonly reduced to the result of divorce, premarital sex, adultery, maternal insufficiencies, and family honor— that is, personal reasons rather than political ones. However, these bombers typically leave behind "martyrdom" videotapes and political messages that speak to their deep political commitments to the Palestinian resistance to Israeli occupation, but such messages are largely ignored in the media and most other accounts of these women (Sjoberg and Gentry 2007: 120, 122–123).

Genocidaires, such as Biljana Plavsic of Serbia and Pauline Nyiramasuhuko of Rwanda, both of whom have been tried by the International Criminal Tribunals for Yugoslavia and Rwanda, respectively, for their roles in fomenting genocide and genocidal rape, have themselves fallen back on gender stereotypes to excuse their actions, constructing themselves as avenging or protective mothers of the nation, while being portrayed as madwomen by others (Sjoberg and Gentry 2007: 155, 165, 152, 167). Such stereotypes denied that both were highly educated, highly placed political women who used their political power to perpetrate political genocide, not victims of maternalism gone awry. As long as the latter is foregrounded, then genocide, as a political act of which anyone is capable given the means and ideologies, is backgrounded. Similarly, as long as women are constructed only as victims, brutal treatment of them will be invited in times of war and "peace."

In short, violence can be "resexed," in Eisenstein's (2007) words, as long as it does not disturb the power of gender to valorize violence, militarism, and war. Moreover, femininity can be militarized without threatening male privilege, and can even bolster it as long as women play "idealized militarized femininity" roles as "capable" but "sanitized" and supportive "'Just Warriors'" who retain the "innocence" and "vulnerability" of "'Beautiful Souls'" (Sjoberg and Gentry 2007: 86).

MEN, MILITARIES, AND GENDER VIOLENCE

In societies where masculinity is associated with power-over and violence, men are under constant pressure to prove their manhood by being tough, adversarial, and aggressive. There are, of course, a variety of forms of male aggression that have been deemed unacceptable or illegitimate within civil societies (such as murder, assault, gang warfare, and, at least in terms of the laws of some countries, wife battering and child abuse). However, in one highly legitimated and organized institution within most societies, men not only can but—to be successful—must prove their masculinity: the military.

State militaries serve many functions. According to world politics wisdom of the (neo)realist variety, militaries serve to protect the borders of states and the citizens within them from outside aggression, inevitable given the anarchic interstate system, which is based on power politics, not the rule of law. In this view, militaries are deemed necessary for the maintenance of national security, either as deterrents to would-be aggressors or as effective fighting machines capable of vanquishing actual aggressors.

More critical world politics perspectives see militaries serving other less laudable functions, such as protecting repressive state elites from rebellion by their own people. This is often described as maintaining the internal security of states at the expense of nonelite citizens. Also, militaries are implicated in maintaining permanent war economies arising from the infamous "military-industrial complex," which organizes a state's economy around producing weapons rather than civilian goods. Under such conditions, the military can become one of the few sites for "employment," not only for the poor and least educated who turn to soldiering or working in weapons plants but also for large numbers of middle-class voters engaged in, for example, research and development activities. More recently, there have been references to the "security-industrial complex" that has arisen since 9/11 in which private industries are organized around producing and purveying intelligence, surveillance, and control systems as extensions of the state and even providing private armies for the state, such as the now infamous Blackwater operation in Iraq. Like the "prison-industrial complex" that has arisen alongside this and in which inmates are not only used as captive slave labor to produce goods for private industries but also are surveilled and controlled at ever higher levels in increasingly private prisons and increasingly worldwide (Sudbury 2005), the security-industrial complex not only organizes the economy but also much of life around the dictates of security at the expense of human rights and welfare.

Still less appreciated or analyzed, even by many critical world politics observers, is the role that the military plays in producing and reproducing masculinity. As Cynthia Enloe has argued, militaries need men to act as "men"—that is, to be willing to kill and die on the behalf of the state (or rivals to it) to prove their "manhood" (Enloe 1983: 212). This remains the linchpin for sustaining vast coercive apparatuses and practices.

Militarized Masculinity

As a social construct, masculinity is not a given but rather is made. Moreover, as we pointed out earlier, there are multiple masculinities, most typically divided up between hegemonic masculinity (associated with elite Western, upper-class, race-privileged, and heterosexual men) and subordinate masculinities (associated with racial minority or global South, lower-class, and sexual minority men). But the nature of hegemonic masculinity also shifts over time as well as across cultures. According to Charlotte Hooper, there have been at least four forms of Western hegemonic masculinity historically: the "Greek citizen-warrior," the "patriarchal Judeo-Christian model," the "honor-patronage" form, and the "Protestant, bourgeois-rationalist" man (2001: 64). She hypothesizes that in the 1990s a new "globalization" man was emerging, particularly in the Anglo-American context. These differing formations, although emerging over time, never cancel each other out. Rather, each morphs from the last so that each model retains elements of previous ones adapted to maintain hegemony in the face of changing socioeconomic, geopolitical, and even technological contexts (Hooper 2001: 65). Thus, although the homosocial martial qualities of the Greek citizen-warrior and the military heroism and risk-taking adventurism bound up in the European aristocratic ideal of the honor/patronage system are downplayed in the more modern bourgeois-rational man— who is all about "reason and self-control or self-denial" (Hooper 2001: 65) to command capitalism rather than armies—aggression and power-over remain common threads. They are simply rechanneled for new arenas of power. The captains of industry and the titans of finance who followed in the age of globalization speak in martial terms, wield economic and technological weapons, and aspire to ruthless takeovers. Such men no longer need hard bodies and physical strength to play out their martial identities, but they carry on the ideal of militarized masculinity nonetheless.

While actual military service as the ultimate test of manhood has been somewhat displaced as hegemonic masculinity could be expressed in other forums, for most men without the highest class privilege and in patriarchal culture more generally, it retains pride of place as the most masculine activity. It has also enjoyed somewhat of a renaissance in the post-9/11 period with the heavy reenactment of the security myth that has re- and hypervalorized male military protection and rescue. As the titans of finance have faltered in the face of the economic crisis of their own making, globalization man is giving way to "security man." As we saw previously, modern militaries actively preserve the association between masculinity and militaries by limiting the participation of women and effeminate or feminized (gay) men. But they also actively construct militarized masculinity through the making of soldiers. As Sandra Whitworth recently chronicled, this involves a whole range of grueling, humiliating, and degrading techniques from boot camp on to break down men's (and a smaller number of women's) sense of individuality and inhibitions about violence and then to build up conformity, "toughness, obedience, discipline, patriotism, lack of squeamishness; avoidance of certain emotions such as fear, sadness, uncertainty, guilt, remorse and grief; and heterosexual competency" (2008: 114). To make a militarized man means "killing the woman" in him (Whitworth 2008: 114).

But as Whitworth also pointed out, these norms of militarized hypermasculinity have some major downsides for military men, especially the many who have been diagnosed with post-traumatic stress disorder (PTSD). Previously referred to as shell shock during the world wars, the more clinical diagnosis of PTSD was applied during the Vietnam War, and it was found that 30 percent of male Vietnam veterans suffered from it (Whitworth 2008: 115). The particularly high rates of it for soldiers coming out of Iraq and Afghanistan, partially as a result of continuous redeployments, are endangering the mystique of the warrior brotherhood and its invincibility. Thus, male soldiers are discouraged from reporting their symptoms and censor themselves for fear of seeming weak and unmanly. Indeed, the Pentagon recently disallowed U.S. soldiers with PTSD, now numbering approximately 300,000, from receiving the Purple Heart in honor of their sacrifice (Alvarez and Eckholm 2009: A1), further pushing sufferers in the closet. Left untreated, the symptoms of "anxiety, fear of death, anger, depression, nightmares" and "hypervigilance" from reliving battlefield memories can also result in "unemployment, alcoholism, and even suicide" as well as divorce, domestic violence, and even murder (Whitworth 2008: 116).

Contemporary military efforts to play down the vulnerability of the male psyche are matched by current military efforts to compensate for the vulnerability of the male body. Armoring military men is not new, but Cristina Masters (2008) has argued that the modifications and extensions of the male body have reached new heights, creating the "cyborg soldier" who will never die and will be willing to kill without remorse. The extreme technologicalization of postmodern warfare seeks to circumvent the comparatively weaker male body, inserting it within machineries of command and control both in and highly distant from the battlefield that are "stronger, faster, more agile, and have much more staying power" (Masters 2008: 95). This displacement of militarized masculinity onto machineries themselves enables such masculinity ideologically to survive the maimings and deaths of flesh-and-blood male bodies, assuring that militarized conflict will not be slowed down by the failings of male bodies and that the maiming and killing of "other" flesh-and-blood bodies will not be seen other than as "blips on radar screens, infrared images, precision-guided targets and numbers and codes on computer screens" (Masters 2008: 99). Thus, militaries are able to retain the mystique of militarized masculinity by disembodying it even as they still rely on male bodies to represent them and do much of their work.

Of course, the reality is that male warriors still die and are maimed psychologically and physically in great numbers as they make up the vast majority of the world's fighters—"the militant many" (Elshtain 1987). According to Joshua Goldstein, although accurate figures are hard to come by, a worldwide survey conducted in 1990 found that males constituted "58 percent of fatalities from war, and 78 percent of other violent deaths" and that "projections of 650,000 deaths in the year 2000 show a similar gender ratio, as do data on all injuries (not just deaths) from violence" (2001: 400). Thus, "male violence" is most perpetrated on other males (Goldstein 2001: 400). However, females aged 15–44 died in war almost as frequently as males in that age group, accounting for 4 percent of war dead compared with 5 percent of males dying in war in 1990 (Goldstein 2001: 400). Current estimates of civilian deaths from violence in the Iraq War range from 90,326 to 98,602 (Iraq Body Count 2009) compared with 4,854 fatalities suffered by U.S. and coalition forces (*Washington Post* 2009), although well over 100,000 such forces (mostly U.S.) have been wounded (iCasualties 2009a) and untold numbers of Iraqi security forces have lost their lives. Similarly, it is estimated that 3,102 Afghan civilians were killed by military violence between 2006 and 2008 (Human Rights Watch 2008) compared with 1,055 coalition casualties (638 of which were U.S. forces) between 2003 and 2009 (iCasualties 2009b). At the same time, almost 5 million Iraqis have become refugees in neighboring countries and internally displaced within Iraq as of 2008 (IOM 2008), constituting a large percentage of the world's 12 million refugees and internally displaced people (IDPs) (UNHCR 2009b). Thus, male combatants pay a heavy price in terms of their lives, their psyches, their bodies, and even their humanity; however, females are increasingly bearing a large brunt of armed conflicts, which goes well beyond dying in them.

Gender Violence

Gender violence typically refers to acts of domestic and sexual violence directed at maintaining gender hierarchies and punishing femininities. It most often means male violence against women, ranging from battering and burning to sexual harassment, assault, mutilation, slavery, trafficking, and torture as well as forced pregnancy and sterilization. However, men also visit gender violence on other men, and women, too, can commit gender violence against other women and men. Women's gender violence occurs less frequently, and because it often involves fewer weapons, it often produces less physical harm. Gender violence also can refer to violence visited upon gays, lesbians, bisexuals, and transgendered peoples targeted for their sexuality (and gender). Although notoriously underreported in national and UN statistics, gender violence is acknowledged by the UN as epidemic throughout much of the world and across cultures, ethnicities, and classes. It is a regular feature of civilian life in heteronormative patriarchal societies, but it is especially rife in military settings. As we have seen, military women suffer gender violence most frequently at the hands of their male comrades, and this is the largest cause of PTSD (increasingly referred to as military sexual trauma, or MST) suffered by women soldiers (Whitworth 2008: 120). Military wives and girlfriends experience domestic violence at the hands of their male partners at three to five times the rate that women in civilian relationships do, and men "who have been in combat are four times more likely to be physically abusive" (Eisenstein 2007: 24). In the United States, rates of domestic and sexual abuse in military families have particularly escalated since 9/11 (Eisenstein 2007: 24).

While widespread gender violence by "friendly" forces against their own could charitably be seen as "unintended consequences" of militarized masculinity, militaries actually institutionalize gender violence against "allied" and "enemy" women. According to Enloe, there are "three 'types' of institutionalized militarized rape: 'recreational rape'— the assumption that soldiers need constant access to sexual outlets; 'national security rape'—when police forces and armies use rape to bolster the state's control over a population; and systematic mass rape as an instrument of open warfare" (Seager 1997: 116). Although recreational rape is a feature of most state militaries, it is particularly associated with the U.S. military, in part because the United States maintains the largest number of foreign military bases. This aspect of the U.S. military gained worldwide attention in September 1995 when two marines and a Navy seaman gang-raped a twelve-year-old Japanese girl in Okinawa (Seager 1997: 116). The storm of protest and anti-U.S. military feelings on the part of the Japanese that this case evoked have not stopped military bases from also being deeply implicated in the business of prostitution.

Many military men have come to expect sexual servicing not just as a perk but as a right and even a necessity during their stints overseas. Given that recreational rape can unleash protest against a foreign military presence (as in the Okinawan case), providing its military men access to legitimate sex (with prostitutes) has been a policy of the U.S. government. As part of Status of Forces Agreements (SOFAs) between the U.S. government and its allies that codify the conditions under which U.S. forces can be stationed in a host territory (Enloe 2000: 92), there are R&R (rest and recreation) agreements that detail the conditions for permitting and controlling the sexual servicing of the U.S. military (Enloe 1993: 154). Perhaps the most notorious site was Subic Bay Naval Base in the Philippines. In the late 1980s, Filipino feminist organizations reported that as a result of high unemployment and extreme poverty, more than 20,000 Filipino women and about 10,000 Filipino children regularly acted as prostitutes for U.S. servicemen at Subic Bay (Enloe 1989: 66). This situation contributed not only to the spread of HIV/AIDS but also to racial tensions and nationalist fervor: Filipinos denounced militarized prostitution as a symbol of their compromised sovereignty. The Subic Bay base was closed in 1991 when the Philippine government revoked its lease, but the nexus between military bases and prostitution and other forms of sex work continues elsewhere.

Katharine Moon's (1997) study of the SOFAs between the United States and South Korea since the Korean War found that the numerous "camptowns" that grew up around U.S. troops stationed there, particularly between the 1950s and 1970s, constituted a "GI's Heaven" where "20,000 registered prostitutes were available to 'service' approximately 62,000 US soldiers by the late 1960's" for as little as two dollars for a half hour sexual encounter (Moon 1997: 30). In the face of rising venereal disease, HIV/AIDS, and racial tensions born of Korean women's disinclination to service military men of color, U.S. and Korean military officials engaged in elaborate measures to "clean up" the camptowns. These efforts were not designed to protect sex workers or to change the postwar economy that left so many primarily rural women, as well as men and children, scrambling to provide "entertainment" for GIs, but rather to make them safer for GIs to continue to be sexually serviced with less fear of disease and racial discrimination. As Moon has argued, in this way, the U.S.–South Korean alliance was preserved on the backs of women literally on their backs.[2]

The Gulf wars in the Middle East have required a different approach to alliance building. In cultural and religious deference to such hosts as Saudi Arabia, the United States issued a "no-prostitution-allowed" policy, but there is evidence that soldiers returning home or redeployed stop along the way for sexual servicing in other ports of call, particularly in Southeast Asia (Enloe 2000: 72). There is no evidence that prostitution or no-prostitution agreements reduce rape, for as Richard Rayner has found, many U.S. military officials and experts continue to believe that rape is a "necessary corollary" to the military's main function—killing (Rayner 1997: 29).

Genocidal rape refers to a systematic program of raping women and girls (and forcing captured "enemy" men to rape each other) to humiliate (feminize) the enemy and to dilute it as a (biological) nation through the impregnation of the enemy's women (Hague 1997: 56). It gained worldwide attention when it was revealed that during the war in Bosnia-Herzegovina that began in 1992, up to 60,000 (mostly Bosnian) women had been raped by 1993, largely by Serb forces (Bunch and Reilly 1994: 36). The massacres and countermassacres engaged in by the Tutsi and Hutu ethnic groups that began in Burundi in 1993 and in Rwanda in 1994 have left well over a million people dead, and it is estimated that between 250,000 and 500,000 women were raped in the Rwandan conflict (NCRW 2006: 40). The current "Rape Capital of the World" is the Democratic Republic of Congo (DRC), where, in 1994, defeated Hutus from the Rwandan conflict fled, followed in 1996 by Tutsi forces allied with now DRC President Kabila (Jones 2008: 16). According to Ann Jones, this spillover from the Rwandan conflict—which also involves armies and militias within the DRC and from other neighboring countries—has been all about a scramble to lay claim to the DRC's rich mineral resources. The main technique employed, however, has been sexual terror of women and girls of all ages through massive and repeated rapes, gang rapes, rapes in captivity, sexual mutilation, and sexual murder, particularly at the hands of the Hutu factions (Jones 2008: 17). Although a peace treaty between the warring factions was signed in 2002, five million have died thus far, 2.1 million of them since 2002. And the rapes continue. As Jones points out, rape is a calculated act of war, for it debilitates women physically by spreading disease; keeps them from working in their fields, which leads to malnutrition; and creates outcast women with no money for themselves or their children, thus undermining families and communities that are left destitute and desolate (2008: 18). Although sexual assaults have been defined as crimes of war since the 1940s, it was not until recently that rape has been prosecuted as a crime of genocide and against humanity (Oosterveld 2005). However, as we address later, this has had little effect on rape as a continuing tool of war. Nor is it having much effect on the fact that women and children (including girls and boys) make up 75 to 80 percent of the world's 50 million refugees and the rapes they commonly experience within refugee camps, not only at the hands of combatants and male refugees but also aid workers and peacekeepers (NCRW 2006: 38).

Although gender violence is most associated with direct violence, it involves considerable structural violence. The sheer costs of military spending ensure that money is not available for meeting human needs for which women are most responsible and that they are most denied. With worldwide military spending at an all-time high of $1.475 trillion, basic social services go wanting. Indeed, it is estimated that only "one third of the world's military spending would satisfy budgetary needs for addressing any and all global problems, from deforestation to HIV and AIDS, from clean water to illiteracy" (WCC 2005: 2). Instead, countries in the global South continue to underspend on basic services such as education and health, devoting on average only 12 to 14 percent of their national budgets to these (WCC 2005: 18), whereas countries in the global North, and especially the United States, continue to overspend on means of destruction. U.S. military spending, which accounts for almost half of all such spending, is "more than the next 46 highest spending countries in the world combined," and "5.8 times more than China, 10.2 times more than Russia, and 98.6 times more than Iran" as well as 55 times more than six states it has branded as "rogue" (Cuba, Iran, Libya, North Korea, Sudan, and Syria) (Center for Arms Control and Non-Proliferation 2008). The rise in military spending since the end of the Cold War—when it declined due to decreases in the former Warsaw Pact spending—is attributable almost entirely to U.S. spending increases for the wars in Iraq and Afghanistan (WCC 2005: 8). As we noted earlier, nine times more has been spent by the United States for its military operations than for its "homeland security" efforts, and there is evidence that funding for social services and environmental protection in the United States was reduced by the Bush administration since 9/11 (WCC 2005: 10), although there are now shifts back to domestic spending for these purposes under the Obama administration.

The largest arms dealers in the world are the permanent members of the UN Security Council (the United States, Russia, France, China, and the UK), who sell primarily to the global South, including countries they have officially deemed human rights violators (WCC 2005: 22–23). At least one-fifth of the global South's debt is attributable to their import of arms, and small arms or light weapons are by far the most traded as they are easily used in civil wars where interstate rules of war are least observed, for gender violence, and by child soldiers, including girls who make up 30 percent of such soldiers in 178 countries (NCRW 2006: 41), and who are pressed into fighting, raping, and being raped (WCC 2005: 24). Meanwhile, "almost all developing countries have consistently failed to meet the UN goal of .07% GDP" to be given for humanitarian and development aid, but "the 'securitization' of aid, in which combating terrorism and combating poverty are treated as the same thing," has been on the increase and has been "funded out of over-stretched aid and development budgets instead of national security budgets" (WCC 2005: 20). Under such conditions, even the modest UN MDGs simply cannot be met.

Given that females make up 70 percent of the world's approximately 1.3 billion people living in absolute poverty (making less than two dollars per day), two-thirds of the world's 800 million illiterates, and the majority of the world's refugees, HIV/AIDS sufferers, land-mine casualties, and sex trafficking, rape, and domestic violence victims (NCRW 2006), military largesse translates into massive structural as well as direct gender violence, enormously affecting women in the global South. Worldwide women's movements and NGOs have long made the connection between war and militarization and the compromising of women's security. Their efforts to bring this to world attention started during the UN Decade for Women when women first held their own tribunals for crimes against women, followed by their promotion of women's human rights at the world human rights conference in Vienna in 1993 and the codification of the connection between armed conflict and gender violence as a violation of women's human rights at the 1995 fourth women's world conference in Beijing (Joachim 2007). Amnesty International and Human Rights Watch also began monitoring and reporting on gender violence in the 1990s, ever since making it a major focus of their human rights campaigns (Joachim 2007: 128), and the genocidal rape in Bosnia and Rwanda also catapulted gender violence and its relationship to armed conflict onto the UN agenda. As explored in the following section, however, although UN action on this has been unprecedented, it has been weak at best, largely upholding gendered divisions of violence, gender violence, and especially the power of gender to privilege militarization and neocolonial or (neo)imperial relations.

GENDERED PEACEKEEPING AND PEACEMAKING

Although part of a longer and wider struggle for women's security from militarized violence, an NGO Working Group on Women and International Peace and Security, consisting of the century-old Women's International League for Peace and Freedom (WILPF), the Women's Caucus for Gender Justice, Amnesty International, International Alert, the Women's Commission for Refugee Women and Children, and the Hague Appeal for Peace in collaboration with UNIFEM, is credited with the final push to have the UN Security Council pass Resolution 1325 in 2000 (Cohn 2008: 187). Although nonbinding, 1325 "calls on" the UN and member countries to do the following: protect women from gender-based violence in war zones and include women (and gender perspectives) in peace negotiations, support their peacemaking initiatives in addition to providing gender-sensitive training to peacekeepers, and engage in gender mainstreaming through UN monitoring of and reporting on the gender dimensions of conflict and conflict resolution, including the impact of armed conflict on women and girls and the roles of women in peacemaking.[3]

Although 1325 was hailed as a breakthrough document, its effects were muted at best. Widespread rapes in the DRC conflict as well as in the Darfur genocide in Sudan and increased reports of rape by peacekeeping forces were featured in subsequent UN Secretary-General studies and reports on women, peace, and security that were mandated by 1325. This acknowledgment of worsening gender violence in war led to the passage of UN Security Council Resolution 1820 in 2008.[4] Although also nonbinding, the text of 1820 reaffirms the principles of 1325, but "stresses" sexual violence as a war crime, "demands" its cessation and no amnesty for its perpetrators, "requests" a policy of "zero tolerance" for sexual violence by UN peacekeepers and in UN refugee camps, and "requests" consultation with women and women's organizations to find solutions to sexual violence.

These resolutions, which were the first to address women, and most notably women as security actors rather than only victims, in the history of the Security Council (Enloe 2007: 129), were preceded by the formation of international criminal tribunals for the former Yugoslavia (ICTY) and Rwanda (ICTR) in 1993 and 1994 respectively. Rape was first prosecuted by a World War II military tribunal that found several Japanese commanders responsible for systematic rapes in Nanking, and the 1946 Fourth Geneva Convention and 1974 UN Declaration on the Protection of Women and Children in Emergency and Armed Conflict speak amorphously to protecting women from war violence (Oosterveld 2005: 68–69). However, the ICTY and ICTR were the first tribunals to begin developing international case law and precedents that spell out a wide range of gender violence (including gender violence perpetrated against men) that is prosecutable as a crime of war and a tool of genocide (Oosterveld 2005: 79). By 1998, these were codified in the Rome Statute of the International Criminal Court (ICC)[5] that recognizes multiple forms of gender violence in armed conflict as crimes against humanity and war crimes and requires gender-sensitive judges and court proceedings that do not retraumatize victims (Oosterveld 2005: 67).

These are significant gender gains in the struggle against gendered insecurities, but they remain problematic on a number of scores. As UNIFEM reports, very few women have served as judges on the ICTY, ICTR, and ICC (2008: 79); women made up just 17 percent of UN Department of Peacekeeping Operations' senior staff; only 1.9 percent of peacekeeping soldiers contributed by member states are women; women remain virtually absent at peace-negotiating tables as participants or even observers; little to no training to prevent sexual violence is provided to peacekeepers; and accountability, compliance, and incentive mechanisms are virtually absent in 1325 and 1820 when compared with those set out in the 2005 Security Council Resolution 1612 on Children and Armed Conflict (2008: 99).[6] Moreover, IGO funding of women's rights organizations overall appears to be declining, not increasing (UNIFEM 2008: 93–94), and the few gender units or advisers deployed for peacekeeping missions are understaffed and underresourced (Whitworth 2004: 131). In addition, those states that are not signatories to the Rome Statute of the ICC, such as the United States, are exempt from having their officials and troops prosecuted by the ICC; much individual military peacekeeper gender violence cannot be proven to rise to the level of crimes against humanity in nongenocidal contexts; SOFAs typically keep peacekeepers as well as militaries immune to prosecution in the host country, and they are rarely if ever tried in their home countries; and civilians and private contractors serving as military or peacekeeping extensions are also immune (Bedont 2005). Finally, there is no international jurisdiction for gender violence perpetrated against one's own comrades-in-arms.

But beneath the failures of these formal mechanisms lie more insidious processes. As feminist IR experts have pointed out (Enloe 1993; Whitworth 2004), donning a "blue beret" sets up contradictions for the primarily military men who become peacekeepers. Military training that inculcates militarized masculinity neither prepares peacekeeping troops for the humanitarian work they are expected to perform nor encourages them to embrace the light weapons they carry or force restraint they must observe. It can also breed male resentment for "missing the 'main' show—conflict and warfare" (Whitworth 2004: 150), but also ensures that peacekeepers (from both the global North and the global South) expect the same perks as other military men, as they "run brothels, assault local women, and kill local citizens" (Whitworth 2004: 152).

On the other side of the coin, as Whitworth argues based on her study of Canadian peacekeeping operations, the UN's new interest in "adding women and stirring" simply grafts on (essentialist) gender analysis, which assumes women will just ease and assist the already predetermined business of peacekeeping and peace negotiations by bringing information on women and "women's issues" into these activities. This predetermined business disregards any considerations of militarized masculinity as a major source of prolonged conflict or such sources of structural violence as neocolonial economic and political relationships and neoliberal economic restructuring that may lie at the heart of the conflict (Whitworth 2004: 133, 137). Instead, this business focuses on "when the fighting broke out" and how to control if not cease it (Whitworth 2004: 133). Thus, rather than causing a rethinking of peacekeeping and peace negotiations, "analyses of women and of gender thus become part of the 'programmatic solutions' that form the UN repertoire of responding to conflict and insecurity around the world, and, in this way, confirm the appropriateness of the repertoire" (Whitworth 2004: 137). In this sense, like gender equality that is subsumed under neoliberal governmentality, gender perspectives on international peace and security are subsumed under a kind of security governmentality. Whitworth concludes that the issue is not so much adding more women to peacekeeping and peacemaking operations, but rather questioning the sole reliance on militaries to do the job of peacekeeping (Whitworth 2004: 183) and, by extension, on military leaders and civilian defense elites to do the job of peacemaking.

Even more problematic, Whitworth points out that peacekeeping itself is a colonial practice. Given that fourteen of the thirty UN peacekeeping operations that were launched between 1988 and 2005 have been in Africa (Hudson 2005), with almost all of the rest in the South as well, contemporary peacekeeping

> comes from an understanding of the places in which those conflicts occur, "conflict-prone third world countries," which are defined by what they lack: the institutions, the liberalism, the rationality, and the order of Western states. Peacekeeping, as part of the contemporary *"mission civilatrice,"* is the means by which that "lack" can be addressed, bringing meaning and order where there are none. Peacekeeping is, in short, part of the "subject constituting project" of the colonial encounter (Whitworth 2004: 185).

Beyond the ironies that the weapons the West sells to the South that enable and increase the brutal conflict there, the colonizing dimensions of peacekeeping not only invite greater militarization of peacekeeping and the conflicts it seeks to quell, but also undermine the peacebuilding efforts of "local" women (and their male allies) that are ignored or discounted.

(DE)MILITARIZING FEMINISM

Given that "*both genders lose in war*, although they lose in somewhat different ways" (Goldstein 2001: 402), we still confront the problem of dealing with the recurring linkages identifying masculinity with aggression and war and femininity with passivity and peace that shore up militarization. Judith Hicks Stiehm (1989) argued that achieving gender parity in the U.S. armed forces might ultimately force an acknowledgment that war is not "manly" and that women can protect themselves. In this view, women's equal participation might destabilize the ways in which the gendered division of violence and the gender inequality upon which it rests contribute to militarization. However, given the historical patterns, gender parity seems an unlikely development in any state military. Moreover, as the jobs of militaries and even peacekeeping forces are increasingly privatized into the hands of essentially paid mercenary forces like Blackwater, such contracting ensures that the "real" business of war will be kept largely in male hands and remain "manly," regardless of some "resexing" of state militaries.

Other feminists have pointed out that although comparatively few women are or will be soldiers on the battlefront, many more serve the military on the home front, working (typically at the lowest levels) for defense and related industries. One could argue that this labor contributes more to life-taking than do individual male and female soldiers on the battlefront. At the same time, as we have seen, women's political violence has become more visible as they gain more political power and enter the ranks of militaries and "terrorist" groups, even though their violence is typically not represented as political violence. At the same time, images and realities of military men's vulnerability are becoming harder to hide and contain, even though there continue to be herculean efforts to do so.

Still other feminists point out that in times of violent conflict, gender dichotomies are not only rigidified but also can lose their rigidity. In contrast to the post-9/11 response in the United States that brought a particularly virulent restaging of gender (and race) binaries and asymmetries, Simona Sharoni (1998) has found that in cases such as "the troubles" in Northern Ireland and the Israeli-Palestinian conflict, women under British and Israeli occupation became significant political actors as patriarchal taboos were lifted in the midst of conflict. This has also occurred in a range of especially Latin American guerrilla or armed national liberation movements against repressive authoritarian governments in which women have been involved in large numbers as politicized and often explicitly feminist actors and combatants (Kampwirth 2002). At the same time, some men, such as imprisoned Irish Republican Army (IRA) members, have developed new understandings of their own vulnerabilities as a result of their prison experiences. As Sharoni (1998) recounts, captured IRA members incarcerated in British prisons learned to protest their treatment in prison out of vulnerability. For example, in resistance to being marked as criminals rather than as political prisoners, they refused to wear prison-issue clothing for over four years, choosing to be naked instead and using only blankets to cover themselves. This is the opposite of and in opposition to the armored man. They also gained new appreciation of feminist perspectives on conflict and peace as a result of working with feminist educators and supporters on the outside who backed their protests. By coming to recognize the interconnections among gender, sexuality, race, class, nationality, and international violence, they thereby learned to eschew militarized masculinity on the understanding that it gets in the way of broad and inclusive struggles for justice and peace that are more nonviolent than violent.

This example brings us to an important distinction—imperialist violence versus resistance to it, whether nonviolent or violent. Since 9/11, feminist debates have shifted to grapple with the militarization of feminism (particularly Western, but especially U.S. feminism) through its appropriation by primarily the Bush administration. In Ann Russo's (2006) analysis of the U.S. Feminist Majority Foundation's (FMF) campaign to stop "gender apartheid" in Afghanistan, she argues that beyond the well-known claim by the Bush administration that the war against Afghanistan was at least partially about liberating Afghan women from the male oppressors of the Taliban, thus, using feminist rhetoric as a stimulus for war, the FMF also actively enabled, supported, and partook in this rhetoric at the expense of Afghan women and women's movements. Although the FMF's pre-9/11 campaign against gender violence could be seen as "counterhegemonic," this campaign ended up colluding with the "project of US imperialism and retaliatory violence as a method of maintaining US power" (Russo 2006: 558). The reasons for this, according to Russo, include the FMF's desire to be taken seriously on the foreign policy stage through pointing to the success of its impact on the Bush administration; its ahistorical reading of the causes of gender violence in Afghanistan, including the Soviet invasion of it and the subsequent U.S. arming of the Taliban; its myopic focus on lifting the burqua and "freeing" women that led the FMF to support the war without consideration of the greater costs that war would visit on Afghan women; and its participation in colonialist and Orientalist thinking. As we pointed out earlier, Orientalism assumes Western superiority and constructs the West as the source of rescue and salvation for the rest, which has justified over the centuries many an invasion and colonization that has caused the havoc from which "others" must be saved. The FMF's alliance with the U.S. State Department in support of the Afghanistan War caused a split between the FMF and the Revolutionary Association of Women in Afghanistan (RAWA), which rejected the invasion and the postinvasion installation of more gender violence–producing patriarchs in the form of the Northern Alliance that they had warned would be the result of the invasion (Russo 2006: 574).

Many other feminists in the West, as well as more generally in the global North and South, have condemned the war in Afghanistan and the "war on terror" more generally (Hawthorne and Winter 2002; Joseph and Sharma 2003; Hunt and Rygiel 2006; Alexander and Hawkesworth 2008). Many U.S. feminists have also chronicled the relentless "war on women" at home and abroad by the Bush administration (Flanders 2004; Finlay 2006), which belied its claims to feminist motivations and puts into serious question assumptions about the relationship between Western modernity and support for gender equality. In contrast, those who do practice "imperial feminism" mitigate against transnational solidarity among women (and with men subjected to imperialism) to resist war and militarism.

As a range of feminist historical scholarship has shown, imperial feminism is not new, whether it is in support of British, Dutch, French, or other empires (McClintock 1995; Midgley 1998; Clancy-Smith and

Gouda 1998; Levine 2004). Features imperial feminism have in common are not only accepting the imperial, masculinist, racist, and heteronormative project of white(ned) men saving white women from racialized men, but also helping to construct, buying into, and representing the imperial, racist, and heteronormative project of white(ned) women saving "brown women from brown men" (Spivak 1988: 297), both of which ensure continued militarism.

Most recently, feminist scholars, along with other critical world politics scholars, have focused their attention on not only U.S. empire, in the form of the military and political unilateralism that particularly the Bush administration enacted (Eisenstein 2004), but also Empire as the current expression of global capitalism, which while most championed by the United States, subsumes even it and the IGOs it dominates under processes of neoliberal governmentality (Hardt and Negri 2000). Although U.S.-fostered securitization of borders and movements seems in contradiction to the open borders that global capitalism requires, the combination of security regimes or globalized militarization with global capitalism allows greater exploitation and oppression. This is not only because globalized militarization causes greater desperation and, thus, more and more at risk or captive and thus cheapened and quiescent labor—as well as a way for private industry to reap enormous profits from war industries—but also because the "war on terror" and global capitalism have been constructed as *the* way to "democracy" and, thus, are not to be questioned.[7] Thus, Empire accepts to some degree feminists and other social movement actors (as well as some "resexing" of male-dominated militaries and occupations) who do not question these twin pillars, for they lend the veneer of democracy to these projects.

Thus, feminists transnationally who do not accept this arrangement, which deradicalizes feminism and other social movements seeking to reduce human insecurities and planetary destruction, have turned their attention to linking and building solidarity against these twin pillars that actually undermine democratization. To resist Empire is to disrupt the gendered division of violence, not by claiming equality to do imperial violence but rather by challenging the power of gender to valorize it. As Arundhati Roy puts it:

Our strategy should be not only to confront Empire, but to lay siege to it. To deprive it of oxygen. To shame it. To mock it. With our art, our music, our literature, our stubbornness, our joy, our brilliance, our sheer relentlessness—our ability to tell our own stories. Stories that are different from the ones we're being brainwashed to believe.

The corporate revolution will collapse if we refuse to buy what they are selling—their ideas, their version of history, their weapons, their notions of inevitability.

Remember this. We be many and they be few. They need us more than we need them (2003: 112).

DISARMING SECURITY

As we indicated at the outset of this chapter, security is always elusive and partial. This does not undercut our argument for the need to confront the crisis of insecurity, which is born of the pursuit of absolute security. The desire for absolute security is the product of hardened masculinist identities that imagine themselves and the world as a series of armed camps set up to preserve their respective autonomies. Whether security can be completely detached from this imagining is an open question, but security has come to mean far more than that (Sutton, Morgen, and Novkov 2008), and it can be pursued without compromising the security of "others" by resisting "othering" itself and recognizing that processes that compromise the security of others compromise the security of a reimagined "self" in solidarity with others.

The newfound attention of "security" IGOs to the compromising of women's security through armed conflict is, on the one hand, welcome, but, on the other hand, has reproduced gender ideologies that construct women as "natural" victims and peace proponents. This "sets up" women to carry the burden of peacemaking and peacebuilding while they lack the material resources and political representation and sway to do so. It also deflects attention from the continued and overwhelming prerogatives of elites, states, and markets to make war and unjust peace. Even the new prosecutions of gender violence in war can have nonhumanitarian effects, including providing additional "fuel for nationalist fervor," resulting in reprisals against women who testify and sustaining conflict (Giles and Hyndman 2004: 13). As we have seen, peacekeeping is also more of a colonizing practice than a peaceful one, and refugees and internally displaced persons are far from safe from not only combatants but also peacekeepers and aid workers. Thus, humanitarian efforts are increasingly being exposed by feminists as part of the "security myth."

Although there are many good reasons to disconnect peace from women (as well as war from men), there remains some value in Spivak's concept of strategic essentialism to resist war and other forms of violence. The notion that women, especially as mothers, are more peaceful has been thoroughly problematized, but the fact remains that women continue to mobilize against war based in part on this very notion. Once into such struggles, they may shift their political identities and recognize that homogenizing notions of womanhood or motherhood are not enough for, and may stand in the way of, transcending or working through political differences and economic and social inequalities. But however women become politicized to resist war together, in doing so they "reject the prevalent relationship to the state (and sometimes with their spouses and partners) and redefine it" (Kaufman and Williams 2007: 30). Thus, identity "myths" can be useful for peace and justice mobilizations as long as they are seen as provisional and political, not foundational or "natural."

Notes

1. By January 2008, 121 U.S. soldiers who had returned from the Iraq and Afghanistan wars had been charged with murder or manslaughter. One-third of those killed were their wives, girlfriends, and children, and one-quarter were largely other servicemen but also servicewomen who were their wives or girlfriends (Sontag and Alvarez 2008).

2. Recently, former sex workers in South Korea have sought an apology and compensation from their government for its role in serving as "'one big pimp'" for the American military, likening their case to that of the "comfort women" who were pressed into serving as prostitutes for the Japanese military during World War II and who also have sought an apology and compensation from the Japanese government (Sang-Hun 2009).

3. See the full text of 1325 from which these recommended actions are drawn, available at the online location included in our Web Resources section.

4. See Web Resources listed at the end of this text for the online location of the full text of UN Security Council Resolution 1820.

5. See Web Resources listed at the end of this text for the online location of the full text of the Rome Statute of the International Criminal Court (ICC).

6. See Web Resources listed at the end of this text for the online location of the full text of UN Security Council Resolution 1621.

7. See Grewal (2005: 202) for an analysis of how security has become the dominant mode of governmentality, using race and gender to "produce figures of risk" who must be disciplined and must adopt self-discipline in order not to threaten the "'security,' happiness and freedom" of those who determine who is "risk-producing" and "at risk."

5

◄○►

Gender and Global
Political Economy

How are women and men positioned and re-positioned in and by global economic processes, and with what effects? What do gendered divisions of labor tell us about how work is defined, valued, and distributed? How does the power of gender affect who has access to and control over symbolic, economic, and environmental resources? There is tremendous variation in how economic processes are operationalized in households, rural and urban communities, nations, and geographic regions. In this chapter, we look at the relationship between gendered inequalities and global political economy (GPE),[1] viewing globalization as a gendered process that reflects both continuity and change. We also consider a contemporary paradox. On the one hand, more women worldwide are seeking and gaining employment, thus becoming income earners and presumably benefiting from the enhanced self-esteem and economic empowerment that formal work affords. On the other hand, the feminization of employment has done little to alter expectations regarding gender divisions of labor or valorizations of masculinized work over women's work, or enabled women in aggregate to significantly increase their control over economic decision-making or environmental resource use. Although gender mainstreaming now features in the World Bank's and other international agencies' economic development policies, the objective is to "integrate women into markets" rather than promote social justice by altering hierarchical gender relations. The power of gender here operates to reproduce divisions of labor and responsibility in social reproduction and formal production that favor short-term neoliberal objectives and sustain

183

commitments to competition and growth—but at the price of long-term crises of social reproduction and environmental sustainability.

With reference to owning economic resources and wielding economic authority, at first glance the positioning of men and women suggests more continuity than change. Gender stereotypes persist in assigning men the primary responsibility for income-generation in households worldwide, and men in aggregate still hold higher-paying and more secure jobs than do women. Men—especially those who are economically, ethnically, racially, and geopolitically privileged—continue to control power-wielding and decision-making authority in economic development planning, corporate investment strategies, and IFIs. These patterns relate to what we have called the *gendered division of labor*: paid-unpaid work, providers-dependents, production-reproduction, and independence in the marketplace versus dependence. We address this in concert with the *gendered division of resources* (culture-nature, active-passive, subject-object, users-resources, advanced-primitive, and exploitation versus stewardship) in this chapter. And, as we continue to show here, the *power of gender* persists through masculinist, racist, classist, and heteronormative assumptions and objectives in economic and geopolitical thinking and practice (despite some economic attention to women and the current economic meltdown). This is most visible when we observe how policymaking remains largely top-down, formulaic, and overreliant on growth and quantifiable indicators, often at the expense of being focused on provisioning, human well-being, and social and environmental sustainability, contributing to what we refer to generally as the *crisis of sustainability*.

But we also note how globalization is disrupting familiar gender patterns and re-positioning women and men by altering assumptions, roles, identities, and livelihoods worldwide. These disruptions are especially visible in relation to economics, in part because gender is so key to unequal divisions of labor and their valorizations, and in part because new technologies are so profoundly altering what is produced, how, where, and by whom worldwide. Some changes are small and incremental, whereas others challenge our deepest assumptions (male breadwinner roles) and most established institutions (patriarchal families where male heads-of-household are the primary "providers"). The effects of these re-positionings and disruptions are complex and defy easy generalizations. As more women enter the paid workforce—some by traveling great distances—this both empowers some women and complicates expectations of hegemonic masculinity for most men. The geographical unevenness of employment opportunities spurs internal and external migrations that alter "traditional" household formations, and diasporas reconfigure ethnic/racialized identifications and alignments. Neoliberal policies have also imposed new disciplining practices that shape the expectations, options, and responses of workers worldwide. The growth imperative of "disaster capitalism" exacerbates old and produces new environmental degradations (Klein 2007). Overvalorization of masculinized activities—literally at the expense of feminized activities and feminized workers—continues to reproduce gendered inequalities and intensifies a polarization of (masculinized) haves and (feminized) have-nots, manifested as well in the masculinized North dumping its disproportionate waste on the feminized South. These stark economic inequalities constitute structural violence and global insecurities, including the insecurity of environmental conditions upon which all else depends.

When we examine how globalization is re-positioning women and men in the workforce, we gain a contemporary picture of what work is available, where and under what conditions, and who does it. When we examine how the power of gender operates, we advance our understanding of how "work" is defined, accounted for, and differentially valorized; how technologies are transforming production, marketing, distribution, and consumption in gendered ways; and how stereotypes of sex and race shape whose bodies and services are sought and "consumed" in pleasure-seeking and care-based industries. In general, our focus on GPE reveals starkly how the power of gender constitutes not only a sexual division of labor that exploits women, but also a gendered, polarized valorization of skills, activities, work, and workers that serves to "naturalize" the exploitation of most of the earth's population and the planet itself.

FEMINIST APPROACHES TO GLOBAL POLITICAL ECONOMY

Economic and work issues raised by feminists include how gendered divisions of labor position men and women differently; how women's domestic, reproductive, and caring labor is deemed marginal to "production" and analyses of it; and how orthodox models and methods presuppose male-dominated activities (paid work, the formal economy) and masculinized characteristics (autonomous, objective, rational, instrumental, competitive). In effect, the extensive (feminized) labor involved in social reproduction and upon which all else ultimately depends is treated as coincidental, as if the rest of the social system could survive without it. As a corollary, "women's work" and feminized qualities are devalued: deemed economically irrelevant (done "for love" not for money), characterized as subjective, "voluntary," "natural," and "unskilled," and either poorly paid or not paid at all. At the same time, feminists criticize mainstream assumptions that all caring labor and social reproduction occurs through heteronormative families and nonconflictual intrahousehold dynamics. Through a mainstream lens—whether academic or policy-making—alternative household forms and the rising percentage of female-headed and otherwise unconventional households are rendered deviant or invisible.[2]

How feminists address and attempt to correct these biases and omissions has varied over time and along numerous dimensions. Many begin by "adding women," which invariably prompts new questions regarding what counts: as relevant data (marriage patterns, family budgets), appropriate sources (family and community records, personal diaries), and germane topics (caring labor, shopping, food preparation, sex work). Attention shifts from a (masculinist) focus on "the main story" of men's activities to the "background" story that underpins and enables men's activities—often with unexpected results. In the early 1970s, for example, Esther Boserup (1970) studied the effects of modernization policies on women in nonindustrialized countries. Paying attention to women's experiences exposed the often deleterious effects of modernization and undercut orthodox claims that development benefited everyone. Subsequent "women in development" (WID) research documented both how policies and practices marginalized women and how women's exclusion jeopardized development objectives.

With its focus on "empirical" gender, WID scholarship initially sought more effective *inclusion* of women in the practices and presumed benefits of development. This orientation was important and productive for revealing inequalities of positioning among women and men. Cumulative research suggested, however, that simply adding women did not address significant problems: the devaluation of feminized labor, the structural privileging of men and masculinity, or the increasing pressure on women to work a triple shift (in familial, informal, and formal activities) to ensure family survival during economic crises. In response, feminists increasingly asked how the power of gender was shaping underlying assumptions, expectations, and even the rules of the game. For many researchers, the liberal, modernist inclinations of WID approaches were gradually displaced by the more constructivist, critical starting points of gender and development (GAD) orientations.[3] GAD scholars problematized the meaning and desirability of development, interrogated the definition of work and how to "count it," exposed the masculinism of unemployed men's reluctance to "help" in the household, challenged constructions of feminism imposed by Western elites, investigated intersections of gender, race, and neocolonialism, and criticized narratives of victimization. These studies marked an opening up of questions, an expansion of research foci, and a complication of analyses.[4]

In the past decade feminists have continued to expose masculinist bias and its effects and expanded the evidence corroborating (and complicating) early feminist critiques. They have deepened the interrogation of foundational constructs (rationality, work, production, capital, value, development) and the critique of neoliberal globalization as masculinist, racist, and imperialist. They have extended their research from more obviously gender-differentiated effects of microeconomic phenomena and national budgets to the less direct effects of macroeconomic policies, including how gender operates even in the abstracted realm of financial markets.[5] The activism of women in the global South raised the profile of women's knowledge and agency, and feminists more generally engaged in rethinking economic "givens" and generating alternative visions of economics based on a more relevant and responsible model of "social provisioning."[6]

Feminists vary in what they identify as corrective practices or priority policies. Strategically, some advocate relatively more acceptable, "doable," and presumably efficacious reforms from within—or not far outside of—conventional frameworks of theory and practice. The adoption of various gender equality policies and measures by international bodies in the 1990s coincided with heightened concerns over the persistence of stark global inequalities and the potential for social deterioration and disruption they posed. A new focus on fighting poverty and on "inclusion" of those most marginalized by globalization appeared in the reports, recommendations, and funding priorities of the UN, World Bank, and other economic development agencies. Feminists welcomed this shift in attention toward women's and social issues and the new opportunities it afforded. Through gender mainstreaming, global networking, and women-oriented NGOs, feminists expanded their capacity to influence policymaking, inform development strategies, direct research agendas, and promote "women's issues." They utilized various approaches to enhance awareness of gender inequalities, deploy human rights discourse to promote women's economic rights, enhance the role of women's agencies, and implement policies more favorable to women's inclusion in market activities.

Most feminists recognize the allure and positive potential of gender mainstreaming policies and the openings they afford. But some also question their underlying premises or efficacy in terms of altering the structural conditions that produce and sustain global poverty. Gender mainstreaming in development agencies has been especially promoted through microcredit initiatives, and these afford a classic example of the pros and cons of "women-targeted" policies.

Microcredit projects disburse small loans to a group of borrowers who collectively share responsibility for repayment. Access to the credit (US $50–150) rotates among members who use it to jump-start or advance entrepreneurial activities, the success of which enables increased earnings, the repayment of the loan, and further reinvestment and accumulation in an upward and out-of-poverty spiral. This strategy targets poor rural women precisely because their lack of any conventional collateral excludes them from access to credit, without which they have no hope of jump-starting a small business, of achieving their entrepreneurial potential and breaking out of the cycle of poverty. Women are also targeted because they are presumed to be better at forging social networks and sustaining the trust necessary for group success, and because their presumed fear of letting the group down will ensure they make an optimal effort toward repayment (Bergeron 2003: 166–167). Finally, women are targeted because of the expectation, and considerable evidence, that they are more likely than men are to use resources in support of family well-being (health, school fees).

The overall effects of this strategy for reducing poverty and/or empowering women are difficult to establish, but it is widely endorsed as a tool for alleviating poverty.[7] On the one hand, microcredit projects direct attention to poor rural women who face limited options and who may be able to realize entrepreneurial benefits from access to these loans. By widening their focus to include issues of social status and the world's poorest women, development agencies draw attention to women as clients of development and provide openings for addressing related gender issues and mobilizing resources (Keck and Sikkink 1998). And in contrast to conventional narratives of devalorization, enthusiasts for microcredit promote positive representations of women's capacities and "traditional" community values. These shifts provide opportunities and openings that target women as agents and beneficiaries; they therefore warrant feminist attention, action, and perhaps their selective endorsement.

On the other hand, microcredit initiatives make a number of problematic assumptions. They presume that the "solution" for ending poverty is to integrate the poor into commercial market activity by ensuring access to financial credit—what Spivak characterizes as "credit-baiting without infrastructural reform" (1999: 418); that poor people can be quickly and easily "rescued" by making small amounts of money available to them; and that poor people have the entrepreneurial skills and wider social system supports necessary for sustainable enterprises, including favorable market conditions. The premise here is that incorporation into circuits of capital enables successful competition and hence prosperity; in other words, capitalism can fix the (poverty) problem that capitalism produces. These initiatives additionally presume that women can simply take on additional work responsibilities, will have the support of family and community members to do so and to prosper, and will be able to control how the money is invested and the profits used. The premise is that institutionalized gender and class inequalities can be overlooked or easily transformed. Although microcredit projects often emerge from laudable intentions, Goetz and Gupta summarize a number of feminist concerns:

> Improvements in women's productivity, mobility, access to markets, literacy, social status, and control of household decisions takes [sic] time,

requires [sic] considerable commitment by development workers, a long-term investment in local-level processes of social changes, as well as a willingness to cope with the sometimes violent and disruptive consequences of challenging class and gender privilege. This is even more true when it comes to changing social attitudes toward women's right of ownership over resources and to assigning value to women's contributions to household well-being (1996: 61).

Critics raise other issues as well. A focus on microfinance avoids asking larger questions regarding the structural causes of poverty and its reproduction through neoliberal policies; the "quick-fix" of microcredit projects shifts support from longer-term and more socially oriented programs addressing the complexity of effective social change; and the foregrounding of quantifiable success indicators (repayment rates) deflects attention from the quality of women's participation and whether and in what ways empowerment actually occurs. We see the power of gender operating in several ways: the framing of development strategies through a "paternalistic colonial lens" (Bergeron 2003:168), the reproduction of gender stereotypes and unchanged distributions of household labor, and simplistic expectations regarding domestic, gender, and class relations in community settings. In these senses, microcredit initiatives exemplify both the promise and flawed delivery of "women-oriented" policies that we reflect on throughout this text: they are a too simplistic answer to complex problems. Such "solutions" to poverty are why the UN's Millennium Development Goals (MDGs) are so behind in being met and why these goals are so insufficient.

WOMEN AND DEVELOPMENT

Gender stereotypes are promulgated by dichotomized categories favored in economic analysis: paid-unpaid work, production-reproduction, skilled-unskilled, formal-informal. These interact with other gendered dichotomies that shape how we think about and valorize work: men's work-women's work, labor for profit–labor for love, working-caretaking, breadwinner-housewife, and so on. We note here that for the most part, these divisions are recent. Prior to modern state-making and industrial capitalism, rigid dichotomies were less familiar because all able-bodied family and community members were expected to contribute, work was therefore a more communal activity, and divisions between public and private spheres, paid and unpaid labor, were not yet institutionalized. Although specific tasks might be gender-coded, the particular coding varied greatly over time and across cultures, and activities in general were valued as necessary and complementary contributions to sustaining families and households. Processes of industrialization, Western modernization, and colonization were key to constituting more rigid, less equal, and thus less complementary conceptions of how labor should be divided between and among sexes, classes, and nations.

This Western division of labor was imposed on many cultures in the Americas, Asia, and Africa from the fifteenth to the twentieth centuries. In many instances, the economic status and well-being of women in diverse cultures were diminished by the patriarchal and political ideologies imposed by capitalist "modernization" processes. For example, farming in many African countries was almost exclusively women's work, and men were responsible for clearing fields, hunting, and warfare. Because Western colonizers assumed land should be "owned" and men should be the "heads of households" and hence the primary earners, they transferred land rights to men (away from women) and ensured that men (rather than women) received agricultural training and technological supports as well as access to cash and credit. Giving some men titles to small plots of land not expropriated by Europeans for plantation agriculture or other uses, and turning men as well as women into farm laborers—either as slaves or minimally paid workers—did not mean empowerment (enhanced capacity) for most colonized men. It favored men's positioning relative to women's, but not relative to those who gained from European colonization. As Gita Sen and Caren Grown observed, "The colonial period created and accentuated inequalities both 'among' nations, and between classes and genders (also castes, ethnic communities, races, etc.) 'within' nations" (1987: 24).

In spite of these earlier colonial interventions, women have continued to be the primary agricultural producers in many less-industrialized nations. Yet Western development strategies featuring aid, loans, and technical assistance have continued to favor landowning men as recipients of assistance, thus disregarding women's vital role in food production, and in many cases worsening the conditions of female farmers. For example, large-scale, highly mechanized farming to produce crops for export has undermined female farming systems that had been central to the maintenance of food self-sufficiency in many countries of the South. This also means that the majority of food is not grown for local or even national consumption but destined for the now global network of food circulation, which is problematic in terms of local health and larger environmental concerns. Moreover, the steady decline of value attributed to agricultural and other (non-oil) primary commodities is devastating for individuals and countries who depend on the sale of primary goods for their economic well-being. Individuals and countries find themselves without sufficient cash for purchasing food and other goods to meet even basic human needs. Top-down and arguably masculinist responses feature accelerating food production through large-scale mechanization, widespread use of chemical fertilizers, and even genetically modifying seeds, plants, and livestock. Although the "green revolution" initiated in the 1960s and more recent efforts have often been technically successful—more food has been produced—they have raised a host of new concerns and especially health and environmental issues.

WOMEN AND NEOLIBERAL GLOBALIZATION

Since approximately the 1970s, globalization has been driven primarily by neoliberal economic policies favored by geopolitical elites (mostly men), and especially, economists trained in the global North and acting as policymakers in international economic institutions (IMF, World Bank, WTO). Advocates of neoliberalism—also known as supply-side economics, the Washington consensus, or market fundamentalism—draw on neoclassical economic theory to argue that markets function most efficiently and productively, and generate the greatest overall prosperity, when they are unfettered by government regulation. Many advocates also claim that unconstrained markets "naturally" foster liberty, democracy, and more peaceful societies. From these assumptions, neoliberal advocates promote a combination of restructuring policies aimed at achieving "freedom" from state-imposed restrictions and opening national borders to create a "world" economy.

The code word of neoliberal capitalism is *liberalization*: ensuring a free market economy by removing governmental interference in and impediments to the "free" flow of money, goods, services, and capital (financial assets). Policy reforms are variously aimed at eliminating such restrictions (while continuing to constrain the movement of workers). *Deregulation* refers to relaxing or removing existing state controls, for example, on wages, prices, and foreign exchange rates, and reducing state regulatory functions, for example, in regard to protecting workers' rights and the environment. *Privatization* refers to replacing the "inefficiencies" of public ownership and control by reducing state ownership and management of enterprises (often those providing public goods and services, such as electricity, transportation, security) in favor of the private sector. Complementing these supply-side reforms are fiscal and monetary *stabilization policies* (to reduce government spending, deficits, and aggregate demand) that involve fewer public-sector jobs and a decrease in state expenditures on social programs (welfare, education, health). Finally, *specialization* in economic activities is promoted—based on the assumption of comparative advantage—and export-oriented policies are favored in pursuit of economic development and growth.

One widely noted effect of neoliberal policies has been the imposition by the IMF of structural adjustment programs (SAPs) in many developing countries. Unfortunately, these programs have eroded whatever gains were made earlier in getting public and private development lending agencies to recognize the importance of women's work and gender issues to successful economic development. Until recently, most critiques of neoliberal restructuring focused on the effects of SAPs in the South, where the costs have been starkly visible (Joekes and Weston 1995; *World Development* 1995; Rai 2002). Many of these countries seek foreign currency loans to finance continued or new debt obligations, and to secure such loans they must accept a variety of neoliberal conditions imposed by World Bank structural adjustment or IMF stabilization programs. Yassine Fall has provided a succinct description:

> Structural adjustment policies are meant to sustain and reinforce conditions that will invite foreign investors to exploit either the labor or natural resources of a country to produce foreign currency for balance of payments purposes and to repay national debt. They encourage the use of a

country's resources for export development rather than for domestic development (again to produce foreign currency to repay debt). They encourage the privatization of services, which reduces the autonomy of local governments and often generates massive unemployment. They encourage cuts in health, education, and social welfare budgets for the purpose of reducing deficits, leaving people, especially women and children who are already impoverished and disadvantaged, in desperate and life-threatening situations (2001: 71).

Because of their initial interest in women and development, feminists have generated the most extensive research on the effects of SAPs. Although there are important differences among countries subject to restructuring, cumulative studies reveal patterns: the enormous social costs of adjustment, increases in income inequality, tendencies toward social polarization that aggravate conflicts, shifts in control over resources, and the "existence of class, gender and ethnic biases in the adjustment process" (Benería 1995: 1844).

Neoliberal globalization is operating to produce similar patterns in "developed" economies, particularly since the end of the Cold War. Former Soviet bloc countries have instituted, also under pressure from Western governments and lending agencies, "shock therapy" programs designed by Western economists to quickly turn socialist economies into capitalist ones. These programs drastically cut and/or privatize government services while also privatizing production to increase productivity, exports, and foreign direct investment. In these countries, working-class women are disproportionately bearing the costs, and economic inequalities are expanding, as unemployment grows and socialized benefits, welfare supports, and medical services that were formerly available are no longer assured. Restructuring is most visibly gendered when we look at its effects on welfare provisioning, which is key to the reproduction of social groups. In large part due to feminist interventions, economic policy analysts now recognize that while the effects of restructuring have been most severe in the global South, there are parallel racialized gender and class effects in the North where cutbacks in public welfare also have their greatest impact on feminized populations: women and the poor.[8]

As economic conditions deteriorate, people seek work wherever they can find it, fueling internal and external labor migrations: to urban areas, export processing zones, seasonal agricultural sites, tourism locales, and anywhere jobs are presumed to exist. People are often "pushed" to move by colonial and capitalist processes that disrupt or destroy former livelihoods. For example, Eurocentric development strategies favor building large-scale industrial and urban infrastructures, often at the expense of small-scale and subsistence farming. This generates primarily male migrations especially to urban areas, mining or oilfield sites, and even distant locations where low- or semiskilled jobs are available. These migrations alter distributions of labor and resources within families, often leaving women full responsibility for agricultural tasks and household survival, or driving them to seek income generation locally or by migrating themselves. Too often, men attempting to find work and survive in distant cities or foreign countries eventually abandon their families, pushing many women into ever more constrained economic choices.[9]

On the "pull" side, women especially are sought as preferred workers where export manufacturing has been established (shaped by colonial histories, uneven capitalist development, and selective foreign direct investment). This preference is premised on familiar stereotypes of women as docile, reliable, and—due to their economic vulnerability—more accommodating, less rebellious, and indeed cheaper labor. Women's employment sometimes displaces men in these jobs, though employment for women tends to be short-lived due to the preference for very young women, the arduous work conditions, and high turnover rates. Moreover, as industry develops, labor-intensive processes decline in favor of capital-and technology-intensive production that generates fewer, and male-dominated, jobs. The overall effect is un- and underemployment in developing countries, further pushing men and women to seek whatever income they can, wherever they can.

In sum, historical inequalities shape whose vulnerability renders them subject to economic migration, what education and training they have received, and what forms of relatively devalorized labor they can access. Consistent with structural vulnerabilities and the nature of "unskilled" jobs available (cleaning, harvesting, domestic service, sex work), these workers tend to be marked (in combination with class) by ethnicity, race, and gender, and the work they find tends to be informal and feminized. In the context of neoliberal globalization, recent migration flows tend to reflect polarized opportunities: at the (masculinized) top an elite pool of highly skilled professionals and technicians flourishes (linked to transnational corporatist opportunities, and the "brain-drain" from developing countries), and at the (feminized) bottom a much larger and generally devalorized pool of semi- or unskilled workers who take whatever work is available (linked to urban areas, corporate agriculture, global cities, and the "care deficit" in the global North).

Being on the move affects personal and collective identities and cultural reproduction, creating new opportunities for some and new problems for others. Traditional family forms and divisions of labor are disrupted, destabilizing men's and women's identities and gender relations more generally. Consider that women now constitute half of all migrants, and where demand is greatest for personal service providers, care work, and domestic labor, women often outnumber men. The enormous care-deficit affects household reproduction transnationally, as women leave their own families to provide care for richer families, where divisions of labor are also reconfigured. Migrants encounter unfamiliar and often hostile environments, and their coping strategies may involve solidifying old or building new allegiances. Identity-based politics becomes a feature of global militarization when men—especially young men— who feel culturally humiliated or economically frustrated seek to "prove" their manhood in conflict situations—as combatants, private security guards, or conflict entrepreneurs. These examples suggest how shifting identities emerge from and carry gendered implications and have complex effects, whether expressed in women-identified communities, nationalist state building, ethnocultural diasporas, anti-immigrant racism, ethnic cleansing, or masculinist fundamentalisms.

PRODUCING CONSENT AND CRISIS

The advent and eventual institutionalization of neoliberal principles marked a turn away from dominant economic policymaking in the post–World War II era. We therefore need to consider how neoliberal ideology and practice became so taken for granted as "the way things are" in recent decades. In the first place, late-twentieth-century electronic and computer technologies dramatically enhanced the global and real-time circulation of information, and deregulation policies enabled unprecedented concentration of media power and control in very few national and transnational agencies and corporations. The result is that private capital and primarily business interests dominate the most powerful media worldwide, with crucial political implications for what news, issues, knowledge, stories, and advertising are broadcast. Although the Internet complicates claims regarding the dominance of broadcast media, the vast majority of the world's people get their information about and develop their understanding of national and global "realities" through the selective lens of these powerful media giants. And the lens they necessarily prefer is profit-oriented, and for the most part it is aligned with neoliberal capitalism. Hence, what most of us "know" beyond our personal experience and local realities emerges from exposure to an intentionally selective and narrow range of information that is shaped not only by commercial interests but inevitably, too, by the race, gender, sexual, and national interests embodied in those who decide what to publicize.

In the second place, business interests increasingly dominate even the most powerful and ostensibly democratic states, with crucial implications for what policies, programs, and national projects are funded and who the eventual winners and losers will be. On one hand, the growing influence of business on governance is the result of state officials internalizing neoliberal principles and ceding public, political authority to private, market-based decision-making. On the other hand, capitalism enables the concentration of resources in a minority of elite "haves" who typically want to have more, and they have more to contribute to the campaigns and lobbying efforts of those who share this agenda. Money is then translated into political power, undercutting democratic principles and further marginalizing "have-nots." When election outcomes, legislation, and priorities are increasingly determined by the rich, citizens effectively get the "best government that money can buy" and the policies that "best" reproduce concentrations of wealth.

Moreover, as we noted in Chapter 3, neoliberal governmentality merges global capitalism with "economic rationality" and instrumental logic as the appropriate criteria for governance. When corporate interests dominate the media, and monied interests dominate governance, people have a dangerously narrow understanding of "reality," and democratic processes have little chance of flourishing. A major consequence—and in spite of long-standing critiques and alternative visions by feminists and others—is that dominant economic and political interests have imposed and to a large extent "normalized" the logic of corporate capitalism as cultural common sense, and have ensured the acceptance of neoliberal ideology and policies as both desirable ("growth provides more for all") and anyway inevitable ("there is no alternative"). This is another way in which economics and politics interact—and in their dominant modalities today—generate entwined global crises.

Once in place, the hegemonic rules of the neoliberal game effectively compel all nations to act like corporate businesses: competing globally with each other for credit, resources, and markets and "cutting costs" to enhance their competitive position. Governments cut costs by cutting back on public expenditures (especially in regard to supporting health, welfare, education and training programs, and maintaining occupational safety and environmental protections, but rarely in regard to militarization), by eroding or prohibiting the power of organized labor and weakening workers' rights, and by restructuring the workforce to produce a lean and mean management system, a smaller core of permanent, secure employees, and a vast pool of informalized and flexibilized workers who are disproportionately women and other economically marginalized groups. One effect of slashing social services is that women's reproductive labor is made even more demanding because they must take on caretaking tasks for which the public sector is abandoning responsibility. As another effect, when public welfare is cut, those most in need of food, medical, and educational assistance—not least to secure employment in the restructured economy—are further marginalized. The general pattern is that neoliberal rules favor private capital and corporate shareholders (embodied primarily in elite males) at the expense of social reproduction, public welfare, and citizen stakeholders, at the same time that the growth imperative of neoliberal capitalism favors accumulation of wealth (for some) over social reproduction and environmental sustainability for all.

When the neoliberal model becomes operative, the market logic of global competition effectively compels all workers to identify with corporate interests. In other words, it becomes rational (within the logic of the system) for workers to effectively "discipline" themselves by accommodating cost-cutting measures and limiting labor demands in hopes of preventing business closures or the movement of jobs to other sites and even overseas. As workers internalize this logic, resistance appears futile; survival requires submission to market dictates and acceptance of ruthless competition as the only apparent choice when playing the only game in town. Discipline is diffuse but effective, as media ensure that workers everywhere are aware of global competition and systemic economic insecurities, and this awareness generates fearful and largely accommodating responses. At the same time, the cultural logic of profit-making respects no boundaries, as marketization penetrates even intimate spheres of social life: bodily functions, sexual relations, biological reproduction. Activities previously considered noncommercial, private, and even sacrosanct are increasingly commodified and drawn into circuits of capital accumulation. Reproductive ova and sperm, infants, human organs, sexualized bodies, intimate caring, sensual pleasures, and spiritual salvation are all for sale.

These developments may be rhetorically "reduced" to instances of "commodification," but they actually constitute enormously complex and ethically fraught quandaries that defy simplistic answers. How are questions of ownership, rights, and responsibilities resolved as private commercial interests transgress formerly "natural" boundaries (of bodies and sexual intimacies), expropriate indigenous knowledge (of plants and societies), and claim dominion over public goods (air, water, outer space)? How does democracy fare as neoliberalism erodes the regulatory capacity and public accountability of states in favor of unaccountable decentralized markets, international agencies, and private interest networks? The emerging questions and unfolding crises confront us with multiple challenges, and there are no easy answers. But as systemic insecurities mount and disturbing outcomes accumulate, we must avoid the familiar and too-easy response of blaming problems on marginalized or "suspect" groups: "irresponsible mothers," "drug-ridden (racialized) inner-city gangs," "job-stealing migrants," "unpatriotic dissidents," "anti-American foreigners," "Muslim extremists," and the faceless—but always also racialized—poor.

To conclude this section, we note that the cumulative effects of neoliberal restructuring and capitalism as a cultural logic are complex, uneven, and controversial. Not all women or historically marginalized groups are disadvantaged by economic restructuring processes. Some individuals with the appropriate skills, training, knowledge, experience, management style, access to credit and/or social class (as well as racial privilege) are able to do well in the restructured global economy. And in some countries of the South, an accelerated ICT sector has generated economic benefits to those with technical and language skills employed by transnational corporations, for instance, in telemarketing operations and computer support services. Nevertheless, we argue here, and demonstrate in the remainder of the chapter, that the overall trends and cumulative effects of neoliberal policies and the cultural logic of capitalism are not conducive to ameliorating economic inequalities, promoting social justice, or improving the environmental health of the planet.

GENDERING TODAY'S GLOBALIZED ECONOMY

Dominant accounts of GPE focus almost exclusively on market-based "productive" activities and the financial arrangements that fuel the economy. Conventional and continuing neglect of reproductive activities exemplifies the power of gender to bias our knowledge of economics by valorizing the (masculinized) public sphere of power and formal (paid) work, at the expense of the marginalized (feminized) family/private sphere of emotional, domestic, and caring (unpaid) labor. Yet all social life and economic production ultimately depend on reproductive activities, which therefore warrant much closer attention.

The Centrality of Reproductive Economic Activities

Socialization involves teaching infants how to behave according to the codes (meaning systems) of a particular culture; it is literally indispensable for the survival of individuals and groups and reproducing the economic order. It teaches us—and we internalize—beliefs regarding gendered identities, roles, and divisions of labor, as well as rules regarding what constitutes "work," who does what work, and how different kinds of work are valued. These lessons are not only about gender but inextricably about race/ethnicity, age, class, religion, nationality, and other axes of difference and differential valorization.

Effective socialization and social reproduction matters structurally for economics because it produces individuals who are ultimately able to "work," and this unpaid reproductive labor (done primarily by women) saves capital the costs of producing key inputs. In this way, capitalism benefits from the patriarchal ideology of states, religions, and heteronormative families that locates women in the home as loving caregivers and assigns them primary responsibility for social reproduction and sustaining the emotional and physical health of family members. Capitalism also benefits from socialization that ensures workers accept as "natural" the hierarchical divisions of labor, differential valorizations of workers and what work they do, and workers' subordination to managers and market-based objectives. In spite of relying on reproductive labor that produces workers, and family relations that relieve work-generated pressures, neoliberal globalization reduces the emotional, cultural, and material resources necessary for the well-being of most women and families. This is key to what we mean by a global "crisis in social reproduction," as women with less time, fewer options, decreased resources, and reduced social services are expected to meet increased labor and nurturing demands, cope with mounting insecurities, and ensure their own and the survival of dependent family members in the context of deepening structural violence (Ehrenreich and Hochschild 2002b; Bakker and Gill 2003; Bakker 2007).

Continuity and Change in Formal and Informal Economic Activities

What are conventionally referred to as "productive" economic activities are the most familiar because economists focus on them as "formal" economic activities—those that typically include earning wages or salaries and in most contexts are recorded by agencies and are in some way regulated and/or taxed by governments. Traditional economic framing distinguishes primary (natural resource, agricultural), secondary (industrial, manufacturing) and tertiary (services, information) production, but these distinctions are increasingly inadequate, especially as ICTs alter what is produced and how.

Changes in primary production are especially marked by technological developments and the steady decline in world prices of and demand for (nonoil) primary products and raw materials. "Declining terms of trade" (lower for primary, sustained or higher for manufactured and high-value-added commodities) are particularly devastating to (feminized) nations where manufacturing capacity is underdeveloped and/or primary production dominates. To compete for credit and markets, states may advertise the availability of "cheap" and/or docile (feminized) labor and nonunionized, environmentally unregulated worksites, or encourage out-migration of workers in hopes of easing unemployment pressures and securing foreign remittances.

Secondary production is being transformed by "deindustrialization." This involves two shifts: first, from material-based and more often unionized factory manufacturing to knowledge-based manufacturing (e.g., computer games), and second, a decline in well-paying, relatively skilled and secure (masculinized) jobs in favor of low-paying, semi- or unskilled and insecure (feminized) jobs. The point here is that manufacturing remains important but declines in value relative to the higher status and earnings of ICT-based work, which reflects a larger global trend in production and employment: from manufacturing to services. Because service jobs tend to be either skilled high-wage (professional-managerial jobs; read "masculinized") or semi-, unskilled, and poorly paid (personal, cleaning, retail, and clerical services; read: "feminized"), this shift amplifies existing income inequalities between males and females, skilled and unskilled workers, and developed and developing nations.

In order to be more competitive by "cutting costs" (especially of labor), firms and nations take measures to render their operations more flexible. "Flexibilization" in general refers to shifts in production processes: to more spatially dispersed networks and decentralized control (the global assembly line; subcontracting), to increasingly casualized (nonpermanent, part-time) and informalized (unregulated, noncontractual) jobs, to small batch, "just in time" (short-term rather than long-term) production planning, and to avoidance or prohibition of organized labor. At the core of flexibilization are efforts to deregulate production processes and labor markets—hence, increasing freedom for management—ostensibly to eliminate inefficient rigidities imposed by regulation and to ensure that the "freedom of the market" is unconstrained. Here the discourse of neoliberalism invokes flexibility as essential for competitive success and as an inherently positive practice and orientation. In contrast, critics argue that flexibilization erodes hard-won workers' rights and constitutes a retreat from the progressive agenda of achieving what the International Labor Organization (ILO) characterizes as "decent work" for all workers.

Cutting back on the workforce is most visible as loss of employment for significant numbers of workers, especially those holding what were previously regarded as full-time, permanent, protected, or secure positions. But a more apt generalization refers not simply to unemployment per se but to the polarization of available employment, with increasing opportunities for those who "fit" the demands of postindustrial or informational capitalism. At the top end are valorized (masculinized and primarily elite male) workers sought for their technical, informational, and knowledge-based skills. At the bottom are those in demand as semi- or unskilled workers: They are valuable to employers and for the accumulation of global capital but are devalorized by their location in feminized jobs. In fact, we argue that flexibilization constitutes *feminization* of employment, understood simultaneously as a material, embodied transformation of labor markets (increasing proportion of women, deteriorating work conditions for men), a conceptual characterization of deteriorated and devalorized labor conditions (less desirable, meaningful, safe, or secure), and a reconfiguration of worker identities (feminized managers, female breadwinners). As jobs require fewer skills, and flexibilization becomes the norm, employers seek workers who are perceived to be undemanding (unorganized), docile but reliable, available for part-time and temporary work, and willing to accept low wages.[10] Gender stereotypes depict women as especially suitable for these jobs, and gender inequalities render women especially desperate for access to income. In short, as more jobs are casual, irregular, flexible, and precarious (read: feminized), more women—and feminized men—are doing them.

Although neoliberal policies have the effect of decreasing formal—especially permanent, secure, decent—employment, they also spur phenomenal growth in "informal"—unregulated, unprotected, and insecure—economic activities. Until recently, conventional accounts paid little attention to informal activities, which were trivialized as remnants of "incomplete modernization" associated with "traditional" (read: non-European) societies. But economists are increasingly aware that informal activities are inextricable from and indeed make possible the "productive" economy, in part because they are inextricable from flexibilization: The outsourcing and subcontracting processes of flexibilization shift production toward less formal, regularized, and regulated work conditions; the erosion of labor power accompanying flexibilization exacerbates the decline in family income that "pushes" more people into informal work; and flexibilization reduces tax revenues, which exacerbates the decline in welfare provisioning, and spurs informal work to compensate in part for this loss.

How to define and measure informal activities is controversial, but all observers agree that the value and extent of these activities have increased dramatically in recent decades and that this phenomenal growth poses a variety of economic, analytical, and normative challenges.[11] Women especially rely on informal activities as a survival strategy to ensure social reproduction: They are overrepresented in informal activities worldwide; the informal economy is the primary source of earnings for women in most developing countries; women are the majority of part-time informal workers in rich countries; and the gender gap that persists globally is even wider in the informal than in the formal economy.[12] In the next sections we expose the power of gender in today's GPE by considering work that blurs formal-informal distinctions.

Homeworkers

The practice of subcontracting or "outsourcing" as key to flexibilized production has generated explosive growth in "homework" or home-based production.[13] Homework is not a residual form of production but in fact integral to industrialization and current restructuring processes: It exposes the blurred boundaries between unpaid housework, paid informal work, and formal waged labor. Global growth in homeworking is attributable to several factors: corporate desires to cut labor and overhead costs by outsourcing production tasks (e.g., sewing, light assembly work) that can be performed by subcontracted laborers in their homes anywhere in the world; large pools of migrant and immigrant workers who are drawn into homework because of racist and sexist discrimination and restrictive immigration laws that prevent them from working in the formal sector; and increasing pressures on women to generate income in support of household survival. These same factors are also associated with the reappearance of sweatshops in the North as well as the South, where (immigrant) women and children toil at sewing machines, typically under unsafe and "hidden" conditions, to produce designer clothing and niche market commodities as part of "just-in-time" production. Women especially are sought for homework because they are considered available and reliable, and their below-subsistence earnings are justified as merely "supplemental" income. Employers may also promote homework as a means of gaining more control over labor by decentralizing and thus undercutting traditional sites of unionization and the development of solidarity among workers. Subcontracting to (female) homeworkers can reap the additional benefit of controlling workers through masculinist ideologies and practices.

The practice of homework differs between rich and poor countries, and within them depending on a variety of local factors. Most homeworkers in the North are married women who have dependent children; they may be poor or middle-class and in urban or rural areas (Dangler 2000: 63). The decline in real wages and benefits due to restructuring has especially fueled the growth of homeworking among working-class families. At the same time, the comparatively advanced infrastructure in the North has increased the number of skilled workers who may prefer working at home. In the South, petty commodity production and informal activities more generally have been and remain significant. In the face of deteriorating economic conditions, declining household incomes ("pushing" women to generate income), limited labor opportunities, and obstacles to wage employment, women undertake homework to ensure the social reproduction of the household and sometimes sheer survival.

In spite of widely varying conditions, we can observe the power of gender to shape patterns in homework. Not least, gendered stereotypes and ideologies render homework an "attractive" option for families and a profitable policy for firms. As one researcher commented, homework "enables women and men to resolve temporarily the contradictions between women's patriarchally defined roles as wives and mothers and the demand for cheap female labor that subsidizes male labor and factories" (Ward 1990: 21). Like informal activities more generally, homework is very poorly paid, and this is justified by characterizing homework as an extension of (unpaid) housework or merely supplementary income. The increasing reliance of the formal economy on the informal economy to produce goods and services under poor working conditions and at extremely low pay rates begins to explain why it is that at a time when women are entering the formal workforce in record numbers, the global phenomenon of the "feminization of poverty" is increasing.

Domestic Labor

In addition to homework, another burgeoning transnational economy of a "domestic" nature is the "maid-trade" (Chin 1998; Anderson 2000; Ehrenreich and Hochschild 2002b), in which gender is not only pervasive but also clearly racialized. Domestic work is called that because it is assumed to occur in a private location—"behind closed doors"— typically a family household or the "temporary home" afforded by commercial accommodations when people are on the move. In addition to the unpaid domestic work of most women in their own homes, class-privileged women and families often seek domestic workers to maintain their homes and care for their children. This transference of domestic labor may be due to employment by the "woman of the house" that precludes her doing it or to sufficient resources that she need not do it herself. In a less familial but still domestic sense, tourist hotels, conference facilities, training and research institutions, and global cities depend on a large number of maids, cooks, and cleaning workers, as well as other service providers.

Domestic work is a rapidly growing global business involving vast networks of people and agencies that facilitate transnational flows, such as money-lenders, airlines, hotels, translation services, training institutions, and banks. It is important to note that payments for domestic work, and especially caregiving work related to a health provision, constitute an important source of foreign remittances for countries of origin[14] and reduce labor costs in receiver countries. In spite of providing socially necessary labor, domestic workers typically reap few benefits and face multiple hardships—especially women who migrate for these jobs. Gender stereotypes associate cleaning and caretaking as women's work; domestic work is understood to be unskilled; it attracts women who need paid work, have little (valued) training, may require housing accommodation, and/or seek work where citizenship status is not monitored. Not surprisingly, domestic workers in private households are often immigrant women. As noncitizens, and even nonnative speakers, they are particularly vulnerable to employer intimidation and abuse occurring in spaces that are understood to be separate from the public gaze and state regulation. Domestic workers who "live in" are especially subject to a variety of exploitative practices: they work long hours and may even be considered "on call" 24 hours a day; they are typically paid very poorly and may have few resources or time for venturing beyond the household; their activities and personal behavior are closely scrutinized; and their live-in status makes them especially vulnerable to sexual exploitation or being construed as "promiscuous or exotic" due to racialized stereotypes (Pettman 1996: 192).

Wives and mothers who pay other (often racialized and migrant) women to do "their" domestic work avoid disrupting gendered divisions of labor within the household, but at the expense of exacerbating class (and often racial and national) divisions among women. While it ostensibly favors the "woman of the house," hiring domestic workers effectively relieves pressure on men to do their share of caring labor, and relieves pressure on states to provide childcare and support social reproduction. These dynamics are further complicated by the fact that many—perhaps most—domestic workers are themselves married women with children, many of whom face the stark choice of either living with their children in poverty or earning desperately needed money by living away from them (Ehrenreich and Hochschild 2002a: 2; Young 2001: 57). Who hires and who serves may reflect colonial histories (black maids of white madams in South Africa) or newer hierarchies of international debt and employment opportunities (Filipino maids in Saudi Arabia). But in all cases it appears that cultural and racial stereotyping occurs in terms of preferred—"suitable" or "trusted"—domestic workers. As Anderson observes, "racist stereotypes intersect with issues of citizenship, and result in a racist hierarchy which uses skin color, religion, and nationality to construct some women as being more suitable for domestic work than others" (2000: 2).

Ehrenreich and Hochschild argue that migration for domestic work is part of a "worldwide gender revolution": As men are increasingly unable to meet traditional breadwinner roles, women are compelled to work outside of the home, which generates the larger question of "who will take care of the children, the sick, the elderly? Who will make dinner and clean house?" (2002a: 3). Domestic work exemplifies the socially necessary labor upon which all else depends. But it is hard to measure objectively, and the commodification of personal, private, and intimate services is also socially and morally controversial. Whether commodified or not, the intangible, emotional aspects of caring labor elude conventional economic theory but are crucial to domestic work—and to paid labor and the economic order more generally. These subjective and cultural aspects extend into an even more controversial regime of labor intimacy: the international political economy of sex.

International Sex Work

There is tremendous variation in how, why, and in what form women (and men)[15] participate in "sex work" (the commercialization of sex). Participation may be on a temporary or part-time basis, as a weekend or full-time job, or intermittently in the many ways made possible by ICTs and especially the Internet. In contrast to the conventional, narrow meaning of "prostitution," sex workers engage in a wide range of activities: as escorts, strippers, exotic dancers, erotic entertainers, people engaging in sexual practices, or being observed in sexual performance. Pornographic videos are tremendously popular and profitable, but prostitution, and the trafficking of women and children for that purpose, feature more prominently in international accounts of sex work.[16] Prostitution is the most frequently studied—and the most sensationalized—version of sex work; as an international industry, it particularly exposes linkages between private fantasies, gender and other sexual stereotypes, economic stratifications, and global markets.

To analyze the international political economy of sex is, however, to enter treacherous terrain: conceptually, for the ethical and political issues at stake; and materially, for the bodies and underground economies involved. The conceptual difficulties center on our discomfort and ambivalence regarding sex as a public topic, whether in terms of research, regulation, or commercialization. Like the commodification of caring and domestic labor, sex for purchase is controversial, and analyzing sex work is particularly problematic for feminists. On the one hand, due to heteropatriarchal identities, ideologies, and practices, it is *female* bodies that are most objectified, manipulated, violated, and physically harmed. This makes the sex industry—including advertising, pornography, videos, prostitution, and trafficking—a particular concern to critics of women's subordination. On the other hand, sex is a profoundly personal and intimate realm of human activity, which cautions against simplistic and moralizing pronouncements regarding appropriate, desirable, or despicable sexual conduct. So whereas the violence entailed in coercing sexual activities or trafficking people for such purposes must be condemned, evaluating the array of sexual activities one might voluntarily engage in—commercially or otherwise—is problematic.

The point here is to recognize the complexity of these issues, and in particular, the cultural diversity regarding sexual norms and the varying, multidimensional and context-dependent reasons for engaging in sex work; also to resist the tendency—well-represented in the literature—to demonize "prostitutes" (more so than their pimps and procurers) and/or neglect the *agency* of women as sex workers.[17] These points are cogently made by Agustín (2007) in her recent study of migrant sex workers and the European social workers and activists dedicated to "helping them." In particular, she exposes the self-importance of middle-class women (normalized by Eurocentric imperialism), their presumption of moral clarity and cultural superiority, and their denial of voice and agency to non-European women while claiming to aid them through "rescue."

This example illustrates how sex workers are devalued by the patriarchal dichotomy pitting good/moral/upright/marriageable women against bad/immoral/fallen/"usable" women, and how the former contribute to the devalorization and silencing of the latter when they reproduce the patriarchal dichotomy. The sex industry exacerbates hierarchies among women in yet other ways. Racially there is a hierarchy among prostitutes reflecting which women are constructed as "sexually appealing" (Asian women represented as exotic and "hospitable") and which are valued as comfortably "European" (women from transitional economies represented as culturally "European," feminine but not feminist). Hanochi also notes hierarchies among sex workers themselves, based on countries of origin and types and "class" of sexual work (2001: 144). More starkly, Pettman reports that although Australian sex workers are likely to insist on condom use, Australian brothels promote their Asian sex workers as available to customers without this protection (1997: 103). These examples reveal that it is not only poverty but masculinist ideologies filtered through stereotypes of race, culture, and nationality that constrain women's economic choices, construe women as sexual servicers, and construct some women as more attractive and some as more "disposable" than others.

The supply side of the sex industry primarily involves women in need of income-generating opportunities, typically in the context of limited employment options, deteriorating economic conditions, and increasing pressures to earn money for oneself or one's family. Some sex workers view their participation as a positive choice, others situate their choice in the context of realistic and limited options, others apparently have very little freedom of choice, and at the extreme are women and children literally coerced into sex work and sometimes trafficked far from home. Definitions of trafficking vary, from literally abducting women to intentionally misleading women who are seeking work and then coercing them into the sex trade by threats of violence against them (or family members), actual violence, and psychological intimidation. Trafficked individuals are subject to many forms of direct and indirect violence, and even for those who escape, returning home may no longer be an option: Families may not welcome a "fallen woman," and marriage prospects may be nonexistent. For most sex workers, there is little public sympathy or assistance; they are stereotyped as "immoral" and held responsible for sex scandals and even the violence committed against them.

As in studies of the international drug trade and illegal immigration, the demand side of the sex industry is rarely questioned or investigated. Masculinist ideologies construct men as naturally eager for and often in pursuit of sex, so that "demand" for women's sexual services—from hospitality hostesses and erotic entertainment to temporary or permanent rights over a woman's body—and a sense of entitlement to women's bodies are taken for granted as "the way things are."[18] Prostitutes face a number of risks, yet the men who seek them out and typically exacerbate those risks are rarely arrested or even stigmatized for their role in the demand side of the sex industry. Women are especially vulnerable if they lack citizenship or are working where "prostitution" is illegal. Pimps, of course, take advantage of these vulnerabilities to threaten and manipulate sex workers, to maintain their sense of insecurity and reliance on pimps, and to reap maximum profits off of women's work.

The sex industry is especially represented as a feature of Southeast Asia, where decades of sex work around U.S. military bases now overlap with sex tourism as a dimension of economic development strategies. As in the case of preferred domestic workers, cultural and racial stereotyping occurs in terms of the most desirable sex workers. Eurocentric gender ideology is infused with racist categorizations of sexualized "natures": white women are often construed as prudish and almost asexual, while black women (and men) are seen as wild and even oversexed. Asian women, however, have been marketed as "perfect" sexual playthings for Western or Westernized men. They are described as childlike and virginal and thus appropriately submissive and nonthreatening; yet they are also presented as extremely responsive and sexually experienced. The combination suggests that Asian women want only to please men and, moreover, know how to do it.

Asian women, however, are only a part of the global sex industry, made more visible by media preoccupations with "exotic" women and sensationalized reporting of trafficked women and children in impoverished countries. In reality, prostitution and sex work more generally exist worldwide. They appear, however, to be increasing as economic conditions deteriorate, ICTs afford novel and elusive activities, and geopolitical developments alter migration flows. Who buys and who sells may vary, but similar to domestic work, in all cases it appears that cultural and racial stereotyping occurs in terms of preferred—desirable, exotic, submissive—sex workers. Ehrenreich and Hochschild offer this explanation:

> Immigrant women may seem desirable sexual partners for the same reason that First World employers believe them to be especially gifted as caregivers: they are thought to embody the traditional feminine qualities of nurturance, docility, and eagerness to please. Some men feel nostalgic for these qualities, which they associate with a bygone way of life. Even as many wage-earning Western women assimilate to the competitive culture of "male" work and ask respect for making it in a man's world, some men seek in the "exotic Orient" or "hot-blooded tropics" a woman from the imagined past (2002a: 9–10).

Interpreting these shifts in formal and informal work is controversial. Some individuals prosper in a less regulated environment, for example, in microenterprises (favored by neoliberal development agencies) where innovation may breed success and multiplying effects; in developing countries where informal activities are crucial for income generation;

and in criminal activities that are big business worldwide. Critics argue that flexibilization and informalization favor capital over labor and hence exacerbate economic inequalities; and more generally, that avoidance of regulations is directly and indirectly bad for wages, workers, the environment, and long-term prospects for societal and global well-being. Feminists expose how these shifts reproduce women as cheap labor, drive women to informal and precarious work as a survival strategy, and exacerbate inequalities among women and within as well as between rich and poor states. Many feminists are also critical of antitrafficking policies (arising primarily out of the Bush administration in recent years) that fail to distinguish between sex work and trafficking; are steeped in moralizing, rescue, and punishment discourses; root the problem in the actions of only "bad" men of the global South; and leave "rescued" women still subject to the neoliberal economic processes that impoverish them and circumscribe their choices.

GENDERED FINANCIAL MATTERS

For three decades, neoliberal policies have been altering not only production processes and the value of "work," but financial arrangements and the value of "money." In brief, and necessarily oversimplified: Deregulation enabled tremendous expansion of cross-border capital flows—of bonds, loans, currencies, equities, and so on—that afforded new opportunities to create profits ("wealth") not through the real economy of production, commodities, consumption and trade, but by trading in capital (financial) assets—in effect making money off of money. What matters is that these processes of wealth creation are based less on exchanges in the "real" economy of goods and services than on *perceptions*—primarily in the minds of male traders and financial investors—of expected revenues and potential risks. Although the bubble of inflated perceptions generates mind-boggling wealth for some, for a while, when it bursts it has devastating effects on the many.

Because it is not generated in the "real" economy and does not conform to conventional economic expectations, the market value of this wealth ("credit money") is in an important sense out of sync with the "real" economy and its "commodity" money. But this does not mean that the real economy (of goods and services, prices and wages) is insulated from the dynamics of global finance. Rather, prices "set" in financial markets, especially through interest and exchange rates (whether these are high, low, or unstable) have effects throughout the socioeconomic order. They shape, for example, whether investments are directed toward trade, financial instruments, or human resources; whether production is labor-intensive or capital-and-technology-intensive; and how labor markets are structured (what types of labor, where located, with what compensation, and under what conditions). When financial matters assume priority, status and decision-making power within businesses, governments, and IGOs shift to those who "manage money" and "know" how to invest. Access to credit becomes decisive for individuals and states and is deeply structured by familiar hierarchies: women, the poor and those who are un- and under-employed face much greater obstacles when credit is sought. Financial markets thus have pervasive effects, and when they are free of governmental regulation, their effects are primarily to enhance concentrations of wealth among elites.

The point to notice here is that the allure of financial trading shifts attention and funding from long-term investments in industry, infrastructure, and human (social) capital, and thus exacerbates the conditions of extreme inequality and crises of social reproduction and sustainability we identify in this text. As the world is currently experiencing, instability of financial markets increases *risks* that are socialized—hurting public welfare because the collectivity pays rather than those who inflated the bubble and variously profited from it. Examining the generation of crises and their effects reveals the power of gender in operation. First, women and gender-sensitive analyses are absent—or at best marginalized—in the decision-making processes and analytical assessments of the financial order. Women are underrepresented in the institutions of global finance, a model of elite agency and (instrumental) economic "efficiency" is deemed common sense, and the masculinism of financial players and their practices is presumed. Second, these exclusions and blinders filter what elite analysts are able—or willing—to "see," especially the dangers of short-term greed and the arrogance of power. They particularly obscure the gendered costs of crises: loss of secure jobs and earning capacity due to women's concentration in precarious forms of employment; lengthened work hours for women as they cushion the impact on household income; decreased participation of girls in education and deteriorated health conditions for women; increased child labor and women's licit and illicit informal activities; and increased structural violence as well as direct violence against women.[19] These costs have important long-term effects: Girls and women are less able to participate as full members of society, and have fewer skills required for safe and secure income-generation, and the intensification of women's work with fewer resources imperils social reproduction more generally. At the same time, entire societies are affected as deteriorating conditions of social reproduction, health, and education have ongoing consequences.

GENDERED POLITICS OF CONSUMPTION

Market processes involve the production of goods and services, the circulation of cash or credit for purchasing them, and the creation of consumer desires that shape what we purchase. A great deal of attention and resources goes into producing both consumer *subjectivities* and a totalizing market *culture* that encourages consumption and the desire for "more." The power of gender operates through marketing, advertising, and deepening the commodification of social life and relations. The politics of advertising—who decides what we "want"—is explicitly about using cultural codes to manipulate consciousness and create ever-changing tastes and fashions. Stereotypes of gender, ethnicity/race, sexuality, and age are used strategically and prominently in advertising to project selective images of bodies, cultures, sexualities, and lifestyles as the "most desired" and "most desirable." Arts and entertainment are also big business on a global scale where selling sex, sensationalism, and stereotypes of "good" and "bad" cultures is a lucrative strategy. Popular music and videos feature sexual themes that are increasingly more explicit, graphic, and violent. Women's bodies continue to be objectified, and their sexual interests are either trivialized or exaggerated into *causes* of male desperation, perversion, and destruction. Demonized peoples are exploited, abused, and even slaughtered with abandon—cast as disposable and categorically disposed of in the name of a "higher" cause.

Although affluent consumption is the privilege of only a small elite, it shapes the desires, choices, and valorization of those without affluence. Pervasive advertising and global media encourage even the poorest to desire consumer goods as an expression of self-worth. Northern desires for cheap goods as well as luxury items—clothes, cars, electronics, flowers, furs, diamonds, gasoline—determine Southern patterns of production, including poorly paid workers, hazardous work conditions, and environmentally unsound practices. Even political activities shift to market-based expressions: Identity-based groups become particular targets of marketing and use consumption as an identity "marker," and political action is increasingly consumer-based as people "vote" through what they do and do not buy. But we might ask: Whose needs, desires, and interests are served by consumerism? Whose bodies and environments are devalorized—rendered disposable—in pursuit of consumerism and the neoliberal commitment to growth (rather than redistribution) that fuels it? These questions become focal as we shift our attention to gendered divisions of resources.

GENDERED RESOURCES

The devalorization of the environment upon which industrial capitalism and more recent neoliberal globalization rest has led to a wide array of resource shortages and maldistributions, ecological degradations, and "natural" disasters, the most serious of which in terms of global impact is the onset of global warming. Although there is finally a global scientific and even global political consensus that global warming is "manmade" by largely industrial pollutants, this has not yet caused a fundamental rethinking of commitments to neoliberal globalization that might curb this ecological meltdown.

Naomi Klein (2007) has recently traced the historical relationship between "free market fundamentalism," initially championed by the Chicago School of neoclassical economists and imposed systematically from South to North and East to West since the Cold War period, and various economic, political, and "natural" disasters. Although she does not provide an epidemiology of the relationship between global warming and such disasters as Hurricane Katrina in 2005 and the Southeast Asian tsunami in 2004, she argues that these "natural" shocks were able to wreak such destruction and loss of human life because of the "policy trinity" of neoliberal globalization—"the elimination of the public sphere, total liberation for corporations, and skeletal social spending" (Klein 2007: 15). The range of social and technological safety nets that would have better protected people and their environments when disasters struck was structurally undermined by a free market ideology that transferred resources from public services and works to private corporate hands. Moreover, she argues that such "natural" disasters, rather than serving as wake-up calls to shift resources back into serving public needs, have actually accelerated private accumulation, deepened human immiseration, and worsened environmental vulnerability. She calls this purposive use of calamities, including environmental ones, to enrich corporations at the expense of human welfare and environmental stability "disaster capitalism," which relies on a neoliberal capitalist "shock doctrine" that works in the following way:

> the coup, the terrorist attack, the market meltdown, the war, the tsunami, the hurricane—puts the entire population into a state of collective shock. The falling bombs, the bursts of terror, the pounding winds serve to soften up whole societies much as the blaring music and blows of the torture cells soften up prisoners. Like the terrorized prisoner who gives up the names of comrades and renounces his faith, shocked societies often give up things they would otherwise fiercely protect (Klein 2007: 17).

We would further argue that this softening up constitutes a feminizing of populations in relation to capital, and racism, classism, and sexism operate to determine who and what is disposable, enabling further extractions of resources and violations of human and civil rights with relative impunity. Indeed, as Klein points out, in the wake of "natural" disasters such as Hurricane Katrina, land developers, corporate contractors, and the politicians who allied with them saw an opportunity to "clean out" the majority poor African American population hardest hit and to start with a "clean slate." Their objective was not to "rebuild" what was lost for the people who lost it, but rather to "reconstruct" selected spaces in ways that were most profitable for private industry and least affordable for those who were dislocated (Klein 2007: 8).

GENDERED DIVISIONS OF RESOURCES

Although the racist and classist dimensions of the vulnerability to and the aftermath of Katrina have been heavily exposed, less well known are its impacts on women specifically. According to a U.S. Institute for Women's Policy Research (IWPR) report (Jones-DeWeever 2008), poor women in New Orleans suffered particularly from further impoverishment and disease but also higher incidences of domestic violence and loss of childcare as well as loss of jobs and health benefits. A United Nations Environment Program (UNEP) report (Seager and Hartmann 2005) also found that 20 percent more women were killed than men in the Southeast Asian tsunami in 2004, in part because they were not warned, could not swim, and/or could not leave the house alone. As WEDO (2008) argues, because women constitute the majority of the poor and suffer most from gender discrimination, they "are the first to lose their homes and their jobs after weather-related disasters, and the last to receive credit, technical help and education on energy and resource conservation." Thus, the majority of the world's women, most of whom inhabit the global South economically and racially, have particular stakes in confronting climate change and reversing the gender, race, and class environmental apartheid and triage that have contributed to it and that are being reimposed in its wake.

As WEDO also points out, poor women are not just on the frontlines of global warming but also central to reversing it. In addition to the fact that women in aggregate have smaller carbon footprints than men in aggregate because they have fewer resources, less control over resources, and "own less than 2 percent of the world's private land" (Ghosh 2007: 444), poor women, as the producers of 60 to 80 percent of food consumed in households and the primary suppliers of water and fuel to households in the global South, have been most active in seeking to conserve and replenish natural resources vital to their families and communities (WEDO 2008). For example, the women's tree-planting Green Belt

Movement in Kenya—for which its founder, Wangari Maathai, received a Nobel Peace Prize—has been planting trees in mountain regions that by 2017 will absorb 375,000 tons of carbon dioxide, while also repairing soil erosion, enabling rainfall retention for farming and electricity, and providing income for poor women (WEDO 2007a). The Green Belt Movement began as a grass-roots women's movement, but this particular project, started in 2006, is being supported by the World Bank's Community Redevelopment Carbon Fund. This "partnership" is a result of linkages that were made between gender inequality and environmental crises by women's movements during the UN Decade for Women and at the UN Environmental Summit in Rio de Janeiro in 1999—linkages that IGOs have only begun to recognize very unevenly. As WEDO (2007a) observes, although "every major global agreement on sustainable development acknowledges the importance of gender equality," the UN Framework Convention on Climate Change (UNFCCC) and the 1997 Kyoto Protocol that facilitates this treaty "are narrowly focused on emissions reductions, rather than social impacts" and social solutions. The largest contributor to greenhouse gases per capita, the United States, has thus far refused to ratify the Kyoto Protocol (yet China as the highest emitter has signed it), and by 2007 only two countries had used a gender perspective in their climate change initiatives reported to UNEP (WEDO 2007a). Moreover, the MDG focused on environmental sustainability has no targets or indicators that address gender inequality as a source of or solution to environmental breakdown, even though there are targets and indicators that address access to clean water and sanitation, reducing emissions, and increasing biodiversity (UNIFEM 2008: 130–131).

Contemporary official resistance to making the connection between gender inequality and global warming has its roots in the rise of Western colonization. This undermined communal land use and women's land rights. In addition, the rise of Western science transformed peoples' notions of nature and instituted a worldview that saw nature strictly as a resource for Eurocentric, "man-made" projects, thus discrediting belief systems associated with "primitive" cultures in which nature was revered as a manifestation of feminine divinity. Early Western science, coupled with Christian ideology, still thought of nature as feminine; but rather than powerful and goddesslike, nature was seen as a passive resource from which European men could take anything they needed or wanted without care for the effects of their interventions. This attitude paved the way for rapacious land-use patterns and technologies, which have led to numerous ecological crises since the advent of the industrial revolution (Merchant 1980). Western gender ideology continues to construe nature as a passive resource to be exploited, controlled, used, and abused. On the flip side, the concomitant racialization of nature as brute and savage during the colonial period has justified efforts to tame it for (white) "man's" purposes ever since. As these ideologies spread, environmental crises have followed, culminating in the contemporary problems of acid rain and global dumping to ozone depletion and global warming.

If we look through the lens of the *gendered divisions of resources*, we see that gender and race ideology contributes to the growth and perpetuation of these problems. The increasingly global aspects of the gendered divisions of resources rest upon dichotomies of culture-nature, active-passive, subject-object, users-resources, advanced-primitive, and exploitation-stewardship. These dichotomies are manifested in the contemporary situation in which women, especially in the global South, have a great deal of responsibility for caring for the environment but little say in how it will be used and for what purposes.

Neoliberal globalization has also ensured that environmental issues are subsumed to the interests of capital, constituting a colonization of nature itself while also naturalizing inequalities. As Nandita Ghosh puts it:

> Promoting market values above all else also reduces complex human relationships with nature to ego-driven, need-based interactions. Nature is also perceived as universal and encompassing of all human society. Here too it is externalized and can be used to justify the "natural" ethnic, sexual, and class oppressions that are always gendered. Both ideologies obfuscate the contributions of human labor to the process by which nature is externalized, produced, and consumed (2007: 446).

This "marketization of nature" also pits "diverse cultures and ecosystems against the privatization and enclosure" of the global resource "commons" (Ghosh 2007: 446), but the neoliberal governmentality or "biopolitics" of Empire intervenes to "control and diffuse a diversity of crises" in the interest of capital (Ghosh 2007: 447) at the same time as whole populations (and one could argue the earth itself) are consigned to what Giorgio Agamben (1998) calls "bare life," a "state of exception" in which legal rights are suspended and bodies are excluded from moral calculus (Ghosh 2007: 448). This enables the continuation of the "shock doctrine" even as IGOs and their member states claim to be addressing environmental crises, but in ways that do not unduly disturb capital or the disposability of gendered, raced, classed, and sexualized bodies.

Gendered Resource Depletion

Although it was only recently that food safety, water access, and energy self-sufficiency became mantras of world politicians and took center stage in debates about global warming and global trade, it was poor, rural women in the global South who first alerted the world about what Gita Sen and Caren Grown (1987) called the "food-fuel-water crises" back in the 1980s. Like the proverbial canaries in the mineshaft, women in subsistence economies bore the initial brunt and continue to be on the front lines of these crises that are due to resource depletion. Women's displacement from the land by large-scale agricultural development for export has contributed to high levels of famine, particularly in Africa. But there are additional consequences of this displacement, contributing not only to continued hunger but also to deforestation and desertification. Women are the main food producers and processors in most of the rural areas of the global South, and they must have access to clean water and firewood for fuel. As their land is lost to corporate farms and as water sources are polluted by agricultural runoff from fertilizers and pesticides or suspended by large-scale dam projects or privatization efforts, rural women and children are forced to travel farther and farther in search of clean water, spending as much as 40 billion hours per year in this pursuit in Africa alone (UNIFEM 2008: 130).

Similarly, as forests are cut down for large-scale agricultural, industrial, tourist, or even residential enterprises, women must go farther afield to look for the firewood needed to cook and to boil water, making it safe to drink. This has exposed them even more to the "firestick" rapes in such places as the DRC and the Darfur region of Sudan. When water and fuel sources are being depleted, not only does food become scarce, but also the basis for ecologically sound agricultural practices is eroded. First, female subsistence farmers are forced to cultivate small plots of land repeatedly rather than engage in crop rotation. Monoculture depletes vital soil nutrients and can eventually even lead to small-scale desertification. Large-scale desertification is the result of the overuse of crop lands by corporate farmers who do not rotate crops, and who overwater and salinate the soil and/or grow crops using methods that destroy fragile topsoil.

Second, when the soil is too depleted to produce crops, rural populations are reduced to consuming the seeds for future crops, destroying their capability to produce their own food. Another alternative is to seek food, as well as fuel and water, farther away from their homes. This pushes rural peoples into marginal and therefore sensitive ecosystems, even conservation areas and parks. Different interests motivate poor rural peoples, who have few alternatives for survival in the short term, and ecologists, who take the longer view toward saving the environment but who do not work on remedies for the unequal distribution of land and resources that forces poor people to seek food, fuel, and water in protected areas.

This unequal distribution of land and resources arises not just from class status but also from gender divisions in a world in which women own less than 2 percent of privately held land. The Western assumption that women are not farmers has led both to the loss of women's land rights and to the failure to provide technological assistance to women who work the land. As we have learned from the unforeseen consequences of high-technology experiments such as the green revolution, not all technology is good or appropriate for every socioeconomic and environmental context. Development mistakes—mistakes for the large number of people impoverished by them—might have been avoided if women farmers in the global South, who are more reliable "natural resource managers," had been consulted about how best to use the land and what technologies are most appropriate (Rodda 1991).

Most women agricultural workers are not formally educated in modern, Western agricultural techniques. However, they work closely with and on the land and have developed significant informal knowledge about ecosystems and appropriate land-use patterns. As farmers, women often know which plants have the most nutritional value and what forms of cultivation lead to the least soil erosion and water consumption. As traditional healers, women often know which plants have medicinal value and what practices sustain the biodiversity of an ecosystem to ensure that such healing vegetation is preserved. As fuel gatherers, women know they are dependent on forests to provide renewable sources of firewood.[20] International and national development planners and agencies that ignore women's knowledge and introduce inappropriate technologies can do much more harm than good.

Globalization forces are constituting an even more serious threat to ecological sustainability and biodiversity as capitalist expansion spreads industries and enterprises into areas that were previously less affected by economic development. Trade liberalization policies, such as Trade-Related Intellectual Property Rights (TRIPs) that were codified in the 1995 General Agreement on Tariffs and Trade (GATT) agreement and are enshrined in the articles of the World Trade Organization (WTO), are essentially allowing transnational pharmaceutical companies to take out patents on seeds and plants that may be used in the industrial production of medical drugs. Vandana Shiva argues that because "intellectual property rights are recognized only as private rights," which exclude "all kinds of knowledge, ideas, and innovations that take place in the 'intellectual commons,'" such as "in villages among farmers and in forests among tribals," rural women, who most often are the custodians of seeds and plants for community medicinal use, not only lose control over these plant materials but also are dispossessed of their knowledge as profit-making enterprises monopolize how this material will be used (1993: 238). The privatization of even genetic materials undermines both public accountability for how the earth and living things on it are used (and abused) and women's capacity for developing more sustainable practices.

Gendered Resource Destruction

Of course, women are not always kind to the environment, especially when they become members of consumer-oriented cultures, which are increasing in number as a result of globalization. Western gender ideology encourages women to adopt a consumer lifestyle through which they can beautify their bodies (according to Western standards), dress fashionably (as defined by male fashion designers), and stock their homes with modern "conveniences" (some of which actually create work). Beauty products are implicated in all manner of ecological harm, ranging from inhumane animal testing of makeup and shampoos to ozone depletion from aerosol spray use. Fur coats are products of the brutal destruction of animals for their pelts. Finally, "keeping up with the Joneses" keeps women (and men) enamored of the idea that they must have more cars, dishwashers, laundry machines, microwaves, refrigerators, computers, and other devices that require much energy to produce and operate, result in a great deal of air and water pollution, and create a significant amount of toxic garbage when they are thrown away to make way for new, improved models.

Whereas middle- and upper-class consumers in "throw-away" societies are heavily implicated in resource waste and environmental pollution, poor and working-class women worldwide suffer the effects of environmental degradation and pollution. The poor and working class are concentrated in crowded and often highly polluted residential areas and largely unregulated, toxic workplaces. For example, women working in Mexico's *maquiladoras* report high levels of illness caused by dust in unventilated garment-industry sweatshops and by open trays of cancer-causing chemicals next to them in electronic-industry workrooms (Kamel 1990: 35). In the rural villages of the global South, women have the greatest exposure to the harmful gases released from their cookstoves (Sivard 1991: 37). Moreover, given the rise in poor, female-headed households, a large number of women and children live in remote rural areas and urban slums, where toxic-waste dumps are common. This situation occurs frequently in countries of the global South that accept toxic refuse from the global North in order to earn foreign exchange. Indeed, Joni Seager reports that as of the early 1990s, there were "at least 1000 attempts to export more than 160 million tons of toxic waste from rich countries to poor since 1986" (1993: 150).

Women's reproductive organs are harmed by exposure to industrial toxins in workplaces and residential communities, resulting in ovarian cancer, infertility, miscarriages, and birth defects (Nelson 1990: 177–179). Recognition of women's susceptibility to industrial toxins has led to some restrictions on where women are allowed to work. However, data on sterility, cancers, and genetic damage indicate that men's reproductive health is also put at risk by working in toxic environments. This suggests that the gendered solution of barring women from certain workplaces is simply an "industrial protection racket" that draws attention away from polluting industries as the real problem (Nelson 1990: 179). Similarly, women's reproductive failures have called attention to the hidden effects of nuclear testing and nuclear power plant emissions and accidents. Yet it is rare that states and industries are held accountable for the extensive reproductive harm and genetic damage their nuclear programs have produced (Seager 1993; Bertell 1985).

Militaries are the worst polluters in the world, according to Seager, who has catalogued the many and extensive harms done to the environment by military installations. This list includes such practices as the production and dumping of toxic wastes from chemical weapons programs, the appropriation of land equal to the size of Turkey in thirteen industrialized countries, the consumption of huge quantities of oil, the emission of large amounts of carbon dioxide and chlorofluorocarbons (CFCs) that cause global warming and ozone depletion, and the destruction of thousands of animals each year in weapons and other tests. The shroud of "national security" in combination with masculine privilege, however, ensures that in "virtually every country, military facilities are exempt from environmental regulations and monitoring requirements" (Seager 1993: 37). The "war on drugs," too, which the U.S. government uses to justify continuous and widespread spraying of carcinogenic herbicides throughout the countrysides of Central and South America and Southeast Asia, is causing untold numbers of birth defects and reproductive disorders in rural women who live in these areas (Seager 1993: 30).

Women as Disposable Resources

As Melissa Wright argues, one of the most economically and "socially useful lies" or "myths" is that of the "disposable third world woman" (Wright 2006: 2–3) who perhaps more than any other is rendered worthless and consigned to "bare life." This lie enables the superexploitation of their laboring bodies while exposing them to a range of bodily harms without rights over their bodies. This accounts for the facts, as detailed in UNIFEM's 2008/2009 report on the world's women, that poor women in the global South have the highest rates of poverty, hunger, maternal mortality, poor maternal health, and HIV/AIDS, and their children are the most subject to high child mortality rates. Reductions in these constitute the bulk of the MDGs, but maternal health "is the most off-track of all MDGs" (UNIFEM 2008: 125). In addition to the heteronormative reduction of women's health to "maternal" health, which assumes that all women are or will be mothers and the only aspect of their health worthy of protection is in relation to their reproductive labor, the broader notion of universal access to reproductive health, including family planning and contraception services, was only recently added as a target to achieve the maternal health MDG. This was as a result of pressure from women's movements and the reality finally recognized that maternal deaths, which have been reduced by only 0.4 percent per year rather than the 5.5 percent annual reduction targeted, could be reduced by one quarter by access to contraceptives and safe terminations (UNIFEM 2008: 127). However, in direct contradiction to this, the percentage of women denied access to contraceptives and family planning services they need increased from 55 percent in 1990 to 64 percent in 2005 (UNIFEM 2008: 127). The combination of further illegalizations of and legal, cultural, and geographical restrictions on contraceptive use and abortions, the rise of state-sponsored religious fundamentalisms, and the U.S. "global gag rule" reimposed under the Bush administration, which denied U.S. funding to any organization that even raises the option of abortion, have conspired to undermine any meaningful progress on the very modest maternal health MDG.[21]

A similar pattern of failing to address underlying causes because they would require women's rights over their bodies and their ability to exercise them can be found in the context of the MDG pertaining to HIV/AIDS. Far from being halted or reversed, women's contraction of HIV/AIDS continues to climb, particularly in sub-Saharan Africa and the Caribbean where it is reportedly most prevalent and where women outpace men in its contraction or in the rates of contraction (UNIFEM 2008: 128). According to UNIFEM, the feminization of HIV/AIDS is highly related to a combination of a relative lack of information and treatment services provided to poor women and the fact that as many as 30 percent of young women are infected by rape (UNIFEM 2008: 128). Yet MDG targets and indicators are silent on such gender dimensions of the pandemic, with the exception of the use of condoms.

The gendered divisions of power, violence, and labor and resources have conspired to construct official blinders, which ensure that especially young women of the global South will continue to be put at tremendous risk through prostitution, rape, poverty, and poor health care, as well as lack of contraceptive services and safe-sex education. These factors, along with a host of other health threats to women ranging from domestic violence and female circumcision to forced sterilizations and preferences for male children in many parts of the global South, have minimized women's power to control their own bodies, making them highly susceptible to contaminants and disease, which they end up passing on to their children, who, in turn, become damaged global resources.

   In short, under the gendered division of resources, women in aggregate but particularly in the global South not only have little access to resources that might make their lives longer and easier but also are treated as resources themselves, to be used, abused, and disposed of when it suits the purposes of powerful men, states, and industries. What most women need and want are rarely considered in the calculus of how resources are defined, divided, and used. Instead, under neoliberal governmentality, they are treated as abject, without agency or rights under a veneer of problem-solving that stigmatizes and colonizes to redirect attention away from global capitalism, militarization, patriarchy, and racism that lie at the heart of global crises. As a result, not just women but the entire planet and its other inhabitants suffer from this far-from-benign neglect. Such purposeful neglect is, nevertheless, still resisted by "people's renewal movements" which

> begin from the premise that there is no escape from the substantial messes we have created and that there has already been enough erasure—of history, of culture, of memory. These are movements that do not seek to start from scratch but rather from scrap, from the rubble that is all around . . . taking what's there and fixing it, reinforcing it, making it better and more equal. Most of all they are building resilience—for when the next shock comes (Klein 2007: 466).

TOWARD RESISTING NEOLIBERALISM

Feminists and other critics of neoliberalism raise a number of concerns. Some areas and sectors have indeed experienced significant growth, but instead of "lifting all boats," the evidence shows that inequalities within and between countries have actually grown (Cornia 2004; Wade 2004; APSA 2008). The selective implementation of liberalization continues to favor the powerful nations of the North, whereas other nations have limited control over protecting domestic industries, goods produced, and jobs provided. Deregulation permitted the hypermobility of "foot-loose" capital and induced phenomenal growth in financial markets and high-risk transactions—that as critics predicted and the current meltdown proves—are unsustainable. Privatization entailed a decline of national-ized industries and decrease in public-sector employment and provision of social services worldwide. Women are disproportionately affected be-cause they are more likely to depend on secure government jobs and on public resources in support of reproductive labor. At the same time and in spite of fewer available resources and more demands on their time, women are expected to fill the gap—thus "solving the problem"—when public provisioning declines. The poorest women and men—who in the global North tend to be ethnic/racial minorities—are especially hurt by reduced public spending because they have the fewest (private) re-sources and hence are most in need of public services and the support they provide.

The picture of GPE presented here reveals a polarization of income and status between masculinized elites and the global majority of femi-nized "others." This generalized analysis also exposed how the cultural code of feminization naturalizes the economic (material) devaluation of feminized work, whether that work is done by women or men who are culturally, racially, and/or economically marginalized. Hence, this chap-ter has illuminated not only how men and women are positioned and being re-positioned globally by gendered divisions to maximize ex-ploitation, but also how the power of gender continues to operate in ways that deflect attention away from such exploitation by naturalizing or depoliticizing it. At the same time, this chapter has exposed how neo-liberal globalization has exacerbated the disposability of resources and bodies, particularly those that are most gendered, racialized, and classed, ultimately threatening the planet itself. In spite of the severity of human exploitation and environmental degradation, we note the continued re-sistance by national and international officialdom to reduce these harms significantly, as this would require fundamental shifts in human relation-ships and in human relationships with the environment, which are pre-cluded by the maintenance of the power of gender.

Vandana Shiva (2005) calls for such a shift in her concept of "Earth Democracy." This is far from the contemporary top-down responses to global crises that are captured by Empire, or neoliberal governmentality coupled with imperialist security governmentality, and that stress corporate-led technological fixes and food-energy-water security only for those who can afford it and through violent means. Instead,

> Earth Democracy allows us to overcome the artificial scarcity and manipulated and manufactured insecurities by seeing and experiencing connections. We begin to see the connections between corporations and corporate states, the connections between the economic wars and military wars, the connections between corporate profits and people's poverty, the connections between globalization and religious fundamentalism. We also start to discover the connections we have to the earth and one another. Exposing the connections of dominant powers enables us to evolve appropriate strategies to transform dead democracies into living democracies. Our ecological and social connectedness enables us to create living economies and living cultures, while building the solidarities which crack open the alliances of the powerful (Shiva 2005: 185).

It is to such resistance and building of solidarity that we now turn to conclude this text. In the final chapter, we also explore what it might mean to de-gender world politics in order to enable more meaningful responses to the crises of representation, insecurity, and sustainability.

Notes

1. We prefer a reference to global political economy (GPE) rather than international political economy (IPE), insofar as GPE draws our attention to increasingly *transnational* processes and requires transdisciplinary perspectives. In contrast to many accounts, we also address discursive shifts, sociocultural changes, and shifting identities as these affect, and are affected by, globalization processes.

2. Overviews of feminist economics include Hewitson 1999; Ferber and Nelson 2003; Barker and Feiner 2004.

3. Rai (2002: 71–73) provides a very useful comparison and discussion of WID and GAD orientations.

4. For recent examples, see Marchand and Runyan 2000; Rai 2002; Mohanty 2003; Peterson 2003; Benería 2003; Parpart and Zalewski 2008.

5. See Truong 1999; *World Development* 2000; Aslanbeigui and Summerfield 2000, 2001; Hooper 2001; Van Staveren 2002.

6. On economics as the study of provisioning see, for example, Nelson 1996; Ferber and Nelson 2003; Power 2004. On feminist economics as offering not only a corrective but alternative and socially progressive understanding of economics see Gibson-Graham 1996; Barker and Feiner 2004. Also see Bergeron 2001 for critiquing the continued

masculinist, racist, and imperial underpinnings of even what some call the post-Washington consensus.

7. For feminist discussions see Goetz and Gupta 1996; Poster and Salime 2002; Bergeron 2003. For enthusiasts, see the Microcredit Summit site, available at http://www.microcreditsummit.org/index.php?/en/about/microfinance_advocacy/ and the World Bank site, available at http://www.cgap.org/p/site/c/home/ (accessed 30 January 2009).

8. The literature is long-standing and extensive; see, for example, Sen and Grown 1987; Vickers 1991; *World Development* 1995, 2000; Bakker 1994; Einhorn and Yeo 1995; and Moghadam 1994, on transition economies of Eastern and Central Europe.

9. Although loss of economic resources is always problematic, Chant (2007) draws on extensive case studies to argue against automatically assuming that women are better off with, than without, men in their households.

10. Gender socialization and stereotyping encourage employers to think of women as more docile than men; and to the extent that women internalize these messages, they may be less assertive than men in general. But this risks reproducing stereotypes and practices, when in fact women are not passive victims in these processes. Research shows that women undertake a variety of resistance activities, as exploitative work experience often has the effect of politicizing women as workers, and control of economic resources favors the empowerment of women. We elsewhere note women's resistance to globalization more generally.

11. Estimates vary, but in 1995, the world's "underground" or informal economy was estimated to be worth US$9 trillion (*Economist* 1999: 59), the equivalent of one-fourth of the "gross global product" for that year; and the value of "housework" to be US$10–15 trillion (UNDP 1995: 6; Tetreault and Lipschutz 2005: 25). Recent studies suggest informal activities constitute more than one-half of all economic output and 75 percent of the gross domestic product of some countries; one-half to three-quarters of nonagricultural work in developing countries is informal, and in Africa accounted for over 90 percent of new jobs in the past decade (ILO 2002b: 5).

12. Virtually all researchers note the problematic nature of data on informality, but these generalizations are widely accepted. See UN 2000; Benería 2003; ILO 2002a; ILO 2002b; Snyder 2005.

13. Dangler (2000) provides an in-depth history of homework as a structural feature of capitalism. Boris and Prügl provide the ILO definition of homework as "the production of goods or the provision of services for an employer or contractor under an arrangement whereby the work is carried out at the place of the worker's own choosing, often the worker's own home" (1996: 5).

14. The data on remittances suggest the financial importance of these flows. Counting only officially recorded transfers, the World Bank expected worldwide remittances to reach $318 billion in 2007 (World Bank 2008: Brief 3: 2). This is twice the level recorded in 2002 and twice as large as official aid to developing countries. Including unrecorded flows would increase the figure significantly, perhaps by 50 percent (World Bank 2005: xiii).

15. Sex workers are not only women (and girls) but also men (and boys), and their customers include not only heterosexual-identified men but also gay-identified men

(and some women, straight and lesbian). As Jacqui Alexander (2005) argues, male sex workers in the Caribbean (and the global South generally) are particular "objects of desire" for white gay tourism and thus subservient to "white gay capital." This is yet another example of how otherwise progressive actors, in this case those who struggle for sexual minority rights at home, engage in colonizing and imperializing practices abroad.

16. Recent studies include Kempadoo and Doezema 1998; Hughes 2000; Hanochi 2001; Agathangelou 2004; Kempadoo 2005; Agustín 2007. Trafficking in women increasingly occurs in connection with transnational criminal networks operating in relation to militarized conflicts and trading in a variety of goods, including drugs, body parts, migrants, precious natural resources, arms, and nuclear materials.

17. Feminists have long debated how to address sex as a politics and especially pornography as a practice. We cannot adequately address the complex issues involved but do acknowledge their importance for how we think about sex and work toward sexual justice.

18. Recent critical summaries with reference to hegemonic Western masculinity, especially for young men, include Kimmel 2008; McCaughey 2008.

19. On gendering global finance and its crises, see Aslanbeigui and Summerfield 2000, 2001; Truong 2000; Floro and Dymski 2000; Van Staveren 2002; Peterson 2003; De Goede 2005.

20. In Mali, for example, certain trees are designated as "women" trees. This means they are reserved for firewood, which is typically harvested from dead branches, and thus the trees are not to be cut down (Rodda 1991: 75).

21. During his first week in office, U.S. President Barack Obama rescinded the Bush administration's global gag rule pertaining to abortion information.

6

◄◦►

Gendered Resistances

FEMINIST RESISTANCE POLITICS

As we have seen in our survey of gender and gendered processes in current world politics and contemporary feminist IR inquiry that has brought these to light, the power of gender continues to foster dichotomizing, stratifying, othering, and depoliticizing in thought and action. These moves produce and maintain crises of representation, insecurity, and sustainability, despite some re-positionings of some women and men on the world stage. Re-positionings, such as those moves that give some women greater access to the means of destruction and more men less access to the means of production, are more the result of the deepening and widening of militarization and economic globalization than of justice-inspired gender equality commitments and policies. Thus gendered divisions of power, violence, and labor and resources are not seriously disturbed by some "resexing" of actors, especially when those actors are still expected to play dutiful or acquiescent roles in support of power-over, militarization, and economic and resource exploitations that are associated with imperial(ist) impulses. Thus, the question is not one of agency alone, but rather whose agency for what?

This concluding chapter explores agency directed to resisting gendered divisions and the power of gender. Rather than offering inventories and anatomies of social movements and their efficacies, we first examine the range of thinking about resistance practices and formations arising out of feminist IR and transnational feminist inquiry. We then provide our ruminations on *de-gendering* world politics to respond to global crises in ways that also promote gender—and more broadly social—justice.

Women and Social Movements

Even as some women gain greater access to formal political power, it is more often the case that critical masses of female political actors who more radically challenge gender dichotomies are found outside of formal power structures. Because they typically organize outside of state apparatuses, these actors tend to be invisible through the state-centric lens on world politics that prevailed until recently. Now that market forces, in the form of private firms and IFIs, are challenging and complicating traditional state prerogatives in world politics, IR has begun to direct attention to what is frequently referred to as "civil society." Neoliberals and neoconservatives tend to conceptualize civil society in terms of the private sector, defined as corporate and individualist interests that are in tension with and seek to maintain autonomy from the state. Critical perspectives tend to view civil society in terms of social movements that resist both state domination and capitalist market exploitation (Macdonald 1994). This latter definition of civil society is making women more visible as actors in world politics. However, only feminist perspectives highlight the central roles that women play in social movement activism.

Women are found in large numbers in social movements for peace, human rights, economic justice, and environmental protection as members of both mixed organizations (which include men and women) and separate organizations (which are women-centered in terms of leadership, focus, and membership, and thus are referred to as women's movements). Until recently, the activities of such social movements have been concentrated below the level of the state and confined within state boundaries. However, as economic, environmental, and social issues increasingly cut across state boundaries due to globalization forces, and as IGOs have become more significant sites for global policymaking and more open to NGO claimants and partnerships, women's movements, and particularly the NGOs that claim to represent them, are becoming more transnational in focus, organization, and impact. These processes are raising the profiles of women's movements in world politics. In this sense, they are part of what is being termed "global civil society," which is seen as either a countervailing balance to or an intervention against state and corporate power (Stienstra 1999: 262).

Women in their social movement roles as nonstate and trans-state actors shift attention from "fitting women into" traditional IR frameworks and toward an understanding that accommodates and empowers women's struggles against the hierarchical consequences of practicing world-politics-as-usual. More often, women's activism not only resists oppressive state and market forces but also often seeks to transform civil society. Indeed, their emphasis on the transformation of civil society is what makes women's movements somewhat distinctive among social movements. Feminists tend to go beyond many critical formulations of civil society by arguing that civil society is not that autonomous from the state and the market, nor does it always resist the negative effects of these forces. All ideals and social movements have potential for variously regressive as well as progressive consequences. Just as there are progressive aspects to civil society, there are also regressive dimensions insofar as civil society reproduces oppressive structures (such as the heteronormative patriarchal family) and ideologies (such as sexism, racism, ablism, and homophobia) inculcated by a range of fundamentalisms. If these oppressive dimensions of civil society are not confronted and changed, it is unlikely that progressive, inclusive, and democratic social movements or global civil society more generally will flourish or that the negative effects of states and markets (reflecting problematic aspects of civil society) will be thoroughly challenged. Thus, even though there are liberating aspects of social movement struggles in which women significantly participate as members and leaders, such movements can perpetuate at the same time that they challenge gendered dichotomies. This caution is especially warranted when there is insufficient attention given to the transformation of civil society in the context of struggles to change states and markets.

Transnational Feminist Movement Debates

As indicated in Chapter 4—and exemplified in the problematics of the FMF campaign against gender apartheid in Afghanistan—there are major ongoing debates about how to resist regressive or imperial tendencies in feminist thought and movements—particularly those that are transnational in character—in order to build more equal and just solidarities to better confront crises of representation, insecurity, and sustainability. At core, anti-imperialist feminisms seek to enhance a "politics of recognition" in which the diverse voices and perspectives of subjugated women and men, or more accurately multiple sexes and genders, are represented equitably and a "politics of redistribution," which challenges the classist, sexist, racist, and heterosexist ways in which the material world is divided up (Fraser 1997). We see the politics of recognition as most central to ameliorating the crisis of representation but also key to challenging the crisis of insecurity, and the politics of redistribution as most central to countering the crisis of sustainability but also key to reducing the crisis of insecurity and enhancing the politics of recognition.

At various times, however, there have been tensions between the politics of recognition and redistribution because one has backgrounded the other. For example, early Marxist feminism was critiqued for focusing on only gendered class relations and material redistributions to solve these inequities without recognition of the need for a greater democratization of struggles to identify and resist not only gendered class exploitation but also other oppressions based on race, sexuality, and nation that intertwined with, variegated, and intensified class stratification. Later, various forms of cultural and ethnic feminisms were critiqued for a relative inattention to class analysis and the politics of material redistribution as they tended to pursue a kind of politics of recognition known as identity politics. Identity politics, while useful to foreground (and thus represent) the experiences and perspectives of a particular subjugated identity group (such as women, Asian women, Latinas, Chicanas, lesbians, and so on), also tended, on the one hand, to essentialize and homogenize such identity groups, and, on the other hand, to so fragment identity into smaller and smaller groupings (young-disabled-lesbian-domestic-Asian American workers) that no common cause could be seen between these groupings of infinite variety. The fragmentation of identity, however, served to draw attention to "hybrid" or "diasporic" identities that resist the forces of essentialism and homogenization and cut across identity groups (Anzaldúa 1999), and thus enable the development of coalition politics. Identity fragmentation (to the point of deconstructing all identities to expose them as always provisional and subject to change) also constitutes a poststructural feminist strategy (as well as a "queering" strategy) to de-naturalize and thus destabilize identities, making them unavailable to be mobilized or used for power and control or to be targets of power and control. Although, for a time, these developments of the politics of recognition overshadowed thinking about the politics of redistribution, today many contemporary feminist theorists and activists are emphasizing both to counter the rise of neoliberal globalization and governmentality and their security apparatuses. Developing and exercising both these politics entails anti-imperialist, antiracist, anti–global capitalist, and antihetero-normative inquiry and political commitments.

Such inquiry and political commitments have been hampered by the ways that some feminist inquiry, both Western and non-Western, is conducted and informs social movements. Chandra Mohanty (2003) has identified practices that mitigate against anti-imperialist feminist thought and action. What she calls the "feminist-as-tourist" model arises from "brief forays into non-Euro-American cultures" in which "particular cultural sexist practices are addressed" through a Western "gaze" (Mohanty 2003: 239). This universalization of gender through a Eurocentric lens both subsumes more complex explanations for oppression under an overarching and ahistorical notion of gender and singles out for critique only certain forms of gender oppression associated with stigmatized local cultural "backwardness" as opposed to "modern" international political and economic forces. This yields social movements that can more easily become supporters and agents of imperial violence in the name of rescue missions. Social movement politics in this mode also tends to conceive of women as experiencing gender oppression in similar ways rather than as differently inflected by race, class, sexuality, and nationality. This cultivates "too easy" assumptions that women share the same experiences and interests, comprising a "global sisterhood" or "nation of women behind borders" (Sylvester 2002). Solidarity is then seen as flowing "naturally" from shared experiences and interests rather than something that needs to be developed through political dialogue and action. As a result, more-privileged women end up speaking for less-privileged ones not only as if women's perspectives were interchangeable, but also under the even more insidious assumption that Western women, in particular, are more "liberated" than others and thus should lead—rather than listen—and forge "the" path for "other" sisters. These perspectives and practices deny the realities on the ground. Consider, for example, that through a more significant embrace of quotas, women in the global South are gaining greater access to positions of formal power than in some of the most "developed" states. At the same time, even the most privileged Western women are subject to (economically motivated) cultural beauty standards and to achieve these involves bodily harm (whether through surgeries, anorexia, or toxic cosmetics). And these women are just as subject to domestic violence as women elsewhere. Yet, progress narratives in the West promote the continuation of colonial mindsets, which find their way into feminist theorizing and social movements that are based on the feminist-as-tourist model. This contributes to crises of representation by failing to practice politics of recognition.

Mohanty's "feminist-as-explorer" model refers to "area studies" approaches (2003: 240–241), which although more detailed, culturally sensitive, and historical in terms of examining women's lives in local, national, and/or regional contexts, still maintain a separation between the West and the non-West. In doing so, this model fails to see connections between global forces and national and local ones and the material conditions shared by the most subjugated women in both the South and North as a result of those global forces. Whether in cases of area studies performed by Western feminists or non-Western nationalist feminists, this cultivates a kind of "cultural relativism" that erases any commonalities among women's struggles (Mohanty 2003: 240). This has the effect of confining social movements within state or regional borders and minimizing potential solidarities across those borders.

Catherine Eschle (2001) argues that these approaches set up a "universalist" versus "particularist" dichotomy from which polarizing debates ensue. The former is most implicated in imperialist impulses and actions; the latter, although also mired historically in Western anthropological practices that legitimated imperial conquest, is alternatively implicated in nationalist, statist, and thus ultimately conservative frameworks (Eschle 2001: 201). Not only does a particularistic approach feed into maintaining an oppositional and static view of "western feminism as unified and necessarily imperialist," but also a notion that those from outside a particular state or region are "inauthentic" knowers and actors who cannot understand or share in struggles outside of the locales from which they come (Eschle 2001: 201–202). Moreover, a vision of feminism organized on the basis of distinct ethnic and cultural identities frequently relies on a prepolitical notion of identity that delegitimizes contestation and dialogue within and across identities. It also marginalizes women who do not fit neatly into a predetermined category (Eschle 2001: 202).

Such women who do not fit may be multiethnic, multinational, or sexual minorities; in this sense, just as a universalistic gender-based feminism undermines a politics of recognition, so too can a particularistic conception of ethnicity or culture-based feminism.

A related conundrum is the dichotomous construction of local versus global and the debates that ensue from this. Particularist advocates tend to privilege local or grassroots struggles as the most "authentic" and least contaminated by global power structures that co-opt and depoliticize social movements. Universalists tend to be most associated with global or international NGOs that lobby IGOs, garnering the majority of resources (although still relatively few compared with states, markets, and IGOs) for their larger-scale and more bureaucratic operations. International women's organizations are not new; they stretch back centuries in the form of women's peace movements, socialist women's *internationales*, and even missionary organizations that attended colonizing processes (Mackie 2001: 180–181). But the recent rise of feminist transnational NGOs has been met with a variety of concerns. First, there is the question of the relationship between the proliferation of contemporary NGOs and the rise of neoliberalism. As noted earlier, the "self-help" ideology of neoliberalism encourages private, voluntaristic, civil society operations to take up the slack—albeit with far fewer resources—for public welfare activities that states have been shedding. This reduces the accountability of states and markets, while also shifting services to unaccountable and relatively poorly resourced private bodies (as well as to underresourced households). Second, to the degree that NGOs are funded by states, IGOs, and most often private corporate foundations, they become more beholden to these interests and their priorities. Third, the "NGO-ization" of social movements, a concept Sonia Alvarez (1999) first coined in relation to Latin American regional women's NGOs she observed springing up during and after the UN Decade for Women, privileges middle-class actors with access to more resources and entrée into corridors of power. At the same time, this NGO-ization leaves behind poorer, more grassroots women who do not have the economic, social, and physical mobility (including foreign, high-theoretical, and bureaucratic language skills) to travel to and be heard at international conferences and sites of power like state and global capitals where lobbying occurs. Moreover, grass-roots movement demands get packaged by NGOs into policy bits that are digestible by states and IGOs and the femocrats within them, thereby taking off their radical edge. In all these senses, it has been argued that the "revolution will not be funded" (INCITE! Women of Color Against Violence 2007).

This local-global split has also been manifested in distinctions sometimes made between transnational feminism(s) and global feminism. The former refers to a more postcolonial conception of transnational linkages between the many struggles of grassroots women of the global South, and the latter is tied to global (or cosmopolitan) feminist NGOs that are dominated by more resourced women from both the North and the South. However, there have also been critiques of a fetishization of the local that is constructed as a more "innocent" space as if there were no power relations at the local level that silence some women over others and may result in parochial approaches that are unmindful of reproducing those power relations and their connections to larger and wider patterns and sources of abuse. Global feminism can be charged with parochialism, as well, in representing only more privileged views or lenses. At the same time, there is worry that transnational feminism risks being reduced to "the romanticization of Third World activism in the global arena" and limits "transnational solidarity to Third World women workers across the First/Third World divide," thereby "becoming the 'other' to western white feminism" (Mendoza 2002: 309). In Breny Mendoza's view, this results from more attention given to cultural critique in much transnational feminist theorizing, which, although is rightly directed to challenging ethnocentrism and confronting racism and heteronormativity as well as sexism, does not address sufficiently "political economic issues" that structure the lives of women in the South and North (2002: 310). This is the result of the politics of recognition overshadowing the politics of redistribution. The latter requires a more thoroughgoing solidarity of more-privileged women (and men) who choose to be against imperialism, racism, global capitalism, sexism, and heterosexism with less-privileged women (and men) who are critiquing and resisting these forces that ultimately threaten the planet and thus all on it.

Combining the politics of recognition with the politics of redistribution will also require coalitional solidarities among women's movements and mixed movements, as Eschle and Maiguascha (2005) have observed with respect to the antiglobalization movement. This movement is most associated with large-scale demonstrations outside various meetings of IFIs and economic elites held in various parts of the world, as well as the huge World Social Forums that have been held in South America, Asia, and Africa in the new millennium. Variously referred to as the antiglobalization, global justice, new *internationale*, or world's peoples movement, it is constituted by congeries of local, national, and transnational social movements from around the world who gather periodically to dialogue with each other, bear witness to, and contest economic globalization and militarized violence. Conceived as a leaderless, memberless, nonorganizational model, which stresses horizontal coalition-building, resists vertical control, and is open to all groups and individuals who wish to build a different world, its main focus, as described in the World Forum Charter of Principles put forward at the first World Social Forum in Porte Alegre, Brazil, in 2001, is as follows:

> The World Social Forum is opposed to all totalitarian and reductionist views of economy, development and history and to the use of violence as a means of social control by the State. It upholds respect for Human Rights, the practices of real democracy, participatory democracy, peaceful relations, in equality and solidarity, among people, ethnicities, genders, and peoples, and condemns all forms of domination and all subjection of one person by another (Sen and Waterman 2009: 70).

These principles attest to the large presence of women and especially feminists in the movement, who made up, with youth, the majority of participants in the first World Social Forum (Eschle 2005: 23), as well as the considerable influence of feminist critiques of inequalities within civil society and global civil society.

Eschle points out, however, the recognition of patriarchy and its relationship to globalization and militarism in movement documents and manifestos was hard won (2005: 23), because of the more orthodox Marxism of predominantly male organizers of forums who could see the struggle only as a class-based one and thereby promoted that limited ideology through their behind-the-scenes leadership of what is supposed to be a leaderless movement (2005: 24). Moreover, as Johanna Brenner has noted, just as some men in Marxist and labor movements attempted to marginalize feminist perspectives and issues such as reproductive rights in critiques of globalization generated at World Social Forums, women in some community-based movements—particularly those that are faith-based or receive funding from the Catholic Church—have been silent on reproductive rights and the rights of sexual minorities even as they have advanced other feminist arguments at these forums, such as calling for attention to domestic violence as bound up in globalization (2009: 34–36). Thus, however much we can assume good intentions, there are no automatic solidarities, and intersectional ones are very hard to achieve in order to bring about both recognition and redistribution in the face of the *longue durée* of gendered divisions of power, violence, and labor and resources that structure global, national, and local spaces in North and South.

In order to build more intersectional coalitions, Mohanty recommends a "feminist solidarity" model for thought and action (2003: 242). This model sees the local and global as mutually constituted and, through comparative analysis, focuses "not just on the intersections of race, class, nation, and sexuality in different communities of women but on mutuality and co-implication, which suggests attentiveness to the interweaving of the histories of these communities" (Mohanty 2003: 242). This enables an alternative mapping of what connects and divides women (and men) based on redirecting attention to "global capitalism, and the uncovering of the naturalization of its masculinist and racist values" (Mohanty 2003: 250) that compromise peoples and the planet. As we have argued, it is the power of gender that breeds the dichotomous thinking that operates to prevent or mitigate this remapping and the more fully developed solidarities that can arise from it. As African American feminist theorist and supporter of coalition-building Bernice Johnson Reagon has famously argued, coalitions are a matter of survival and can be built only through praxis or acting together on particular projects at particular times (Reagon 2000; Gilmore 2008). They are not entered into because participants are like each other, like each other, or are safe from each other, but because "that's the only way you can figure you can stay alive" (Reagon 2000: 344) in the face of the widespread crises of representation, insecurity, and sustainability that affect all but the most privileged and that need to be resisted collectively in both small and large ways.[1] And although, as another African American feminist, Audre Lorde (2008) famously argued, it is problematic to "dismantle the Master's house" with the "Master's tools," even the tools that are implicated in neoliberal governmentality can be used for dismantling and rebuilding projects, because such tools arose, albeit in more deradicalized and distanced form than was intended, from social movement analysis and agitation.

Feminist Resistance Projects in Global Perspective

There are easily millions of small and larger women's and feminist resistance projects directed in some way to challenging gendered divisions of power, violence, and resources and the crises of representation, insecurity, and sustainability they have spawned. Throughout this text, we have pointed to a few of them. Here we focus on a handful of those that have used global gender instruments instituted only recently to take them beyond the sorely circumscribed intent and use of them by IGOs and states. This is not to overshadow the many historical and contemporary equality, peace, labor, and environmental movements within and across states that feminists continue to document as sources of resistance, some of which preceded world forums and others that do not make use of global gender policy instruments and may not be represented at World Social Forums. Nor is it to dismiss the very real power relations within, between, and among social movements and NGOs. Rather, we offer these examples as suggestive that the dichotomies of universalist-particularist, local-global, and transnational feminism–global feminism are not as operant on the ground. Instead we see a mixing of strategies and actors engaged in ongoing coalitional struggles to build solidarity across internal and external borders through demanding much greater accountability from states and markets and in civil society.

As Suzanne Zwingel (2005) points out, there have been numerous efforts to "bring CEDAW home" by local, national, and transnational women's movements. In the vast majority of states in which CEDAW has been ratified—with the most notable exception of the United States—feminists have had to organize long and hard to get their states to adopt the legal provisions required by CEDAW even after lobbying long and hard for the ratification of it. Zwingel argues that the degree to which CEDAW can be brought home is dependent upon "first, the degree to which political institutions enable the representation of women's interests within public policy formations; second, the existence of transnational governmental or non-governmental activism that supports the appropriation and implementation of international norms; and third, the level of cultural affinity with the Convention" (2005: 408). In the case of Finland, which was alone among the Nordic states in not having a gender equality law when it ratified CEDAW, femocrats in the Council for Equality, a national women's policy agency, played upon the Finnish government's relative openness to women's interests and representation and its self-identity as space for socioeconomic equality to shame it into creating gender-equality legislation by marshalling evidence from their femocrat contacts in other countries and at the global level that Finland was an outlier, particularly in the Nordic context (Zwingel 2005: 409). Chile first complied with CEDAW by creating a women's policy agency, SERNAM (Servicio Nacional de la Mujer). But in the relative absence of women in formal political positions at the national level and prevailing ideologies of "gender complementarity," which justify keeping women in their places, rather than equality, SERNAM forged relationships with women's local NGOs and networks to bring some aspects of reproductive health onto the legislative agenda, including sex education and sterilization (Zwingel 2005: 410). As Zwingel notes, these local NGOs and networks advocated the more radical agenda of reproductive rights, including abortion, which SERNAM did not promote, but invocations of CEDAW by both SERNAM and networks of local movements pushed the right wing back to some degree, including enabling the legalization of divorce (2005: 410–411). CEDAW has also spawned the development of transnational NGOs dedicated to disseminating information on CEDAW to women's groups at all levels and monitoring its implementation. Organizations like the International Women's Rights Action Watch (IWRAW) in the United States and sister organizations like the IWRAW Asia Pacific located in Malaysia are part of the "transnational community of gender experts." However, networks of local groups and NGOs that work with these organizations and are not part of national or international elites benefit from and use the intersectional interpretation of CEDAW that IWRAW offices provide through connecting gender, race, and class discrimination and, in turn, make such CEDAW interpretations relevant and responsive to "the particular shape of gender hierarchies in their own contexts" (Zwingel 2005: 412–413). Thus, the otherwise dead law of CEDAW is made live and is constantly reinterpreted to further radicalize its meanings and implementation from diverse women's perspectives at all levels of organizing.

A similar process has been observed in the case of UN Security Council Resolution 1325. For example, Carol Cohn (2008) has reported that women's organizations in Kosovo and Afghanistan have translated the document into multiple languages used in their home countries, further translating UN-speak into understandable and useful language for grassroots women. Such practices are also occurring in Afghanistan, the DRC, El Salvador, Iraq, Liberia, and Rwanda. in part because of connections made in transnational workshops focused on implementing 1325 (Cohn 2008: 190–191). Were it not for DRC women's lobbying of the UN peacekeeping mission there, there would not be even the one gender adviser finally put into place (Cohn 2008: 190). In 2007, more than 150 Iraqi women's organizations signed a letter, sent to the U.S. Speaker of the House and the UN Secretary-General, which charged that the postinvasion constitutional process in Iraq was neither inclusive nor observant of CEDAW, 1325, or Security Council resolutions on Iraq specifically. Not only were secular women largely excluded from the drafting process of the Iraq constitution, but also personal status law was being subsumed under Islamic law with the help of Islamic women legislators who have been the only beneficiaries of the recently introduced women's quota of 25 percent in the Iraqi parliament (Al-Ali and Pratt 2009: 135–137). This letter has fallen on deaf ears, but it exposes the hypocrisy of U.S. unilateralism and its claims on behalf of democracy and gender equality and speaks to the widespread mobilizations of Iraqi women against the continued occupation and war. Moreover, continued dialogue and mobilization around 1325 are exposing its multiple problematics. These include the idea of protecting only women and only in war while leaving the prerogatives of war and the war system in place; making no connections between men and masculinities and war and thus doing nothing to address changing masculinities or men's participation in war; and leaving intact the idea that women are "more naturally" peaceful rather than widening responsibilities for all, elites and global civil society alike, to end war. As Cohn observes:

> While I do not think one can begin to understand war without gender; while I understand gender, war, nationalism, ethnicity, religion, capitalist forms of production, and consumption (how long should I make this list?) as mutually constitutive, I fear that "Women-as-peacemakers" places too much of war on gender. And in so doing, actually leaves the dominant political and epistemological frameworks untouched.
>
> I fear it is the easy way out. That it obscures all the parts of the war system, including, perhaps paradoxically, the working of gender regimes themselves (2008: 202).

We will return later to the challenges of breaking down the power of gender that undergirds war, but here our point is that policies such as 1325 are undergoing radical contestations and reformulations in the hands of local, national, and transnational women's movements that use them.

As further evidenced by the World Social Forums and calls for "Earth Democracy" arising from them and the many social movements that comprise the antiglobalization movement,[2] resistance politics has not ended under neoliberal governmentality: Its assumptions and rules continue to be contested. Those who practice resistance politics also make use of other tools associated with global capitalism, particularly the Internet. Although digital divides continue between men and women, rich and poor, ethnic majorities and ethnic minorities, and North and South, the explosion of transnational, national, and even local organizing would not have been possible without ICTs. Cyberfeminism has enabled UN gender architectures, transnational and national feminist NGOs, and even grassroots women's organizations to monitor policies, exchange information, and build solidarity networks on an unprecedented scale. As Wendy Harcourt (1999) points out, far from homogenizing and controlling women, the Web has opened up new political spaces for diverse women who can bypass discriminatory spatial structures and represent themselves and their struggles in less mediated ways, while also contesting exclusivist constructions of cultural and national identity. This is not to dismiss the commercial control, violence promotion, and disembodiment in which the Web is deeply implicated, but it does raise a "tale" of another Internet that is being reappropriated to engage in a feminist "postcolonial politics of representation on-line" in order to change oppressive circumstances in "off-line" lives (Franklin 2004). However, as Gillian Youngs (2005) points out, "cybercitizenship" remains quite unequal, requiring a politics of redistribution in relation to ICTs as well.

Feminist resistance directed to challenging the crises of representation, insecurity, and sustainability also takes other symbolic forms that do not require large-scale mobilizations or technological access. Women have used the few resources available to them to pioneer many forms of protest that have gained global recognition: These include donning the veil in protest of Western imperialism, as women did in the Iranian Revolution; engaging in guerrilla theater, as the U.S. feminist peace protest group CODEPINK[3] does; setting up women's peace camps outside nuclear weapons installations, as the women of Greenham Common in Britain pioneered; holding silent vigils to protest those "disappeared" by military dictatorships, for which the Argentinean Mothers of the Plaza de Mayo are famous; staging silent street protests against the Israeli occupation of Palestine, which was started by Women in Black (and which now has chapters in twenty-eight countries protesting war and violence); or hugging trees to save them, for which the local Chipko women's movement in India is internationally known.

Feminist scholars, too, have been a part of the deconstruction and reconstruction of world politics, engaging in a range of theoretical, material, and discursive interventions. In our conclusion of this text, we consider insights from feminist IR and related scholarship that illuminate, without resolving, how the power of gender in world politics might be challenged. The stakes are high and the road is long, but the more ways to travel it, the better.

TOWARD DE-GENDERING WORLD POLITICS

After three decades of feminist IR analysis and activism, what have we learned? How do major changes in world politics in recent decades confirm, complicate, and contest feminist IR and related feminist lenses? As we write, the world faces old and new challenges, particularly in terms of global security and political economy. The post-9/11 climate of fear and uncertainty—exacerbated by the U.S.-led "war on terror"—generates hypermasculine thinking and acting. The more recent collapse of financial arrangements in the United States, with devastating effects worldwide, generates economic perplexity and a frantic search for fixes. In these contexts, realities and representations of uncertainty, chaotic conditions and looming crises operate, not surprisingly, to amplify desires for clarity, creating predictability and imposing social order. As we argue throughout this text, there are indeed multiple crises, and collective longing for easy answers and quick fixes is understandable. But the message of this text is cautionary, urging a fundamental transformation in ways of identifying, thinking, and acting that requires much more than any quick fix. We have argued that the power of gender as a meta-lens and hegemonic worldview itself is key to producing crises of global proportion. The problem then is that paths of least resistance—conventional ways of responding—are not only inadequate but part of, indeed productive of, the problem. Hence, deconstructing the power of gender is a necessary component of addressing these crises and transforming world-politics-as-usual. This is obviously no simple or short-term project but one that we delay or sideline at great risk. It is urgent that we get on with asking not only "How do we fix this problem?" but also "How do we transform the systems that produce and reproduce these problems?"

In concluding this text, we consider how its lessons might illuminate and potentially guide the development of alternative lenses and transformational politics. Recognizing that we are never "outside" of the system we critique means that no perspective can avoid complicity or claim innocence. The choice is not about whether we participate in the institutional practices constituting our life worlds but only how, in what ways, with what effects? Do we take paths of least resistance that inexorably reproduce world-politics-as-usual, or attempt to be critically aware of structural violence and wary of too easy analyses and quick fixes? What have we learned that might help us construct, however provisionally, forms of anti-imperialist feminism that avoid appropriations and impositions?

In a recent text on feminist methodologies, Brooke Ackerly and Jacqui True identify several ways in which feminist IR is distinguished from mainstream and other critical IR scholarship: It is "grounded in the human experience," "attentive to gender and other social constructions to identify emancipatory potential (and not practice forms of oppression in research)," "self-reflective," and "cognizant of the ongoing nature of the processes under study and the research process" (2006: 255–256). As such, feminist IR sees itself as collective inquiry that seeks to be supportive of and accountable to the struggles of subjugated collectivities; this process entails not only privileging examinations of material oppressions and resistances, but also deconstructing oppressive discursive practices and reconstructing alternative conceptual frameworks for rethinking world politics. We engage some of these reconceptualization strategies in addressing the question of de-gendering world politics, remembering they are only potential signposts on the road to change, not prescriptive directions.

De-Gendering Power

When we recognize how much coercive power it takes to run this inequitable system, we begin to see why feminists argue that the deployment of coercive power is ultimately destructive of those who rule as well as those who are ruled. Disabling people—especially women—by depriving them of even the most basic needs so that the few can accumulate wealth and weaponry destroys genuinely popular support for states, international organizations, and their leaders. In the absence of popular support and consent as the sources of legitimacy for those in power, coercion is the only mechanism available to insecure rulers, who must rely on dividing, impoverishing, and degrading people and the planet to maintain their power. Therefore, "we" (referring here and throughout this conclusion to congeries of individuals, collectivities, and coalitions who make the political choice to challenge world-politics-as usual) must question not only the validity but also the efficacy of "power-over" as the mechanism for organizing world politics or solving world problems.

Effectively questioning power-over entails challenging the power of gender as a lens that privileges top-down masculinist, colonizing, and often coercive power that is associated with public (state, governmental) authority and institutions, at the expense of private (civil society and familial) sources of knowledge and potential authority. While doing so, we must also avoid romanticizing or interpreting as more "authentic" the experience or knowledge emanating from civil society or familial locations. Perhaps most crucial for avoiding the imperial impulse is recognizing that no single or universal answer to complex problems will be adequate, and may be disastrous. Hence, de-gendering also involves vigilance against the too-easy answers of "problem-solving" policy responses that are promulgated by elite decision-makers—whether in state governments, IGOs, NGOs, corporations, agencies, social movements or communities—rather than addressing what keeps (re)producing systemic problems.

One alternative to coercive power is the more feminist concept of enabling power. In this model, conflicts of "difference"—as constituted through a self-other opposition and zero-sum lens—are addressed and ideally resolved not by force or its threat but in nonviolent interaction and mutual learning. Lily Ling, for example, has coined the idea of "postcolonial learning" to refer to the need of the "Self" to "concede that its own survival and subjectivity *depend* on learning from the Other" (2002: 23). As she points out, such learning often takes place in the wake of "conquest and desire" when "Self and Other collide, overlap, and contradict" (Ling 2002: 16). Postcolonial learning "does not necessarily bring forth a better world," but it does "democratize knowledge and power" (Ling 2002: 23) in ways that make it difficult to maintain hierarchical dualisms as Self and Other partake of each other and negotiate hybridized understandings. Although the costs of "the arrogance and security affected by conquerors" weigh most heavily on the conquered, such arrogance and (in)security production also "prohibits learning" on the part of the conquerors, "shackling them to a bewildering stagnation amidst constant change" (Ling 2002: 22). Ling attributes blocks to postcolonial learning in part to the "hypermasculinity" of particularly great powers in both West and East (2002: 234). This, along with hypermasculine fears of hyperfemininity, mitigates against shifts in state as well as human subjectivities.

Feminist theorizing about the high degree of reciprocity, interconnectedness, and hybridity typifying most social relations and encounters recognizes that they take place in contexts of contingency and ambiguity.

The concept of enabling power denies neither the need for autonomy nor the complexities of social interaction, but it does deny that a depiction of only hostile and competitive forces at work in the world is accurate or adequate. Christine Sylvester describes this model of enabling power as "relational autonomy" and contrasts it with the masculinist and imperialist ideal of "reactive autonomy" (valuing independence over interdependence and order over justice), which permeates the practice of international relations:

> In liberal political theory, the cast of masculine reactive autonomy appears in stories of abstract social contracts entered into, seemingly, by "orphans who have reared themselves, whose desires are situated within and reflect nothing but independently generated movement" [citation deleted]. Realist international relations theory follows this mold, even as it focuses on those anarchic spaces that elude social contract; for it depicts states as primitive "individuals" separated from history and others by loner rights of sovereignty—backed up, for good measure, by military hardware—and involved in international conventions and institutions only on a voluntary basis (1992: 157).

The reactive autonomy model in effect erases most social reality, especially the webbing that constructs meaning and order, as well as the practices of social reproduction that ensure everyday life and generational continuity. Reactive autonomy assumes that social order and cooperative relations are virtually impossible without some forms of hierarchy and coercion. This mindset, or lens, encourages paths of least resistance that at best institutionalize a balance of forces, and at worst rely on direct coercion. In contrast, relational autonomy assumes that cooperation typifies human relations when they are relatively equal and is destroyed in the presence of inequality, "othering," and coercion.

Moving toward a relational autonomy model for world politics would move us toward de-gendering world politics more deeply than we could simply by adding women (and other subjugated groups) to existing power structures. On the one hand, without deeper institutional changes, simply adding women can generate (still unrepresentative of all women) tokens whose presence may fuel complacency rather than sustained efforts at transforming representational politics. And simply adding women to public power without adding men to domestic labor and caretaking, and also holding elite men (and women) responsible for undermining webs of care, effectively exacerbates the crisis of social reproduction. On the other hand, adding women cannot take the form of a simple reversal that merely privileges feminine "care" over masculine "coercion." In such a reversal, not only gender dichotomies but also features of the feminine concept of care that oppress women would remain in place. Specifically, because caring has historically been a demand imposed upon subordinated groups and is, in this sense, inextricable from relations of inequality, a care model may offer insights on, but not solutions to, oppressive social relations. Caring that exclusively takes the form of sacrificing self or group interests is just another framing of inequality.

Emphasizing relational autonomy as a model of international relations would assist women in terms of a redistribution of resources to ease their lives, but we also need to facilitate women's autonomy (sometimes of the reactive sort) through the realization of gender equality that entails a politics of recognition. Full equality, not only *between* men and women but also *among* women and *among* men, cannot be achieved unless all men have an equal responsibility for (social) reproductive or relational work (from the household through to the international arena) and diverse (in terms of race, class, sexuality, and nation) women have an equal say in how the world is organized.

Kathleen Jones (1993) posits a concept of "compassionate authority" (not to be confused with the Bush-ism of "compassionate conservativism") that foregrounds "humanizing authority." In the face of contemporary crises and the threats they pose, compassionate authority involves a

> shift away from the paternalism and the male protection racket as inefficient and heartless forms of social coordination no matter who practices them. Our understanding of authority changes if authoritative roles include female symbolism. Practices of leadership are altered toward a network model, and the relationship between leaders and followers shifts from a command-obedience structure based on fear of loss of protection toward a more consensual egalitarian model. Leadership and political ac-

tion stimulates a move from efforts to destroy alternatives to those celebrating the birth of alternatives as new beginnings (Jones 1993: 240).

While there is a "strategic essentialism" at work here, the process of redefining authority opens up the possibility for transforming who can lead, what the basis of leadership could be, how it could be more equal and consensual, and what shifts in direction it could take.

De-gendering power then involves multiple moves, and not least a turn away from power-over to enabling power. It involves recognizing that interdependence, differing perspectives and uncertainty in outcomes are inescapable aspects of the human condition; we must acknowledge and address them rather than pursue the illusion of simple answers, and top-down, market-oriented fixes so endemic to neoliberal governmentality that seeks to dispel politics understood as contestation of dominant scripts. We need to pursue a politics of recognition that acknowledges and empowers subjugated voices and marginalized alternatives; and a politics of redistribution that enables more democratic participation by the many and not just the elite few. Unless we de-gender power, we leave the crisis of representation in place, effectively "disposing" of identities, voices, and alternatives that lack requisite resources or do not comfortably "fit."

De-Gendering Violence

The assumption that violence is largely the result of anarchic international relations—in contrast to supposedly "peaceful" domestic communities—obscures the question of the amount of and the way in which violence is deployed from the personal and local to the national and global levels. We know that domestic violence—the euphemism for the wide range of physical and emotional abuse suffered mostly by wives and children in families, but also can refer to the everyday violence inflicted on a range of peoples subjugated by gender, race, sexuality, and national origin—is widespread throughout the world. Hence, it makes little sense to argue that the level and frequency of violent conflict is what separates international relations from domestic relations. A more productive starting point would be to see domestic and international violence as intimately connected and from that starting point investigate how and why this is the case and what the systemic implications are. Through this lens, international violence and the crisis of insecurity we identify in this text are bound up with historically institutionalized and deeply internalized constructions of gender and heteronormativity (that are always raced and classed). The power of gender establishes paths of least resistance in regard to gender performance that are so naturalized they are difficult even to see and so internalized and normalized that they are even harder to defy. As we noted earlier, whether and to whatever extent we individually resist, none of us avoids gender socialization or lifelong pressures to conform to dominant gender norms and expectations.

The model of masculinity that is currently hegemonic encourages males to assume assertive, arrogant, aggressive, and power-over ways of thinking and acting that effectively produce conditions of conflict, othering, competition, and structural violence. In addition, military security policies and practices can be seen, in part, as the pursuit of masculinist reactive autonomy that can tolerate no interdependent relations. This model and its demands do less to empower men than subject them to crippling emotional (and physical) states and unrelenting pressure to "prove" their manhood, when, in reality, any claims to such status are fragile and precarious. Insofar as this model is valorized, women aspire to it as well—in part to enjoy the status and unreconstructed authority it affords and in part to realize its material benefits, such as higher pay.

But adding women to militaries where violence is constitutive raises different issues from adding them to positions of formal political authority. The aggressive and hypermasculinized climate of militaries is particularly hostile to feminized identities and bodies, so that women and feminized men are not and arguably cannot be treated as equal, no matter how well-intentioned individual agents and policies might be. Merely increasing women's presence in militaries without also analyzing the power of gender will simply "resex" militaries to a certain degree without challenging the masculinism and imperialism of the war system and the ways of thinking and acting it engenders. Similarly, merely defining peace as the absence of the direct violence of war simply obscures the deep structural inequalities that both give rise to and are the result of violence. Sustaining sexism, racism, classism, heterosexism, and gendered nationalism has heretofore been vital to sustaining militarism and the "us" and "them" mentality that goes along with it. Thus, any serious attempt to end war must involve significant alterations in local, national, and global hierarchies.

With reference to the crisis of insecurity, the power of gender as a meta-lens naturalizes us-them as a necessarily hierarchical and oppositional dichotomy, which then fuels arrogance, distrust, fear, and often violence. Ultimately, it divides the human community into unequal and opposed beings who must resort to violence to settle disputes. This violent process may alter who the winners and losers are, but it rarely reduces systemic inequalities and keeps reproducing violence. By adopting the lens of reactive autonomy, IR practitioners—even without intending to—reproduce expectations of hostile and competitive behavior, which in turn generate uncooperative and defensive responses. This is how we find ourselves caught in self-perpetuating, vicious cycles such as arms races and "wars on terror" that produce more expressions of "terror" through hypermasculinist "othering" and outlawing all dissent. In contrast, the model of relational autonomy encourages mutual respect and cooperation. For this model to flourish in IR would require that we not only alter our lenses but also make profound changes in our individual and collective practices.

Simona Sharoni (2006) calls for an analytical approach and praxis of "compassionate resistance" to resist imperialist state violence. Arising out of her own scholarship on and resistance work in the context of the Palestinian-Israeli conflict, compassionate resistance refers to "analysis and targeting of oppressive systems and policies" but with "empathy," not only for those on the receiving end of violence, but also for those who are caught up in supporting and/or acting on behalf of oppressors because of uncritical acceptance of structural and ideological pressures (Sharoni 2006: 289). This "humanizes" conflicts while still maintaining clarity about the wrongs of them and who commits those wrongs. Rejecting the more liberal idea of "compassionate listening" between oppositional parties to reduce enmity because it assumes an "equal playing field, " Sharoni argues that compassion cannot be forged without oppressors taking responsibility for concrete acts that have led to unequal power relations on the ground and in a given encounter between those in conflict (2006: 289). This means that "one cannot speak of compassion between Palestinians and Israelis without specific reference to the Israeli occupation of the West Bank and the Gaza Strip and to such oppressive practices as the Apartheid Wall, checkpoints and home demolitions" (Sharoni 2006: 289). However, compassionate resistance can flow when people become aware of their positions in and relationship to the conflict" (Sharoni 2006: 289–290) including deep complicity in it, and make conscious decisions about solidarity work against systems of power, privilege, and control as a result.

Another kind of analytical strategy advocated by Cynthia Weber (1999) is "queering" the national security state. In her "queer" reading of U.S.-Caribbean relations, she finds that invasion and colonizing practices of the United States were fueled by its self-imagination as the male lover who imagines the Caribbean as the feminine object of "his" affections. Unable to maintain the affections of Cuba after "her" revolution against neocolonial rule, the United States, Weber argues, had "his" heterosexual prowess wounded, leading to a relative loss of "phallic" power that it has attempted to camouflage ever since. By seeing international relations as intersexual relations, Weber hopes to expose the very fragile (and, in fact, lost) hegemonic masculinity upon which the United States projects its power, and in the process, prompt a rethinking of U.S. self-identity based on phallic power projection and its violent effects.

Feminist activism against violence in its various forms has a long history and many diverse expressions. Cynthia Cockburn (1998 and 2007) has traveled widely to interview and work with women engaged in producing and negotiating solidarities in the context of often extremely violent conditions. Standing among and with antiwar activists, she asks, "Why does war persist; why, given its recurring horrors, is it still thinkable?" She argues that whatever else the particulars reveal, the cultivation of masculinities in and outside of militaries is key to the reproduction of violence as simply an acceptable way of being. In her words, "War as institution is made up of, refreshed by and adaptively reproduced by violence as banal practice. . . . Masculinity in its various forms is an important content of that cycle: masculinity shapes war and war shapes masculinity" (Cockburn 2007: 248). In concluding her 2007 book, she captures the power of gender—and its violence—in her own terms: "War is the most violently coercive form taken by othering, the space in which differentiation becomes lethal. Its means, the means of coercion, are fearful in the extreme. But it is the othering itself that is the problem. Assuring the self by objectifying, excluding, diminishing, confining, oppressing and exploiting an other" (Cockburn 2007: 258). In this sense, war, and its contemporary form, Empire, is the absence of politics, for it shuts down dialogue and contestation in favor of domination and the inculcation of thoroughgoing complicities in it. The "security myth" ultimately holds all hostage to its dictates and constant replay.

There is nothing simple or easy about identifying and institutionalizing alternatives to violence-as-usual. Generating alternatives presumes as a starting point both a politics of recognition that cultivates respect rather than othering, and a politics of redistribution that minimizes inequalities and grievances that so often fuel conflicts. More specific anti-imperialist strategies entail an emphasis on dialogic, transversal, discursive, and activist restructurings of valorized and devalorized identities of states, nations, and people, coupled with analyses of class, race, gender, nation, and sexuality stratifications and violences that produce and are produced by virulent us-them and self-other dichotomies. Unless we de-gender violence, we leave structural violence in place, producing and reproducing not only "others" who are "disposable" but also violent practices of "disposal."

De-Gendering Labor and Resources

Whereas the desirability of adding women to institutions designed for direct violence (and especially imperialist means and ends) is hotly debated, adding women (and other less economically privileged people) to the public realm of political power-wielders and the business world of economic income earners would seem a less contestable feminist goal. And, of course, feminists have worked long and hard to promote these projects. However, as we have seen, neoliberalism so marketizes and circumscribes political institutions and human relations and subjectivities that gaining such footholds does not necessarily translate into feminist gains more broadly defined as the development of social justice. It also has leavened gendered economic inequalities downward, with some women increasingly enjoying some of the benefits of access to higher political and economic positions, but many men "falling down" economically. This "race to the bottom" for many men and "staying at the bottom" for many women is not the kind of equality that feminists envision. Far more people (women and subordinated men) should be "moving up," but this cannot occur without wider (not just women's) responsibilities for taking care of social reproduction upon which all else depends.

With reference to the crisis of sustainability, the power of gender operates to valorize productive over reproductive, formal over informal, and paid over unpaid labor. This has left women primarily responsible for serving others and ever willing to put family survival ahead their own (despite small and problematic efforts to get men to shoulder more of this work), but it has also ensured that social reproduction more generally is devalorized and underresourced by those at the top. As Kate Bedford (2008) and Amy Lind (forthcoming) observe, the World Bank has begun to "target" men in the global South to become better fathers and husbands to better contribute to social reproduction in the household in the face of widespread poverty and violence. Beyond the heteronormative assumptions of this approach that reproduce paternalism and deny that many households are female-headed and not always heterosexual, this tactic demonizes poor men and deflects attention from primarily elite men's economic policies (proffered by the World Bank and other IFIs) that systematically undermine social reproduction worldwide.

Even if increasing more diverse women's presence at the top of corporate and IFI hierarchies might translate into more humane and gender-sensitive labor and social reproduction policies, the fact remains that few women and few men can actually be at the top of pyramidal hierarchies. Increasing the number of women in higher-paying, male-dominated occupations may increase some women's wages and status. But that would not necessarily lead to challenging the global gendered dichotomy between productive and reproductive labor, which renders the latter "nonwork." Also, drawing poor rural women into circuits of capital through microcredit might enable some entrepreneurial women to prosper. But none of these moves disrupt the logic of capital accumulation or the growth imperative it establishes. They do not lead to questioning what is produced, why, and under what circumstance, nor whose bodies are exploited in the process, whose backyards surrendered to the waste produced, or how actual resources are distributed. Yet these are the underlying problems generating the crisis of sustainability, and to address them we need transformative strategies.

In addition to others just cited, it is necessary to undermine the gendered dichotomy of "modern" and "traditional" that pervades the thinking and practices of development agencies. The power of gender creates an association between "women's work" and "primitive" economic and technological practices found in non-Western societies. This association tends to discredit the knowledge and agency of women in development processes, and devalues the quite complex, self-sufficient, and ecologically sustainable economic activities and technologies in which many women (and some men) engage in traditional societies. Undermining this association and the devaluation of both women and traditional cultures that it entails require questioning the kind of progress that masculinism and modernity have brought to us.

Moving beyond the power of gender involves questioning as well the premises of neoliberal capitalism: the imperative of growth, commodification of the life world, and pursuit of profits for some at the expense of well-being for all. By making visible the costs of current economic priorities, as well as who (most women and all marginalized peoples) and what (the environment) bear the brunt of these costs, states and corporations would find it harder to justify a great deal of what they claim is wealth-generating activity. Such costs include the realities that few are benefiting from the wealth that many workers are producing and that the formal sector of so-called productive work is dependent on the reproductive and informal sectors, rather than the reverse. Keeping the reproductive and informal sectors undervalued is "functional" only for those few at the top who reap greater profits as a result of this under- or devaluation.

Instead of having an equal say in what and how resources are to be used, women and people of the global South more generally are treated as resources themselves. Noting that "added resources" give added power to "states to do things that they could not have done previously," Christine Sylvester argues that "women are non-recognized resources for realist states, occupying positions ranking with oil, geography, industrial capacity, and military preparedness as contributions to power" (1992: 169). In fact, all states (and corporations) appropriate women's (and many men's) bodies and labor to extend their resource base and thus their power within and outside state borders. Yet this fact is concealed by the gendered division of resources. However, when a gender-sensitive lens is used to view world politics, the positions of women in a state's and a corporation's resource base are revealed, permitting women to specify strategies of resistance against this appropriation of their bodies and labor.

Individual women, too (particularly middle- and upper-class women in the global North), have a responsibility to change and curb their consumption patterns. These women benefit—in the form of cheap consumer goods—from the cheap labor of primarily poor and racialized women (and feminized men) of the global South. They do so, however, at the expense of creating international solidarity among women (and men) to struggle against the global gendered division of labor and the exploitative practices of neoliberal capitalism. Ultimately, de-gendering labor will involve increasing not only the presence of women in male-dominated occupations and institutions at all levels but also recognizing the power of gender to perpetuate differential valorization of skills, bodies, identities, jobs, and resources in ways that reproduce and cumulatively deepen inequalities.

Respect for nature as a partner in, not a slave to, the world community must be accompanied by respect for the needs of the vast majority of women and peoples of the global South to enjoy a much greater share of the world's resources. At the same time, it is incumbent on those who struggle for equity in parenting, work, consuming, soldiering, office-holding, decision-making, and property-owning to concern themselves with transforming these activities in ways that are not ecologically harmful. We must engage a politics of redistribution to ensure more equitable access to and control over resources, and a politics of recognition to address shifting identities borne of global migrations and the citizenship claims they raise. Both entail rejecting the symbolic and material valorization of hegemonic masculinity at the expense of all that is feminized. Unless we de-gender labor and resources, we individually and collectively face an ever-deepening and widening crisis of sustainability. On the one hand, feminizing employment without enlarging responsibility for care undermines social reproduction, and exploitative production processes—especially the dangerous, debilitating, and demeaning work that is the survival option for too many—create "disposable" people and even countries. On the other hand, excessive and irresponsible growth "disposes" of natural resources, creates "disposable" waste that further degrades the environment, and depletes the resources upon which we all depend.

De-Constructing the Power of Gender

In concluding this text, we observe that the early feminist insight, asking "where are the women?" remains a productive starting point. This "add women" lens provides telling data on the differential positions and re-positionings of women and men, and in the process, improves our knowledge of men and reveals problems and instabilities not foreseen when women are left out of the picture. Noting how re-positionings are patterned provides a more realistic picture of world politics and enables us to make better sense of "what is going on." In effect, asking the "woman question" in a systematic fashion leads inevitably to asking the "man question." And, as myriad feminist studies across the disciplines confirm, asking these questions leads to complicating sex itself as a constitutive binary and refiguring gender too as not naturally "given" but historically constructed and culturally varying.

Asking feminist questions about the hierarchical relationships between "men" and "women" further disrupts dichotomized thinking, as it leads to seeing there are no generic women or men but rather gendered identities cross-cut by other dimensions of difference—especially ethnicity/race, nationality, and sexuality—so that hierarchies exist among women and men as well as between men and women. In these senses, the "woman question" remains an important and productive starting point because it leads us to more complex and contested terrain. In this text, it leads from "adding women" to recognizing intersectionality and adopting a postcolonial feminist lens. For us, a crucial key is exposing and deconstructing the power of gender as a meta-lens that naturalizes and reproduces essentializing, dichotomizing, stratifying, and depoliticizing thought and action. We have argued that the power of gender constitutes a resilient and adaptive lens, one that is taken for granted and naturalized because beliefs in, and identities based on, a simplistic binary of sex are deeply internalized, and at the same time, there are powerful incentives for conforming to the paths of least resistance they constitute.

One objective in preceding chapters was to present a contemporary picture of global positionings and re-positionings of women and men.

The patterns that appear suggest in some ways an extraordinary shift in awareness of gender inequalities and a corollary commitment to improving hierarchical relationships between men and women through policy reorientations. We note here how these successes confirm the importance of visionary ideals, activist energies, and social movements—in this case women's and feminist movements—for altering social imaginaries and achieving large-scale change. At the same time, we observe that the power of gender as a meta-lens remains too often in place, limiting changes to "adding women" in problematic ways. First, in spite of inclusive rhetoric, only some (typically elite) women get added, which exacerbates hierarchies among women and effectively pits subordinated groups against each other. Second, construing women as a generic group homogenizes their experiences and interests, rather than recognizing differences among women and the necessity of dealing with these through dialogue and in struggle. Third, "framing" women (and particularly women of the global South) exclusively as victims or in need of help renders them a group to be "rescued," rather than listening to them, learning from them, and/or recognizing their agency. Fourth, when essentializing stereotypes are deployed to promote raising the status of women (as incorruptible leaders, natural peacemakers), they often become tools for demonizing some men (as incorrigible tyrants, violence-prone rogues). Fifth, women as the object of policy recommendations become the solution to problems, rather than altering the institutional practices and underlying systems that continuously generate problems. For example, feminizing employment enables women to serve more effectively as "buffers" ensuring family survival during economic crises, but only by increasing the workload for women and altering expectations for only poor men. Constituting women as the problem fixers not only increases their burdens and responsibilities, but also deflects attention away from what causes and reproduces systemic inequalities and who benefits from them. In this sense, the easy fix of "adding women" leaves governmentality, the war system, and global capitalism in place, and fails to hold states, militaries, and corporations accountable for the crises of representation, insecurity, and sustainability they induce.

In short, and however well-intended, simply "adding women" without transforming the power of gender is not only inadequate for addressing

inequalities between women and men but too often exacerbates inequalities among women (and among men). We observe this in the "new politics of gender equality" at the international level, where gender equality
is separated from other forms of equality, with the effect of increasing
other forms of inequality that disadvantage women in other ways while
also increasing subordinated men's resistance to gender equality.

Obviously, a great deal must change before world politics is de-gendered.
Toward that end we have identified some suggestive signposts, but these
are only a beginning. They emerge from a wide-ranging but necessarily
partial investigation of world-politics-as-usual, in which our attention
has focused on the deeply problematic power of gender as a meta-lens
and hegemonic worldview. The dichotomizing, stratifying, and depoliticizing effects of this meta-lens both produce and normalize global
power structures and crises, hence precluding meaningful advances in
social equality and justice. De-gendering world politics requires then
that we disrupt and transform these processes, which entails a serious rethinking of what it means to be human and how we might organize ourselves in more cooperative and mutually respectful ways. It requires no
less than deconstructing the power of gender.

Overall, these changes are less a matter of identifying and promulgating
policies than of individually and collectively remaking human society by
reconstructing our identities, beliefs, expectations, and institutions. This
is the most difficult and complex of human projects, but history shows
that we are capable of such revolutionary transformations.

In one sense, we have no choice. Contemporary global processes
force us to develop new understandings of who "we," as humans, are
and how "we," as global citizens and planetary stewards, must act. In
another sense, we willingly seek systemic transformations because we
desire more than diffusely imposed discipline, globalized fear, and
commodified life worlds. We demand lives of meaning and value, and
the actualization of justice. And whatever our commitments to justice,
we cannot pursue them if we retain the power of gender as a meta-lens
that produces and at the same time normalizes inequalities and hence
injustice. There is no single or simple strategy to follow, but crucially
important is a commitment to re-politicizing thought and action to *resist* what continually divides the world, yet binds it to deadening and
destructive patterns.

Notes

1. Kathleen Staudt's (2008) extensive study of and participation in women's cross-border organizing against femicide at the U.S.-Mexico border shows the extreme obstacles presented by "the border" to that organizing despite such proximity, but she argues that borderlands—as hybrid spaces where the intersection of local, national, and global is so visible—are particularly important sites for the development of coalition politics "on the ground."

2. For numerous examples of explicitly and implicitly feminist struggles against globalization, see Naples and Desai 2002; Waller and Marcos 2005; Moghadam 2005; and Hawkesworth 2006.

3. See Web Resources listed at the end of this text for the online location of CODEPINK and other select feminist NGOs. The Boston Consortium on Gender, Security, and Human Rights is a good source for learning about women engaged in peacebuilding projects in the global South, and other sites offer a wealth of information about contemporary struggles of women (at times, with men) for peace and economic, political, social, and environmental justice.

Web Resources

Select Gender, Gender-related, and other Relevant Intergovernmental Organization (IGO) Policies/Documents

Beijing Platform for Action (BPA)—Fourth World Conference on Women (September 1995)
http://www.un.org/womenwatch/daw/beijing/platform

Convention on the Elimination of All Forms of Discrimination Against Women (CEDAW)
http://www.un.org/womenwatch/daw/cedaw

United Nations Convention on the Rights of the Child (November 20. 1989)
http://www.unhchr.ch/html/menu3/b/k2crc.htm

International Convention on the Elimination of All Forms of Racial Discrimination (December 21, 1965)
http://www2.ohchr.org/english/law/cerd.htm

Gender-related Development Index (GDI) and Gender Empowerment Measure (GEM)
http://hdr.undp.org/en/statistics/indices/gdi_gem

Gender Mainstreaming: A Tool for Change—A European Community of Practice
http://www.gendermainstreaming-cop.eu

United Nations Millennium Development Goals (MDGs)
http://www.un.org/millenniumgoals

United Nations Economic and Social Council Resolution 1997/2 (Gender Mainstreaming)
http://www.un.org/womenwatch/daw/documents/ecosoc1997/
eresAgreedConclusions1997–2.pdf

United Nations Security Council Resolution 1325 (October 31, 2000)
http://www.un.org/events/res_1325e.pdf

United Nations Security Council Resolution 1621 (September 6, 2005)
http://www.peacewomen.org/un/sc/1325_Monitor/RW/Res/1621(2005).pdf

United Nations Security Council Resolution 1820 (June 19, 2008)
http://www.state.gov/documents/organization/106577.pdf

Rome Statute of the International Criminal Court (ICC) (July 17, 1998)
http://untreaty.un.org/cod/icc/index.html

United Nations Global Initiative to Fight Human Trafficking (UN.GIFT)
http://www.ungift.org

European Commission—Justice and Home Affairs—Human Trafficking
http://ec.europa.eu/justice_home/doc_centre/crime/trafficking/wai/doc_crime_
human_trafficking_en.htm

European Union—External Relations—Human Rights & Democratisation—Human Trafficking
http://ec.europa.eu/external_relations/human_rights/traffic/index.htm

United Nations Convention Relating to the Status of Refugees (July 28, 1951)
http://www.unhchr.ch/html/menu3/b/o_c_ref.htm

United Nations Convention Relating to the Status of Stateless Persons (September 28, 1954)
 http://www.unhchr.ch/html/menu3/b/o_c_sp.htm
Universal Declaration of Human Rights (December 10, 1948)
 http://un.org/Overview/rights.html
United Nations Framework Convention on Climate Change (UNFCCC) / Kyoto Protocol
 http://unfccc.int/2860.php

Select Gender and Gender-related Intergovernmental Organizations (IGOs)

Joint United Nations Program on HIV/AIDS (UNAIDS)
 http://www.unaids.org
United Nations Development Fund for Women (UNIFEM)
 http://www.unifem.org
United Nations Division for the Advancement of Women (UNDAW)
 http://www.un.org/womenwatch/daw
United Nations Fund for Population Activities (UNFPA)
 http://www.unfpa.org/
United Nations Inter-Agency Network on Women and Gender Equality (IANWGE)
 http://www.un.org/womenwatch/ianwge/index.html
United Nations International Research and Training Institute for the Advancement of Women (UN-INSTRAW)
 http://www.un-instraw.org
United Nations Office of the Special Adviser to the Secretary-General on Gender Issues and Advancement of Women (OSAGI)
 http://www.un.org/womenwatch/osagi

Other Select Intergovernmental Organizations (IGOs)

Food and Agriculture Organization of the United Nations (FAO)
 http://www.fao.org
International Monetary Fund (IMF)
 http://www.imf.org
International Organization for Migration (IOM/OIM)
 http://www.iom.int/jahia/jsp/index.jsp
Inter-Parliamentary Union (IPU)
 http://www.ipu.org
Office of the United Nations High Commissioner for Refugees (UNHCR)
 http://www.unhcr.org
Organization for Economic Cooperation and Development (OECD)
 http://www.oecd.org
United Nations (UN)
 http://www.un.org
United Nations Development Program (UNDP)
 http://www.undp.org
United Nations Economic and Social Council (ECOSOC)
 http://www.un.org/ecosoc
United Nations Educational, Scientific, and Cultural Organization (UNESCO)
 http://portal.unesco.org
United Nations Environment Program (UNEP)
 http://www.unep.org

World Bank
     http://www.worldbank.org
World Health Organization (WHO)
     http://www.who.int
World Trade Organization (WTO)
     http://www.wto.org

Select Gender and Gender-related Nongovernmental Organizations (NGOs) and Information

Amnesty International (AI)
     http://www.amnesty.org
AI—Stop Violence Against Women
     http://www.amnesty.org/en/campaigns/stop-violence-against-women
Arab Women's Solidarity Association United (AWSA United)
     http://www.awsa.net
Association for Women's Rights in Development (AWID)
     http://www.awid.org
BLACKGIRL INTERNATIONAL
     http://www.blackgirl.org
Boston Consortium on Gender, Security, and Human Rights
     http://www.genderandsecurity.org
Center for Reproductive Rights
     http://reproductiverights.org
Center for Women's Global Leadership
     http://www.cwgl.rutgers.edu
CODEPINK
     http://www.codepink4peace.org
Development Alternatives with Women for a New Era (DAWN)
     http://www.dawnnet.org
Equal Representation in Government and Democracy (ERGD): 50–50 by 2020®
     http://www.ergd.org
Feminist Majority Foundation (FMF)
     http://feminist.org
Feminist Theory and Gender Studies Section (FTGSS) of the International Studies Association
     http://www.femisa.org, http://ftgss.blogspot.com
Global Fund for Women
     http://www.globalfundforwomen.org
Green Belt Movement
     http://www.greenbeltmovement.org
Human Rights Watch
     http://www.hrw.org
Human Rights Watch—Women's Rights
     http://www.hrw.org/en/category/topic/women%E2%80%99s-rights
Institute for Women's Policy Research (IWPR)
     http://www.iwpr.org
Instituto Social y Político de la Mujer (ISPM)
     http://www.ispm.org.ar

International Center for Research on Women (ICRW)
http://www.icrw.org
International Community of Women Living with HIV/AIDS (ICW)
http://www.icw.org
International Feminist Journal of Politics (IFjP)
http://www.tandf.co.uk/journals/titles/14616742.asp
International Women's Rights Action Watch (IWRAW)
http://www1.umn.edu/humanrts/iwraw
International Women's Tribune Centre (IWTC)
http://www.iwtc.org
Isis Women's International Cross Cultural Exchange (Isis-WICCE)
http://www.isis.or.ug
MADRE
http://www.madre.org
National Council for Research on Women (NCRW)
http://www.ncrw.org
Navdanya—Research Foundation for Science, Technology, and Ecology (RFSTE)
http://www.navdanya.org
Pan Pacific and Southeast Asia Women's Association (PPSEAWA)
http://www.ppseawa.org
PeaceWomen: A Project of the Women's International League for Peace and Freedom
http://www.peacewomen.org
Revolutionary Association of the Women of Afghanistan (RAWA)
http://www.rawa.org
WIDE Network
http://www.wide-network.org
Women Against Fundamentalism
http://www.womenagainstfundamentalism.org.uk
Women in Black
http://www.womeninblack.org
Women in International Security (WIIS)
http://www.wiis-brussels.org
Women Living Under Muslim Laws (WLUML)
http://www.wluml.org
Women Nobel Laureates
http://nobelprize.org/nobel_prizes/lists/women.html
Women's Environment and Development Organization (WEDO)
http://www.wedo.org
Women's International League for Peace and Freedom (WILPF)
http://www.wilpf.int.ch
Women's Research and Education Institute (WREI)
http://www.wrei.org
World Social Forum/Fórum Social Mundial
http://www.forumsocialmundial.org.br

References

Ackerly, Brooke A. 2008. *Universal Human Rights in a World of Difference.* Cambridge: Cambridge University Press.

Ackerly, Brooke A., Maria Stern, and Jacqui True, eds. 2006. *Feminist Methodologies for International Relations.* Cambridge and New York: Cambridge University Press.

Ackerly, Brooke A., and Jacqui True. 2006. "Studying the Struggles and Wishes of the Age: Feminist Theoretical Methodology and Feminist Theoretical Methods," in Brooke A. Ackerly, Maria Stern, and Jacqui True, eds., *Feminist Methodologies for International Relations,* pp. 241–260. Cambridge and New York: Cambridge University Press.

Agamben, Giorgio. 1998. *Homo Sacer: Sovereign Power and Bare Life.* Trans. Daniel Heller-Roazen. Stanford, CA: Stanford University Press.

Agathangelou, Anna. 2004. *The Global Political Economy of Sex: Desire, Violence, and Insecurity in Mediterranean Nation States.* New York: Palgrave Macmillan.

Agustín, Laura Maria. 2007. *Sex at the Margins: Migration, Labour Markets, and the Rescue Industry.* London and New York: Zed Books.

Al-Ali, Nadje, and Nicola Pratt. 2009. *What Kind of Liberation? Women and the Occupation of Iraq.* Berkeley: University of California Press.

Alexander, Karen, and Mary E. Hawkesworth, eds. 2008. *War and Terror: Feminist Perspectives.* Chicago: University of Chicago Press.

Alexander, M. Jacqui. 2005. *Pedagogies of Crossing: Meditations on Feminism, Sexual Politics, Memory, and the Sacred.* Durham, NC: Duke University Press.

Alvarez, Lizette, and Erik Eckholm. 2009. "Purple Heart Is Ruled Out for Traumatic Stress." *New York Times,* January 8: A1, A19. Available at http://www.nytimes.com/2009/01/08/us/08purple.html (accessed February 9, 2009).

Alvarez, Sonia. 1999. "Advocating Feminism: The Latin American Feminist NGO 'Boom.'" *International Feminist Journal of Politics* 1(2): 181–209.

American Political Science Association (APSA). 2008. "The Persistent Problem: Inequality, Difference, and the Challenge of Development." Report of the Task Force on Difference, Inequality, and Developing Societies, July. Available at http://www.apsanet.org/~globalinequality/imgtest/ThePersistentProblem.pdf (accessed February 6, 2009).

Andersen, Margaret L. 1983. *Thinking About Women: Sociological and Feminist Perspectives.* New York and London: Macmillan.

Anderson, Bridget. 2000. *Doing the Dirty Work? The Global Politics of Domestic Labour.* London: Zed Books.

Antrobus, Peggy. 2006. "Gender Equality in the New Millennium: Goal or Gimmick?" *Caribbean Quarterly* 52(2/3): 39–50.

Anzaldúa, Gloria. 1999. *Borderlands/La Frontera: The New Mestiza.* 2d ed. San Francisco: Aunt Lute Books.

Araújo, Clara, and Ana Isabel García. 2006. "The Experience and the Impact of Quotas in Latin America," in Drude Dahlerup, ed., *Women, Quotas, and Politics*, pp. 83–111. London and New York: Routledge.

Ashley, Richard. 1989. "Living on Borderlines: Man, Poststructuralism, and War," in James Der Derian and Michael J. Shapiro, eds., *International/Intertextual Relations: Postmodern Readings of World Politics*, pp. 259–322. Lexington, MA: Lexington Books.

Aslanbeigui, Nahid, and Gale Summerfield. 2000. "The Asian Crisis, Gender, and the International Financial Architecture." *Feminist Economics* 6(3): 81–104.

———. 2001. "Risk, Gender, and Development in the 21st Century ." *International Journal of Politics, Culture, and Society* 15(1): 7–26.

Bakker, Isabella. 2007. "Social Reproduction and the Constitution of a Gendered Political Economy." *New Political Economy* 12(4): 541–556.

———, ed. 1994. *The Strategic Silence: Gender and Economic Policy*. London and Atlantic Highlands, NJ: Zed Books.

Bakker, Isabella, and Stephen Gill, eds. 2003. *Power, Production, and Social Reproduction: Human In/Security in the Global Political Economy*. Basingstoke, Hampshire; New York: Palgrave Macmillan.

Barker, Drucilla K., and Susan F. Feiner. 2004. *Liberating Economics: Feminist Perspectives on Families, Work, and Globalization*. Ann Arbor: University of Michigan Press.

Bedford, Kate. 2008. "Governing Intimacy in the World Bank," in Shirin M. Rai and Georgina Waylen, eds., *Global Governance: Feminist Perspectives*, pp. 84–106. Basingstoke and New York: Palgrave Macmillan.

Bedont, Barbara. 2005. "The Renewed Popularity of the Rule of Law: Implications for Women, Impunity, and Peacekeeping," in Dyan Mazurana, Angela Raven-Roberts, and Jane Parpart, eds., *Gender, Conflict, and Peacekeeping*, pp. 83–108. Lanham, MD: Rowman and Littlefield.

Benería, Lourdes. 1995. "Toward a Greater Integration of Gender in Economics." *World Development* 23(11): 1839–1850.

———. 2003. *Gender, Development, and Globalization: Economics as If All People Mattered*. New York: Routledge.

Benhabib, Seyla, and Drucilla Cornell, eds. 1987. *Feminism as Critique: On the Politics of Gender in Late-Capitalist Societies*. Cambridge: Polity.

Bergeron, Suzanne L. 2001. "Political Economy Discourses of Globalization and Feminist Politics." *Signs: Journal of Women in Culture and Society* 26(4): 983–1006.

———. 2003. "Challenging the World Bank's Narrative of Inclusion," in Amitava Kumar, ed., *World Bank Literature*, pp. 157–171. Minneapolis: University of Minnesota Press.

Bertell, Rosalie. 1985. *No Immediate Danger: Prognosis for a Radioactive Earth*. London: Women's Press.

Boris, Eileen, and Elisabeth Prügl, eds. 1996. *Homeworkers in Global Perspective: Invisible No More*. New York and London: Routledge.

Boserup, Esther. 1970. *Woman's Role in Economic Development*. New York: St. Martin's Press.

Brah, Avtar. 2002. "Global Mobilities, Local Predicaments: Globalization and the Critical Imagination." *Feminist Review* 70: 30–45.

Brenner, Johanna. 2009. "Transnational Feminism and the Struggle for Global Justice," in Jai Sen and Peter Waterman, eds., *World Social Forum: Challenging Empires*, pp. 26–37. 2d ed. Montreal and New York: Black Rose Books.

Brittan, Arthur. 1989. *Masculinity and Power*. Oxford and New York: Basil Blackwell.

Brown, Sarah. 1988. "Feminism, International Theory, and International Relations of Gender Inequality." *Millennium Journal of International Studies* 17(3): 461–475.

Brown, Wendy. 1988. *Manhood and Politics: A Feminist Reading in Political Theory.* Totowa, NJ: Rowman and Littlefield.

Bunch, Charlotte and Niamh Reilly. Center for Women's Global Leadership (CWGL). 1994. *Demanding Accountability: The Global Campaign and Vienna Tribunal for Women's Human Rights.* New York: United Nations Development Fund for Women (UNIFEM) and Center for Women's Global Leadership (CWGL).

Carollo, Russell, Jeff Nesmith, and Elliot Jaspin. 1997. "Army Treated Rape as Lesser Crime." *Dayton Daily News*, January 12: A1.

Carver, Terrell. 1996. *Gender Is Not a Synonym for Women.* Boulder, CO: Lynne Rienner Publishers.

Center for Arms Control and Non-Proliferation. 2008. "In Context: US Military Spending Versus Rest of the World." Available at http://www.globalissues.org/article/75/world military-spending (accessed February 22, 2009).

Chan-Tiberghien, Jennifer. 2004. "Gender Skepticism or Gender-Boom? Poststructural Feminisms, Transnational Feminisms, and the World Conference Against Racism." *International Feminist Journal of Politics* 6(3): 454–484.

Chant, Sylvia. 2007. *Gender, Generation, and Poverty: Exploring the "Feminization of Poverty" in Africa, Asia, and Latin America.* Cheltenham and Northhampton, MA: Edward Elgar.

Chappell, Louise, and Lisa Hill. 2006. *The Politics of Women's Interests: New Comparative Perspectives.* London and New York: Routledge.

Chin, Christine B. N. 1998. *In Service and Servitude: Foreign Female Domestic Workers and the Malaysian "Modernity" Project.* New York: Columbia University Press.

Chowdhry, Geeta, and Sheila Nair, eds. 2002. *Power, Postcolonialism, and International Relations: Reading Race, Gender, and Class.* London and New York: Routledge.

Chowdhury, Najma, and Barbara J. Nelson et al. 1994. "Redefining Politics: Patterns of Women's Political Engagement from a Global Perspective," in Barbara J. Nelson and Najma Chowdhury, eds., *Women and Politics Worldwide*, pp. 3–24. New Haven, CT: Yale University Press.

Clancy-Smith, Julia, and Frances Gouda, eds. 1998. *Domesticating the Empire: Race, Gender, and Family Life in French and Dutch Colonialism.* Charlottesville, VA: University Press of Virginia.

Clausewitz, Carl von. 2004. *On War.* Whitefish, MT: Kessinger Publishing.

Cockburn, Cynthia. 1998. *The Space Between Us: Negotiating Gender and National Identities in Conflict.* London: Zed Books.

———. 2007. *From Where We Stand: War, Women's Activism, and Feminist Analysis.* London: Zed Books.

Cohen, Cathy J., Kathleen B. Jones, and Joan C. Tronto, eds. 1997. *Women Transforming Politics: An Alternative Reader.* New York: New York University Press.

Cohn, Carol. 2008. "Mainstreaming Gender in UN Security Policy: A Path to Political Transformation?" in Shirin Rai and Georgina Waylen, eds., *Global Governance: Feminist Perspectives*, pp. 185–206. Basingstoke and New York: Palgrave Macmillan.

Collins, Patricia Hill. 1991. *Black Feminist Thought: Knowledge, Consciousness, and the Politics of Empowerment.* New York: Routledge.

Connell, R. W. 1987. *Gender and Power.* Cambridge, UK: Polity Press.

———. 1995. *Masculinities.* Berkeley: University of California Press.

Cook, Rebecca, ed. 1994. *Human Rights of Women: National and International Perspectives.* Philadelphia: University of Pennsylvania Press.

Cornia, Giovanni Andrea, ed. 2004. *Inequality, Growth, and Poverty in an Era of Liberalization and Globalization.* Oxford: Oxford University Press.

Crenshaw, Kimberlé. 1991. "Mapping the Margins: Intersectionality, Identity Politics, and Violence Against Women of Color." *Stanford Law Review* 43: 1241–1299.

Dahl, Robert A. 1961. *Who Governs? Democracy and Power in an American City.* New Haven, CT: Yale University Press.

Dahlerup, Drude. 2006a. "Conclusion," in Drude Dahlerup, ed., *Women, Quotas, and Politics,* pp. 293–307. London and New York: Routledge.

———. 2006b. "Introduction," in Drude Dahlerup, ed., *Women, Quotas, and Politics,* pp. 3–31. London and New York: Routledge.

D'Amico, Francine. 1997. "Policing the U.S. Military's Race and Gender Lines," in Laurie Weinstein and Christie C. White, eds., *Wives and Warriors: Women and the Military in the United States and Canada,* pp. 199–234. Westport, CT: Bergin and Garvey.

D'Amico, Francine, and Peter R. Beckman. 1994. "Introduction," in Peter R. Beckman and Francine D'Amico, eds., *Women, Gender, and World Politics: Perspectives, Policies, and Prospects,* pp. 1–14. Westport, CT: Bergin and Garvey.

Dangler, Jamie Faricellia. 2000. "The Periodic Resurgence of Non-Factory-Based Production," in Faruk Tabak and Michaeline A. Crichlow, eds., *Informalization: Process and Structure,* pp. 47–68. Baltimore, MD, and London: Johns Hopkins University Press.

De Goede, Marieke. 2005. *Virtue, Fortune, and Faith: A Genealogy of Finance.* Minneapolis: University of Minnesota Press.

Devlin, Claire, and Robert Elgie. 2008. "The Effect of Increased Women's Representation in Parliament: The Case of Rwanda." *Parliamentary Affairs* 61(2): 237–254.

The Economist. 1999. August 28.

Edkins, Jenny. 1999. *Poststructuralism and International Relations: Bringing the Political Back In.* Boulder, CO: Lynne Rienner Publishers.

Ehrenreich, Barbara, and Arlie R. Hochschild. 2002a. "Introduction," in Barbara Ehrenreich and Arlie R. Hochschild, eds., *Global Woman: Nannies, Maids, and Sex Workers in the New Economy,* pp. 1–14. New York: Metropolitan Books.

———, eds. 2002b. *Global Woman: Nannies, Maids, and Sex Workers in the New Economy.* New York: Metropolitan Books.

Einhorn, Barbara, and Eileen Janes Yeo, eds. 1995. *Women and Market Societies: Crisis and Opportunity.* Aldershot and Brookfield, VT: Edward Elgar.

Eisenstein, Zillah R. 2004. *Against Empire: Feminisms, Racisms, and the West.* London: Zed Books.

———. 2007. *Sexual Decoys: Gender, Race, and War in Imperial Democracy.* London: Zed Press; New York: Palgrave.

Eisler, Riane. 2007. *The Real Wealth of Nations: Creating a Caring Economics.* San Francisco: Berrett-Koehler Publishers.

Eisler, Riane, David Loye, and Kari Norgaard. 1995. *Women, Men, and the Global Quality of Life.* Pacific Grove, CA: Center for Partnership Studies.

Elshtain, Jean Bethke. 1987. *Women and War.* New York: Basic Books.

———. 1992. "Sovereignty, Identity, Sacrifice," in V. Spike Peterson, ed., *Gendered States: Feminist (Re)Visions of International Relations Theory,* pp. 141–154. Boulder, CO: Lynne Rienner.

Enloe, Cynthia. 1983. *Does Khaki Become You? The Militarisation of Women's Lives.* Boston, MA: South End Press.

————. 1989. *Bananas, Beaches, and Bases: Making Feminist Sense of International Politics.* Berkeley: University of California Press.

————. 1990. "Womenandchildren: Making Feminist Sense of the Persian Gulf Crisis." *Village Voice*, September 25: 29ff.

————. 1993. *The Morning After: Sexual Politics at the End of the Cold War.* Berkeley, CA: University of California Press.

————. 2000. *Maneuvers: The International Politics of Militarizing Women's Lives.* Berkeley, CA: University of California Press.

————. 2007. *Globalization and Militarism: Feminists Make the Link.* Lanham, MD: Rowman and Littlefield.

Epstein, Cynthia Fuchs. 1988. *Deceptive Distinctions.* New Haven, CT: Yale University Press.

Equal Representation in Government (ERGD). 2009. "Women Prime Ministers and Presidents." Available at http://ergd.org/Premiers.htm (accessed February 8, 2009).

Eschle, Catherine. 2001. *Global Democracy, Social Movements, and Feminism.* Boulder, CO: Westview Press.

————. 2005. "Constructing 'the Anti-Globalisation Movement,'" in Catherine Eschle and Bice Maiguascha, eds., *Critical Theories, International Relations, and the "Anti-Globalization Movement,"* pp. 17–35. London and New York: Routledge.

Eschle, Catherine, and Bice Maiguascha, eds. 2005. *Critical Theories, International Relations, and the "Anti-Globalization Movement."* London and New York: Routledge.

Fall, Yassine. 2001. "Gender and Social Implications of Globalization: An African Perspective," in Rita Mae Kelly et al., eds., *Gender, Globalization, and Democratization*, pp. 49–74. Lanham, MD: Rowman and Littlefield.

Faludi, Susan. 2007. *The Terror Dream: Fear and Fantasy in Post-9/11 America.* New York: Metropolitan Books, Henry Holt and Co.

Farrell, Amy, and Patrice McDermott. 2005. "Claiming Afghan Women: The Challenge of Human Rights Discourse for Transnational Feminism," in Wendy S. Hesford and Wendy Kozol, eds., *Just Advocacy? Women's Human Rights, Transnational Feminisms, and the Politics of Representation*, pp. 33–55. New Brunswick, NJ, and London: Rutgers University Press.

Fausto-Sterling, Anne. 1992. *Myths of Gender: Biological Theories about Women and Men.* 2d ed. New York: Basic Books.

————. 2000. "The Five Sexes, Revisited." *The Sciences* 40(4): 19–23.

Ferber, Marianne A., and Julie A. Nelson, eds. 2003. *Feminist Economics Today: Beyond Economic Man.* Chicago: University of Chicago Press.

Ferguson, Ann. 1984. "On Conceiving Motherhood and Sexuality: A Feminist Materialist Approach," in Joyce Trebilcot, ed., *Mothering: Essays in Feminist Theory*, pp. 153–182. Totowa, NJ: Rowman and Allanheld.

————. 1989. *Blood at the Root: Motherhood, Sexuality, and Male Dominance.* London: Pandora.

Finlay, Barbara. 2006. *George W. Bush and the War on Women: Turning Back the Clock on Progress.* London and New York: Zed Books.

Flanders, Laura, ed. 2004. *The W Effect: Bush's War on Women.* New York: Feminist Press at City University of New York (CUNY).

Floro, Maria, and Gary Dymski. 2000. "Financial Crisis, Gender, and Power: An Analytical Framework." *World Development* 28(7): 1269–1283.

Focal Point for Women in the Secretariat. 2001. "Statistics." *Network: The UN Women's Newsletter* 5 (August) (3). Available at http://www.un.org/womenwatch/osagi/network/fall2001.htm (accessed February 8, 2009).

Foucault, Michel. 1991. "Governmentality," in Graham Burchell, Colin Gordon, and Peter Miller, eds., *The Foucault Effect: Studies in Governmentality*, pp. 87–104. Chicago: University of Chicago Press.

Franklin, M. I. 2004. *Postcolonial Politics, the Internet, and Everyday Life: Pacific Traversals Online.* London and New York: Routledge.

Fraser, Nancy. 1997. *Justice Interruptus: Critical Reflections on the "Postsocialist" Condition.* New York: Routledge.

Friedenwall, Lenita, Drude Dahlerup, and Hege Skjeie. 2006. "The Nordic Countries: An Incremental Model," in Drude Dahlerup, ed., *Women, Quotas, and Politics*, pp. 55–82. London and New York: Routledge.

Ghosh, Nandita. 2007. "Women and the Politics of Water: An Introduction." *International Feminist Journal of Politics* 9(4): 443–454.

Gibson-Graham, J. K. 1996. *The End of Capitalism (As We Knew It): A Feminist Critique of Political Economy.* Cambridge, MA: Blackwell Publishers.

Giddings, Paula. 1984. *When and Where I Enter: The Impact of Black Women on Race and Sex in America.* New York: Bantam Books.

Giles, Wenona, and Jennifer Hyndman. 2004. "Introduction: Gender and Conflict in a Global Context," in Wenona Giles and Jennifer Hyndman, eds., *Sites of Violence: Gender and Conflict Zones*, pp. 3–23. Berkeley: University of California Press.

Gilmore, Stephanie, ed. 2008. *Feminist Coalitions: Historical Perspectives on Second-Wave Feminism in the United States.* Urbana and Chicago: University of Illinois Press.

Goetz, Anne Marie, and Rina Sen Gupta. 1996. "Who Takes the Credit? Gender, Power, and Control over Loan Use in Rural Credit Programs in Bangladesh." *World Development* 24(1): 45–64.

Goldstein, Joshua S. 2001. *War and Gender: How Gender Shapes the War System and Vice Versa.* Cambridge: Cambridge University Press.

Grant, Rebecca. 1994. "The Cold War and the Feminine Mystique," in Peter R. Beckman and Francine D'Amico, eds., *Women, Gender, and World Politics: Perspectives, Policies, and Prospects*, pp. 119–130. Westport, CT: Bergin and Garvey.

Grewal, Inderpal. 2005. *Transnational America: Feminisms, Diasporas, Neoliberalisms.* Durham, NC, and London: Duke University Press.

Grewal, Inderpal, and Caren Kaplan, eds. 1994. *Scattered Hegemonies: Postmodernity and Transnational Feminist Practices.* Minneapolis and London: University of Minnesota Press.

Grewal, Inderpal, and Caren Kaplan. 2001. "Global Identities: Theorizing Transnational Studies of Sexuality." *GLQ* 7(4): 663–679.

Guerrero, M. A. Jaimes. 1997. "Exemplars of Indigenism: Native North American Women for Decolonization and Liberation," in Cathy J. Cohen, Kathleen B. Jones, and Joan C. Tronto, eds., *Women Transforming Politics: An Alternative Reader*, pp. 205–222. New York: New York University Press.

Hague, Euan. 1997. "Rape, Power, and Masculinity: The Construction of Gender and National Identities in the War in Bosnia-Herzegovina," in Ronit Lentin, ed., *Gender and Catastrophe*, pp. 50–63. London and New York: Zed Books.

Hanochi, Seiko. 2001. "Japan and the Global Sex Industry," in Rita Mae Kelly et al., eds., *Gender, Globalization, and Democratization*, pp. 137–148. Lanham, MD: Rowman and Littlefield.

Harcourt, Wendy, ed. 1999. *Women@Internet: Creating New Cultures in Cyberspace.* London and New York: Zed Books.

Harding, Sandra. 1986. *The Science Question in Feminism.* Ithaca, NY: Cornell University Press.

————. 1991. *Whose Science? Whose Knowledge? Thinking from Women's Lives.* Ithaca, NY: Cornell University Press.

Hardt, Michael, and Antonio Negri. 2000. *Empire.* Cambridge, MA: Harvard University Press.

Hawkesworth, Mary E. 2006. *Globalization and Feminist Activism.* Lanham, MD: Rowman and Littlefield.

Hawthorne, Susan, and Bronwyn Winter, eds. 2002. *September 11, 2001: Feminist Perspectives.* North Melbourne, Australia: Spinifex.

Hesford, Wendy S., and Wendy Kozol, eds. 2005. *Just Advocacy? Women's Human Rights, Transnational Feminisms, and the Politics of Representation.* New Brunswick, NJ: Rutgers University Press.

Hewitson, Gillian J. 1999. *Feminist Economics: Interrogating the Masculinity of Rational Economic Man.* Cheltenham, UK: Edward Elgar.

Hoogensen, Gunhild, and Bruce O. Solheim. 2006. *Women in Power: World Leaders Since 1960.* Westport, CT, and London: Praeger.

Hooper, Charlotte. 1998. "Masculinist Practices and Gender Politics: The Operation of Multiple Masculinities in International Relations," in Marysia Zalewski and Jane Parpart, eds., *The "Man" Question in International Relations,* pp. 28–53. Boulder, CO: Westview Press.

————. 2001. *Manly States: Masculinities, International Relations, and Gender Politics.* New York: Columbia University Press.

Hudson, Heidi. 2005. "Peacekeeping Trends and Their Gender Implications for Regional Peacekeeping Forces in Africa: Progress and Challenges," in Dyan Mazurana, Angela Raven-Roberts, and Jane Parpart, eds., *Gender, Conflict, and Peacekeeping,* pp. 111–133. Lanham, MD: Rowman and Littlefield.

Hughes, Donna M. 2000. "The 'Natasha' Trade: The Transnational Shadow Market of Trafficking in Women." *Journal of International Affairs* 53(2): 625–652.

Human Rights Watch. 2008. "Afghanistan: Civilian Deaths from Airstrikes." Available at http://www.hrw.org/en/news/2008/09/07/Afghanistan-civilian-deaths-airstrikes (accessed January 14, 2009).

Hunt, Krista, and Kim Rygiel, eds. 2006. *(En)gendering the War on Terror: War Stories and Camouflaged Politics.* Burlington, VT: Ashgate.

iCasualties. 2009a. "Iraq Coalition Casualty Count." Available at http://icasualties.org/oif (accessed January 14, 2009).

iCasualties. 2009b. "Operation Enduring Freedom." Available at http://icasualties.org/oef (accessed January 14, 2009).

INCITE! Women of Color Against Violence. 2007. *The Revolution Will Not Be Funded: Beyond the Non-Profit Industrial Complex.* Cambridge, MA: South End Press.

International Labor Organization (ILO). 2002a. *Decent Work and the Informal Economy* (Report VI). Geneva: ILO. Available at http://www.ilo.org/public/english/standards/relm/ilc/ilc90/pdf/rep-vi.pdf (accessed February 8, 2009).

————. 2002b. *Women and Men in the Informal Economy: A Statistical Picture.* Geneva: ILO. Available at http://www.ilo.org/public/english/region/ampro/cinterfor/temas/informal/genero/doc.htm (accessed February 8, 2009).

International Organization for Migration in Iraq (IOM). 2008. "Iraq Displacement and Return: 2008 Mid-Year Review." Available at http://www.iom-iraq.net/Library/Iraq%20Displacement%20and%20Return%20Mid-Year%20Review%202008.pdf (accessed February 3, 2009).

Inter-Parliamentary Union (IPU). 2006. "Women in National Parliaments." Available at http://www.ipu.org/wmn-e/arc/classif300906.htm (accessed October 10, 2008).

Iraq Body Count. 2009. "Iraq Body Count." Available at http://www.iraqbodycount.org (accessed January 14, 2009).

Jagger, Alison M. 1983. *Feminist Politics and Human Nature.* Totawa, NJ: Rowman and Allenheld.

Jeffords, Susan. 1989. *The Remasculinization of America: Gender and the Vietnam War.* Bloomington and Indianapolis: Indiana University Press.

Joachim, Jutta M. 2007. *Agenda Setting, the UN, and NGOs: Gender Violence and Reproductive Rights.* Washington, DC: Georgetown University Press.

Joekes, Susan, and Ann Weston. 1995. *Women and the New Trade Agenda.* New York: UNIFEM.

Johnson, Allan G. 2005. *The Gender Knot: Unraveling Our Patriarchal Legacy.* Philadelphia, PA: Temple University Press.

———. 2006. *Power, Privilege, and Difference.* 2d ed. Mountain View, CA: Mayfield.

Jones, Ann. 2008. "A Crime Against Society." *The Nation,* December 29, pp. 16–20. Available at http://www.thenation.com/doc/20081229/jones (accessed March 11, 2009).

Jones, David E. 1997. *Women Warriors: A History.* London and Washington, DC: Brassey's.

Jones, Kathleen B. 1993. *Compassionate Authority: Democracy and the Representation of Women.* New York and London: Routledge.

Jones-DeWeever, Avis. 2008. "Executive Summary," in Avis Jones-DeWeever, Institute for Women's Policy Research (IWPR), *Women in the Wake of the Storm: Examining the Post-Katrina Realities of the Women of New Orleans and the Gulf Coast.* Available at http://www.iwpr.org/pdf/GulfCoastExecutiveSummary.pdf (accessed March 17, 2009).

Joseph, Ammu, and Kalpan Sharma, eds. 2003. *Terror, Counter-Terror: Women Speak Out.* London and New York: Zed Books.

Kamel, Rachel. 1990. *The Global Factory.* Washington, DC: American Friends Service Committee.

Kampwirth, Karen. 2002. *Women and Guerilla Movements: Nicaragua, El Salvador, Chiapas, Cuba.* University Park: Pennsylvania State University Press.

Kaufman, Joyce P., and Kristen P. Williams. 2007. *Women, the State, and War: A Comparative Perspective on Citizenship and Nationalism.* Lanham, MD: Lexington Books.

Keck, Margaret, and Karen Sikkink. 1998. *Activists Beyond Borders: Transnational Advocacy Networks in International Politics.* Ithaca, NY: Cornell University Press.

Kempadoo, Kamala, ed. 2005. *Trafficking and Prostitution Reconsidered: New Perspectives on Migration, Sex Work, and Human Rights.* Boulder, CO: Paradigm Publisher.

Kempadoo, Kamala, and Jo Doezema, eds. 1998. *Global Sex Workers.* New York: Routledge.

Kimmel, Michael. 2008. *Guyland.* New York: Harper Collins.

Klein, Naomi. 2007. *The Shock Doctrine: The Rise of Disaster Capitalism.* New York: Metropolitan Books, Henry Holt and Co.

Knapp, Gudrun-Axeli. 2005. "Race, Class, Gender: Reclaiming Baggage in Fast Travelling Theories." *European Journal of Women's Studies* 12(3): 249–265.

Laclau, Ernesto, and Chantal Mouffe. 1985. *Hegemony and the Socialist Strategy: Toward a Radical Democratic Politics.* London: Verso.

Levine, Philippa, ed. 2004. *Gender and Empire.* Oxford and New York: Oxford University Press.

Lind, Amy. forthcoming. "Queering Globalization: Sexual Subjectivities, Development, and the Governance of Intimacy," in Marianne H. Marchand and Anne Sisson Runyan, eds., *Gender and Global Retructuring: Sightings, Sites, and Resistances.* 2d ed. London and New York: Routledge.

Ling, L.H.M. 2002. *Postcolonial International Relations: Conquest and Desire between Asia and the West*. London: Palgrave.

Lips, Hilary. 1991. *Women, Men, and Power*. Mountain View, CA: Mayfield.

Lorde, Audre. 2008. "The Master's Tools Will Never Dismantle the Master's House," reprinted in Alison Bailey and Chris Cuomo, eds., *The Feminist Philosophy Reader*, pp. 49–50. New York: McGraw-Hill.

Lovenduski, Joni, ed. 2005. *State Feminism and Political Representation*. Cambridge and New York: Cambridge University Press.

Macdonald, Cameron Lynne, and Carmen Sirianni, eds. 1996. *Working in the Service Society*. Philadelphia, PA: Temple University Press.

Macdonald, Laura. 1994. "Globalizing Civil Society: Interpreting International NGOs in Central America." *Millennium* 23: 227–285.

Macfarquhar, Neil. 2008. "In a First, Gay Rights Are Pressed at the U.N." *New York Times*, December 19: A22. Available at http://www.nytimes.com/2008/12/19/world/19nations .html?partner=permalink&exprod=permalink (accessed February 3, 2009).

Mackie, Vera. 2001. "The Language of Globalization, Transnationality, and Feminism." *International Feminist Journal of Politics* 3(2): 180–206.

Marchand, Marianne H., and Anne Sisson Runyan, eds. 2000. *Gender and Global Restructuring: Shifting Sites and Sightings*. London: Routledge.

Masters, Cristina. 2008. "Bodies of Technology and the Politics of the Flesh," in Jane L. Parpart and Marysia Zalewski, eds., *Rethinking the Man Question: Sex, Gender and Violence in International Relations*, pp. 87–108. London and New York: Zed Books.

Matland, Richard E. 2006. "Electoral Quotas: Frequency and Effectiveness," in Drude Dahlerup, ed., *Women, Quotas, and Politics*, pp. 275–292. London and New York. Routledge.

McCall, Leslie. 2001. *Complex Inequality: Gender, Class, and Race in the New Economy*. New York: Routledge.

McCaughey, Martha. 2008. *The Caveman Mystique: Pop-Darwinism and the Debates over Sex, Violence, and Science*. New York: Routledge.

McClintock, Anne. 1995. *Imperial Leather: Race, Gender, and Sexuality in the Colonial Contest*. New York: Routledge.

McIntosh, Peggy. 2007. "White Privilege and Male Privilege," in Vera Taylor, Nancy Whittier, and Leila J. Rupp, eds., *Feminist Frontiers*, pp. 9–15. 7th ed. Boston: McGraw-Hill.

Mendoza, Breny. 2002. "Transnational Feminisms in Question." *Feminist Theory* 3(3): 295–314.

Merchant, Carolyn. 1980. *The Death of Nature: Women, Ecology, and the Scientific Revolution*. San Francisco: Harper and Row.

Midgley, Claire, ed. 1998. *Gender and Imperialism*. Manchester: Manchester University Press.

Mies, Maria, Veronika Bennholdt-Thomsen, and Claudia von Werlhof. 1988. *Women: The Last Colony*. London and New York: Zed Books.

Moghadam, Valentine M. 2005. *Globalizing Women: Transnational Feminist Networks*. Baltimore, MD: Johns Hopkins University Press.

———, ed. 1994. *Democratic Reform and the Position of Women in Transitional Economies*. Oxford and New York: Oxford University Press.

Mohanty, Chandra Talpade. 1991. "Under Western Eyes: Feminist Scholarship and Colonial Discourses," in Chandra Mohanty, Ann Russo, and Lourdes Torres, eds., *Third World Women and the Politics of Feminism*, pp. 51–80. Bloomington and Indianapolis: Indiana University Press.

————. 2003. *Feminism Without Borders: Decolonizing Theory, Practicing Solidarity*. Durham, NC, and London: Duke University Press.

Montagu, Ashley. 1974. *The Natural Superiority of Women*. New York: Collier Books.

Moon, Katharine H. S. 1997. *Sex Among Allies: Military Prostitution in U.S.-Korea Relations*. New York: Columbia University Press.

Nanda, Serena. 1998. *Neither Man Nor Woman: The Hijras of India*. New York: Wadsworth.

Naples, Nancy, and Manisha Desai, eds. 2002. *Women's Activism and Globalization: Linking Local Struggles and Transnational Politics*. New York: Routledge.

National Council for Research on Women (NCRW). 2006. *Gains and Gaps: A Look at the World's Women*. New York: NCRW.

Nelson, Julie A. 1996. *Feminism, Objectivity, and Economics*. London: Routledge.

Nelson, Lin. 1990. "The Place of Women in Polluted Places," in Irene Diamond and Gloria Feman Orenstein, eds., *Reweaving the World: The Emergence of Ecofeminism*, pp. 173–188. San Francisco: Sierra Club Books.

Nelson, Mariah Burton. 1994. *The Stronger Women Get, the More Men Love Football*. New York: Avon Books.

Nikolic-Ristanovic, Verna. 1996. "War and Violence Against Women," in Jennifer Turpin and Lois Ann Lorentzen, eds., *The Gendered New World Order: Militarism, Development, and the Environment*, pp. 195–210. New York: Routledge.

Okin, Susan Moller. 1979. *Women in Western Political Thought*. Princeton: Princeton University Press.

Oliver, Kelly. 2007. *Women as Weapons of War: Iraq, Sex, and the Media*. New York: Columbia University Press.

Okojo, Kamene. 1994. "Women and the Evolution of a Ghanaian Political Synthesis," in Barbara J. Nelson and Najma Chowdhury, eds., *Women and Politics Worldwide*, pp. 285–297. New Haven, CT: Yale University Press.

Ong, Aihwa. 2006. *Neoliberalism as Exception: Mutations of Citizenship and Sovereignty*. Durham, NC, and London: Duke University Press.

Oosterveld, Valerie. 2005. "Prosecution of Gender-based Crimes in International Law," in Dyan Mazurana, Angela Raven-Roberts, and Jane Parpart, eds., *Gender, Conflict, and Peacekeeping*, pp. 94–117. Lanham, MD: Rowman and Littlefield.

Parpart, Jane L., and Marysia Zalewski, eds. 2008. *Rethinking the Man Question: Sex, Gender, and Violence in International Relations*. London: Zed Books.

Pateman, Carole. 1988. *The Sexual Contract*. Cambridge: Polity.

Peters, Julia, and Andrea Wolper, eds. 1995. *Women's Rights, Human Rights: International Feminist Perspectives*. New York and London: Routledge.

Peterson, V. Spike. 2003. *A Critical Rewriting of Global Political Economy: Integrating Reproductive, Productive, and Virtual Economies*. London and New York: Routledge.

————. 2007. "Thinking Through Intersectionality and War." Special Issue on "Race, Gender, Class, Sexuality, and War." *Race, Gender, and Class* 14(3/4): 10–27.

Peterson, V. Spike, and Laura Parisi. 1998. "Are Women Human? It's Not an Academic Question," in Tony Evans, ed., *Human Rights Fifty Years On: A Radical Reappraisal*, pp. 132–160. Manchester: University of Manchester Press; New York: St. Martin's Press.

Pettman, Jan Jindy. 1996. *Worlding Women: A Feminist International Politics*. London and New York: Routledge.

————. 1997. "Body Politics: International Sex Tourism." *Third World Quarterly* 18(1): 93–108.

Phillips, Anne. 1991. *Engendering Democracy*. University Park: Pennsylvania State University Press.

Phoenix, Ann, and Pamela Pattynama, eds. 2006. Special Issue on "Intersectionality." *European Journal of Women's Studies* 13(3).

Pierson, Ruth Roach, ed. 1987. *Women and Peace: Theoretical, Historical, and Practical Perspectives*. London and New York: Croom Helm.

Poster, Winifred, and Zakia Salime. 2002. "The Limits of Microcredit: Transnational Feminism and USAID Activities in the United States and Morocco," in Nancy A. Naples and Manisha Desai, eds., *Women's Activism and Globalization*, pp. 189–219. New York: Routledge.

Power, Marilyn. 2004. "Social Provisioning as a Starting Point for Feminist Economics." *Feminist Economics* 10(3): 3–20.

Prügl, Elisabeth. 1999. *The Global Construction of Gender: Home-Based Work in the Political Economy of the Twentieth Century*. New York: Columbia University Press.

Rai, Shirin M. 2002. *Gender and the Political Economy of Development*. Cambridge: Polity.

———. 2008. "Analyzing Global Governance," in Shirin Rai and Georgina Waylen, eds., *Global Governance: Feminist Perspectives*, pp. 19–42. Basingstoke and New York: Palgrave Macmillan.

Randall, Vicky. 1987. *Woman and Politics: An International Perspective*. 2d ed. Chicago: University of Chicago Press.

Rayner, Richard. 1997. "The Warrior Besieged," *New York Times Magazine*, June 22: pp. 24–29. Available at http://query.nytimes.com/gst/fullpage.html?res=9C07E0D6113FF931A15755C0A961958260&sec=&spon=&partner=permalink&exprod=permalink (accessed February 8, 2009).

Reagon, Bernice Johnson. 2000. "Coalition Politics: Turning the Century," in Barbara Smith, ed., *Home Girls: A Black Feminist Anthology*, pp. 343–355. New Brunswick, NJ, and London: Rutgers University Press.

Richardson, Laurel W., and Verta A. Taylor, eds. 1983. *Feminist Frontiers: Rethinking Sex, Gender, and Society*. Reading, MA: Addison-Wesley.

Rodda, Annabel. 1991. *Women and the Environment*. London: Zed Books.

Roscoe, Will. 2000. *Changing Ones: Third and Fourth Genders in Native North America*. London: Palgrave Macmillan.

Roy, Arundhati. 2003. *War Talk*. Cambridge, MA: South End Press.

Ruddick, Sara. 1984. "Preservative Love and Military Destruction," in Joyce Trebilcot, ed., *Mothering: Essays in Feminist Theory*, pp. 231–262. Totowa, NJ: Rowman and Allanheld.

Russo, Ann. 2006. "The Feminist Majority Foundation's Campaign to Stop Gender Apartheid: The Intersections of Feminism and Imperialism in the United States." *International Feminist Journal of Politics* 8(6): 557–580.

Said, Edward. 1979. *Orientalism*. New York: Vintage Books.

———. 1993. *Culture and Imperialism*. New York: Knopf.

Sang-Hun, Choe. 2009. "Ex-Prostitutes Say South Korea and the U.S. Enabled Sex Trade Near Bases," *New York Times*, January 8: A6.

Sapiro, Virginia. 1983. *The Political Integration of Women: Roles, Socialization, and Politics*. Urbana: University of Illinois Press.

Seager, Joni. 1993. *Earth Follies: Coming to Feminist Terms with the Global Environmental Crisis*. New York: Routledge.

———. 1997. *The State of Women in the World Atlas*. 2d ed. New York: Penguin Books.

———. 2009. *The Penguin Atlas of Women in the World*. 4th ed. New York: Penguin Books.

Seager, Joni, and Betsy Hartmann. 2005. *Mainstreaming Gender in Environmental Assessment and Early Warning*. Nairobi, Kenya: United Nations Environment Program (UNEP).

Available at http://www.unep.org/DEWA/products/publications/2005/Mainstreaming_Gender.pdf (accessed March 11, 2009).

Sen, Gita and Caren Grown, eds. Development Alternative with Women for a New Era (DAWN). 1987. *Development, Crises, and Alternative Visions: Third World Women's Perspectives.* New York: Monthly Review Press.

Sen, Jai, and Peter Waterman, eds. 2009. *World Social Forum: Challenging Empires.* Montreal: Black Rose Books.

Sharoni, Simona. 1995. *Gender and the Israeli-Palestinian Conflict: The Politics of Women's Resistance.* Syracuse, NY: Syracuse University Press.

———. 1998. "Gendering Conflict and Peace in Israel/Palestine and the North of Ireland." *Millennium: Journal of International Studies* 27: 1061–1089.

———. 2006. "Compassionate Resistance: A Personal/Political Journey to Israel/Palestine." *International Feminist Journal of Politics* 8(2): 288–299.

Shiva, Vandana. 1993. "GATT, Agriculture, and Third World Women," in Maria Mies and Vandana Shiva, eds., *Ecofeminism,* pp. 231–245. London: Zed Books.

———. 2005. *Earth Democracy.* Cambridge, MA: South End Press.

Sivard, Ruth Leger. 1991. *World Military and Social Expenditures.* Washington, DC: World Priorities.

———. 1996. *World Military and Social Expenditures.* Washington, DC: World Priorities.

Sjoberg, Laura, and Caron E. Gentry. 2007. *Mothers, Monsters, Whores: Women's Violence in Global Politics.* London and New York: Zed Books.

Smith, Dan. 1997. *The State of War and Peace Atlas.* London: Penguin Books.

Smith, Hilda L., and Berenice A. Carroll. 2000. *Women's Political and Social Thought: An Anthology.* Bloomington: Indiana University Press.

Snyder, Karrie Ann. 2005. "Gender Segregation in the Hidden Labor Force: Looking at the Relationship between the Formal and Informal Economies." *Gender Realities* 9: 1–27.

Sontag, Deborah, and Lizette Alvarez. 2008. "Across America, Deadly Echoes of Foreign Battles." *New York Times,* January 13: A1, A14–15.

Spivak, Gayatri Chakravorty. 1987. *In Other Worlds: Essays in Cultural Politics.* London and New York: Methuen.

———. 1988. "Can the Subaltern Speak?" in Cary Nelson and Lawrence Grossberg, eds., *Marxism and the Interpretation of Culture,* pp. 271–313. Urbana and Chicago: University of Illinois Press.

———. 1998. "Gender and International Studies." *Millennium: Journal of International Studies* 27(4): 809–831.

———. 1999. *A Critique of Postcolonial Reason: Toward a History of the Vanishing Present.* Cambridge, MA: Harvard University Press.

Squires, Judith. 2007. *The New Politics of Gender Equality.* Basingstoke and New York: Palgrave Macmillan.

Squires, Judith A., and Jutta Weldes. 2007. "Beyond Being Marginal: Gender and International Relations in Britain." *British Journal of Politics and International Relations* 9(2): 185–203.

Staudt, Kathleen. 2008. "Gender, Governance, and Globalization at Borders: Femicide at the US-Mexico Border," in Shirin Rai and Georgina Waylen, eds., *Global Governance: Feminist Perspectives,* pp. 234–253. Basingstoke and New York: Palgrave Macmillan.

Steans, Jill. 2006. *Gender and International Relations.* 2d ed. New Brunswick, NJ: Rutgers University Press.

Stiehm, Judith Hicks. 1989. *Arms and the Enlisted Woman.* Philadelphia, PA: Temple University Press.

Stienstra, Deborah. 1999. "Of Roots, Leaves, and Trees: Gender, Social Movements, and Global Governance," in Mary K. Meyer and Elisabeth Prügl, eds., *Gender Politics in Global Governance*, pp. 260–272. Lanham, MD: Rowman and Littlefield.

Sudbury, Julia, ed. 2005. *Global Lockdown: Race, Gender, and the Prison-Industrial Complex*. New York: Routledge.

Sutton, Barbara, Sandra Morgen, and Julie Novkov, eds. 2008. *Security Disarmed: Critical Perspectives on Gender, Race, and Militarization*. New Brunswick, NJ: Rutgers University Press.

Sylvester, Christine. 1992. "Feminists and Realists View Autonomy and Obligation in International Relations," in V. Spike Peterson, ed., *Gendered States: Feminist (Re)Visions of International Relations Theory*, pp. 155–178. Boulder, CO: Lynne Rienner.

———. 1994. *Feminist Theory and International Relations in a Postmodern Era*. Cambridge: Cambridge University Press.

———. 2002. *Feminist International Relations: An Unfinished Journey*. Cambridge: Cambridge University Press.

Tetreault, Mary Ann, and Ronnie D. Lipschutz. 2005. *Global Politics as If People Mattered*. Lanham, MD: Rowman and Littlefield.

Tickner, J. Ann. 1993. *Gender in International Relations*. New York: Columbia University Press.

———. 2001. *Gendering World Politics: Issues and Approaches in the Post–Cold War Era*. New York: Columbia University Press.

———. 2006. "Feminism Meets International Relations: Some Methodological Issues," in Brooke Ackerly, Maria Stern, and Jacqui True, eds., *Feminist Methodologies for International Relations*, pp. 19–41. Cambridge: Cambridge University Press.

Truong, Thanh-Dam. 1999. "The Underbelly of the Tiger: Gender and the Demystification of the Asian Miracle." *Review of International Political Economy* 6(2): 133–165.

———. 2000. "A Feminist Perspective on the Asia Miracle and Crisis." *Journal of Human Development* 1(1): 159–164.

United Nations (UN). 1995. *The World's Women 1995: Trends and Statistics*. New York: United Nations.

———. 2000. *The World's Women 2000: Trends and Statistics*. New York: United Nations.

United Nations Development Program (UNDP). 1995. *Human Development Report 1995*. New York: Oxford University Press.

———. 1997. *Human Development Report 1997*. New York: Oxford University Press.

———. 2007a. "Table 28: Gender-related Development Index," in UNDP *Human Development Report 2007/2008*, pp. 326–329. Available at http://hdr.undp.org/en/media/HDR_20072008_GDI.pdf (accessed December 5, 2008).

———. 2007b. "Table 29: Gender Empowerment Measure," in UNDP *Human Development Report 2007/2008*, pp. 330–333. Available at http://hdr.undp.org/en/media/HDR_20072008_GEM.pdf (accessed December 5, 2008).

United Nations Development Fund for Women (UNIFEM). 2008. *Progress of the World's Women 2008/2009: Who Answers to Women?* New York: UNIFEM. Available at http://www.unifem.org/progress/2008/media/POWW08_Report_Full_Text.pdf (accessed February 6, 2009).

United Nations Division for the Advancement of Women (UNDAW). 1989. "Women and Decision-Making," UN Doc. EGM/EPPDM/1989/WP.1/Rev.1. Vienna: United Nations.

United Nations High Commmissioner for Refugees (UNHCR). 2009a. "Statement by António Guterres, UN High Commissioner for Refugees, to the UN Security Council," New York, 8 January. Available at http://www.unhcr.org/admin/ADMIN/496625484.html (accessed March 11, 2009).

———. 2009b. Press Release, "High Commissioner Guterres Briefs Security Council on Global Protection Challenges." New York, January 8. Available at http://www.unhcr.org/news/NEWS/49661c7e4.html (accessed March 11, 2009).

Van Staveren, Irene. 2002. "Global Finance and Gender," in Jan Aart Scholte and Albrecht Schnabel, eds., *Civil Society and Global Finance,* pp. 228–246. London: Routledge.

Vickers, Jean. 1991. *Women and the World Economic Crisis.* London and New York: Zed Books.

Vickers, Jill. 2006. "The Problem with Interests: Making Political Claims for Women," in Louise Chappell and Lisa Hill, eds., *The Politics of Women's Interests,* pp. 5–38. London and New York: Routledge.

Wade, Robert H. 2004. "Is Globalization Reducing Poverty and Inequality?" *World Development* 32(4): 567–589.

Waller, Marguerite, and Sylvia Marcos, eds. 2005. *Dialogue and Difference: Feminisms Challenge Globalization.* New York and Basingstoke: Palgrave Macmillan.

Ward, Kathryn B. 1990. "Introduction and Overview," in Kathryn B. Ward, ed., *Women Workers and Global Restructuring,* pp. 1–24. Ithaca, NY: ILR Press of Cornell University.

Washington Post. 2009. "Faces of the Fallen." Available at http://projects.washington post.com/fallen (accessed January 14, 2009).

Weber, Cynthia. 1999. *Faking It: U.S. Hegemony in a "Post-Phallic" Era.* Minneapolis and London: University of Minnesota Press.

Weiner, Jim. 1996. "Army Expands Sex Inquiry: One Sergeant Pleads Guilty." *New York Times,* November 13: A1, A16.

Whitworth, Sandra. 2004. *Men, Militarism, and UN Peacekeeping: A Gendered Analysis.* Boulder, CO: Lynne Rienner.

———. 2008. "Militarized Masculinity and Post-Traumatic Stress Disorder," in Jane L. Parpart and Marysia Zalewski, eds., *Rethinking the Man Question: Sex, Gender, and Violence in International Relations,* pp. 109–126. London and New York: Zed Books.

Woehl, Stephanie. 2008. "Global Governance as Neoliberal Govenmentality: Gender Mainstreaming in the European Employment Strategy," in Shrin Rai and Georgina Waylen, eds., *Gender and Global Governance: Feminist Perspectives,* pp. 64–83. Basingstoke and New York: Palgrave Macmillan.

Women's Environment and Development Organization (WEDO). 2007a. "Changing the Climate: Why Women's Perspectives Matter" (Factsheet). Available at http://www .awid.org/eng/Issues-and-Analysis/Library/Changing-the-Climate-Why-Women-s-Perspectives-Matter (accessed February 5, 2009).

———. 2007b. "50/50: Getting the Balance Right in National Cabinets" (Factsheet). Available at http://www.wedo.org/wp-content/uploads/5050_cabinetsfactsheet021.pdf (accessed February 5, 2009).

———. 2008. "Women: Essential to Climate Change Solutions" (Factsheet). Available at https://www.wedo.org/wp-content/uploads/wdaccmediafactsheet.pdf (accessed March 17, 2009).

World Bank. 2005. *Global Economic Prospects: Economic Implications of Remittances and Migration 2006.* Washington, DC: World Bank.

———. 2008. *Migration and Remittances Factbook.* Washington, DC: World Bank.

World Council of Churches (WCC). 2005. *World Military Expenditures: A Compilation of Data and Facts Related to Military Spending, Education, and Health.* Geneva, Switzerland: WCC Coordination Office for the Decade to Overcome Violence. Available at http://overcomingviolence.org/fileadmin/dov/files/wcc_resources/dov_documents/MilitarySpendingReport.pdf (accessed February 8, 2009).

World Development. 1995. Special Issue: Gender, Adjustment, and Macroeconomics. 23(11): 1825–2017.

———. 2000. Special Issue: Growth, Trade, Finance, and Gender Inequality. 28(7): 1145–1390.

Wright, Melissa. 2006. *Disposable Women and Other Myths of Global Capitalism.* New York and London: Routledge.

Young, Brigitte. 2001. "Globalization and Gender: A European Perspective," in Rita Mae Kelly et al., eds., *Gender, Globalization, and Democratization,* pp. 27–47. Lanham, MD: Rowman and Littlefield.

Youngs, Gillian. 2005. "Ethics of Access: Globalization and the Information Society." *Journal of Global Ethics* 1(1): 69–83.

Yuval-Davis, Nira. 1997. *Gender and Nation.* London: Sage.

———. 2006. "Intersectionality and Feminist Politics." *European Journal of Women's Studies* 13(3): 193–209.

Zalewski, Marysia, and Jane Parpart, eds. 1998. *The "Man" Question in International Relations.* Boulder, CO: Westview Press.

Zine, Jasmin. 2006. "Between Orientalism and Fundamentalism: Muslim Women and Feminist Engagement," in Krista Hunt and Kim Rygiel, eds., *(En)gendering the War on Terror: War Stories and Camouflaged Politics,* pp. 27–49. Burlington, VT: Ashgate.

Zwingel, Susanne. 2005. "From Intergovernmental Negotiations to (Sub)National Change: A Transnational Perspective on the Impact of CEDAW." *International Feminist Journal of Politics* 7(3): 400–424.

About the Authors

V. Spike Peterson is a professor in the Department of Political Science at the University of Arizona, where she holds courtesy affiliations in women's studies, Institute for LGBT Studies, and international studies.

Anne Sisson Runyan is a professor in and the former head of the Department of Women's, Gender, and Sexuality Studies at the University of Cincinnati, where she holds affiliations with political science and the Taft Research Center.

Index